Genealogy *and* Computers

for the

Advanced Researcher

PULLING IT ALL TOGETHER

- Research in the Field
- Tracing Ancestors Abroad
- Word Processing with PAF™
- Designing and Publishing Your Genealogy

Karen Clifford

CLEARFIELD COMPANY

Printed for
Clearfield Company, Inc. by
Genealogical Publishing Co., Inc.
Baltimore, Maryland
1995

International Standard Book Number: 0-8063-4561-6

Made in the United States of America

To my daughter,

Tamra, who gave me two

great gifts for Christmas,

time to finish this book,

and a granddaughter

to share our

joy!

TABLE OF CONTENTS

CHAPTER ONE

CHAPTER TWO

CHAPTER THREE

CHAPTER FOUR

CHAPTER FIVE

CHAPTER SIX

CHAPTER TEN

CHAPTER ELEVEN

CHAPTER TWELVE

CHAPTER THIRTEEN

CHAPTER FOURTEEN

INTRODUCTION

The purpose of this text is to help you complete the project you started in *Genealogy & Computers for the Complete Beginner* and its sequel, *Genealogy & Computers for the Determined Researcher*. Those books introduced you to the world of Family History and how to use computer technology to complete your family history project faster, neater and more economically than was ever before possible.

The books also intended to make the results better by introducing you to sources and methods which could be applied as you trace your own family line and come upon various stumbling blocks. I hope you enjoyed the casual approach used to teach professional research methods and techniques. In this last book of my series I will continue to make complex topics understandable.

You will take your home sources, research, computer files, pictures, maps, reports and graphs and consolidate them into a finished family history that can be shared with your family and friends. Your final product may be an article, report, book, video or audio recording.

Because most people want to wait to publish their first family history when they find their ancestor who first came to this country, I've also included introductory techniques for making a connection to your ancestor's country of origin.

Even a family with modest means can produce a family history today that is more professional than the most wealthy person could have produced ten years ago. Now it is more a matter of knowledge and dedication than finances. This book will provide the knowledge, so let's get started by defining what it is that we want to accomplish.

CHAPTER ONE

Defining Your Family History Objectives

This Chapter will cover:

- Gaining confidence to start writing
- Deciding who your audience will be
- Identifying what problem you will try to solve
- Selecting the family to write about
- Deciding on a time perspective
- Choosing a writing style
- Locating background materials
     - Oral histories
     - On-site research
     - Hiring help

Gaining Confidence to Start Writing

Although there appears to be "magic" in a good book, you won't need a genie to create a wonderful family history. Writing is a learned skill. It is a craft. If you stick to it, you will succeed; but there is no "right" way to do such an intensely personal work. This chapter is meant to aid you in your goal to write a family history by passing on some techniques to get your family history started, keep the momentum moving, put the transitions in place, and bring it to a conclusion.

Some people write on paper, some type directly to the page, some enter into the computer, while others dictate into a dictaphone. Basically, writing should contain a "warmth" and interest in the subject. It should be free from clutter. A real secret is to strip each sentence to its shining meaning. Simplify...simplify...simplify. This requires writing, editing, and writing again. This is where a computer really comes into its own. With a computer you can edit without completely rewriting.

Do not fear writing in the first person. If you feel more relaxed writing this way, do it. Be yourself when you write and you will naturally stand out as a living example of your family.

Trust your own judgement. Different families require different approaches. You will need to ultimately decide the correct approach, the right voice, and the best format.

Take pride in your organizational skills of putting this work together. The story needs to flow, to be linear and sequential for ease of understanding, but with a certain amount of tension or suspense to intrigue the reader. These characteristics can be added bit by bit until you have built a perfect structure for your family history.

Read a variety of prepared family histories found in local libraries; in specialty libraries such as the Family History Library in Salt Lake City, Allen County Public Library in Fort Wayne, Indiana or local family history centers; or in hundreds of society and library publications. This will provide you with ideas on how to write your own history. Watch for introductions, conclusions, transitions, graphics, and layout. Jot down ideas you like and what you hope to avoid.

Some of the best examples for this project can be found in periodicals. These family histories must of necessity be short, concise, and appealing to compete with other items in the period-ical. Many are available on microfilm or fiche on indefinite loan at local family history centers or at local genealogy or historical societies. Notice the difference between these and those written in book form.

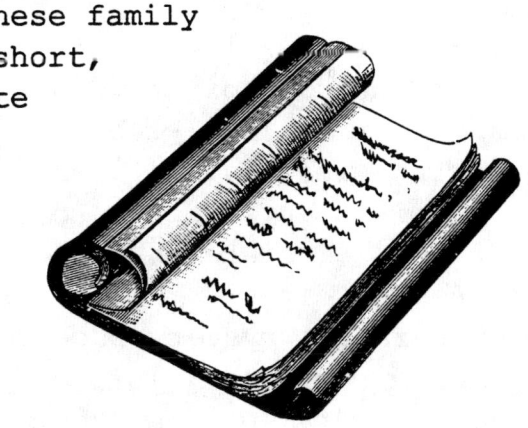

Deciding Who Your Audience Will Be

Decide who will want to read your history or who you will want to read it.

Also decide the time and place you will be writing from, for example are you going from present to the past or from the past to the future.

We are emotionally moved by the sound of voices. Tell your story in the language of the time and place where your ancestors lived and it will bring them to life.

Identifying What Problem You Will Try to Solve

Nearly all writing is ultimately a question of solving a problem. It might be a problem of organizing information, an approach or attitude to something, or a statement of facts. Perhaps it is a long-sought-after family mystery such as the missing identity of a grandfather. Think back to the goals you were trying to accomplish when you started your research, and write about that challenge.

Selecting the Family to Write About

With so many interesting ancestral lines to work on, it is hard for some writers to limit their writing to a manageable limit. Perhaps you might select lines with common localities or common experiences (such as the German lines or the Civil War lines).

Try not to do all the lines at once as you are beginning your first writing project. Limit yourself to one or two lines or you might feel like this fellow who was totally overwhelmed by the project.

4

Decide on a Time Perspective

It is most helpful to decide in advance if you are going to write *past to present* or *present to past*. This means deciding beforehand if you are telling your narrative from your modern perspective or from the viewpoint of the oldest ancestor and then moving forward in time.

Have an outline of who you wish to cover and when. Decide if you will be telling your story using present or past tense verbs. Your story will be unified if you select one tense and stick to it.

Choosing a Writing Style

Unity is also achieved by mood.

Your approach might be casual and chatty or have a certain formality. What does not work is to mix the two. Decide, therefore, if you want to be involved or detached, humorous or serious. Will your style be one of a reporter providing information or that of a caring friend or relative?

Introduction. The most importance sentence in any story is the first one. It must lead the reader to the second sentence and so forth until the interest in the story captures him. The next sentence to work on is the last sentence of each paragraph because it launches you into the next paragraph. Try a twist of humor or surprise. Below are some thoughts to get you started:

1. Begin with an interesting statement.

2. State your goal or purpose.

3. Place the individual in his/her historical setting.

4. Giving a brief pedigree chart overview.

5. Include some humor.

Transition phase. Help the reader move from place to place with transitions. Many words will do:

"but,"
   "yet,"
      "however,"
         "nevertheless,"
            "still," "instead,"
               "thus," "therefore," "meanwhile,"
                  "now," "later," "today,", "yesterday," and
                     "subsequently."

Another technique is to keep your sentences and your paragraphs short. This gives "air" or visual pauses to your writing and allows the reader's mind to rest and ponder the information presented.

Graphics. Placing appropriate visual aids in your writing will be more effective than pages of written words. Try:

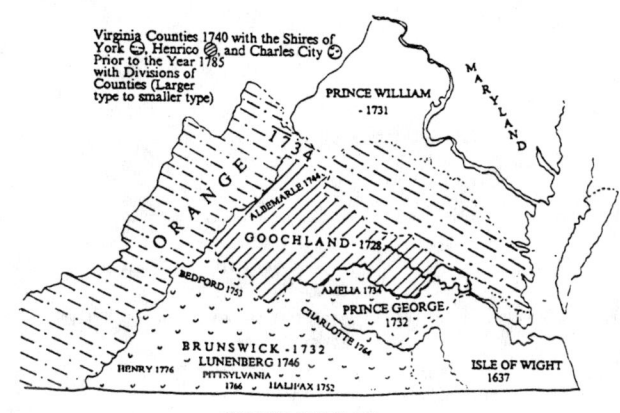

Maps. Draw your own maps listing places specifically mentioned in your history. It is also interesting to place the ancient localities in modern settings so others in the family may locate them.

Charts and Tables. Charts and tables often help to explain analysis of data between families of the same surname.

1820 CENSUS HISTORY

State of _Indiana_   County of _Sullivan_

Household of	MALES						FEMALES				
Surname, Given Name Page/Township	0-10	10-16	16-18	16-28	26-45	45 & up	0-10	10-16	16-26	26-45	45& up
Smith, George p. 21 Beaver	0	0	1	0	1	1	0	0	0	1	1
Smith, George p. 223 Kent	0	0	0	1	0	0	0	0	1	0	0
Smith, George p. 41 Vernon	Jim Pete 2	Tim 1	Matt 1	John 1	0	Geo. 1	0	Sue Elie 2	May 1	? 1	0
Smith, George p. 42 Vernon	0	0	0	Geo. 1	0	0	0	0	Marg 1	0	0

COLONIAL WARS

King Philip's War	1657-76
King William's War European name: War of the Palatinate	1689-97
Queen Anne's War European name: War of Spanish Succession	1702-13
King George's War European name: War of Austrian Succession	1744-48
French & Indian War European name: Seven Years' War	1754-63

Revolutionary War	1775-83

Pedigree charts are easier to follow than narrative descriptions of family lineages. Time tables of events help others to understand the historical setting.

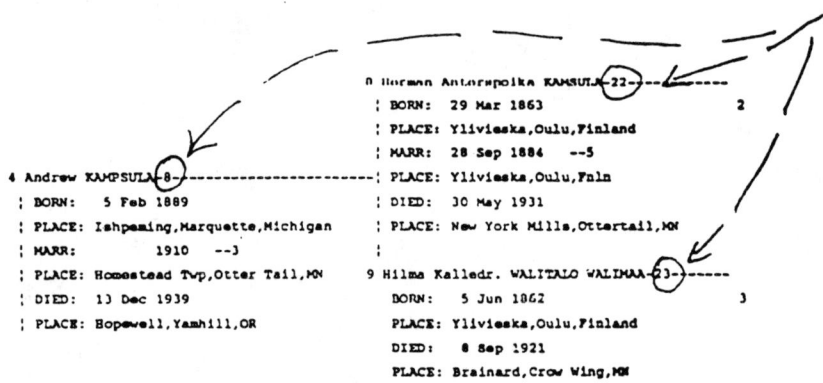

```
                                                 0 Herman Antonpoika KAMSULA-22---
                                                 ; BORN:  29 Mar 1863              2
                                                 ; PLACE: Ylivieska,Oulu,Finland
                                                 ; MARR:  28 Sep 1884  --5
       4 Andrew KAMPSULA-8-)------------------------; PLACE: Ylivieska,Oulu,Fnln
       ; BORN:   5 Feb 1889                          ; DIED:  30 May 1931
       ; PLACE: Ishpeming,Marquette,Michigan         ; PLACE: New York Mills,Ottertail,MN
       ; MARR:         1910  --3                      ;
       ; PLACE: Homestead Twp,Otter Tail,MN       9 Hilma Kalledr. WALITALO WALIMAA-23-)-----
       ; DIED:  13 Dec 1939                          BORN:    5 Jun 1862              3
       ; PLACE: Hopewell,Yamhill,OR                  PLACE: Ylivieska,Oulu,Finland
                                                     DIED:    8 Sep 1921
                                                     PLACE: Brainard,Crow Wing,MN
```

Pictures. A book containing pictures is always more pleasing to the eye than those without. Pictures might include snapshots of the family church, gravestones, business, or homesite as well as family portraits. Technology is now available to "scan" pictures directly into a computer so they will be placed into the history when it is printed.

If pictures are going to be produced of a different type of paper and inserted all at one spot in the center of the book, this should be decided ahead of time.

8

Clip Art. For those who do not have pictures, many copyright free clip art books are available to add interest to your histories. By looking at this book, you'll see how effective a picture can be. Chapter Two will cover more on this topic.

Sketches. If you like to sketch, this is a wonderful way to add interest to your family history. Consider, for example, sketches of the family home, the surrounding woods, rivers, or other historical settings. Color sketches do not reproduce well, but black ink sketches reproduce beautifully.

Detail. Don't use too many dates. Rather, provide references which lead the reader to attached pedigree charts and family group records or listings. A good rule of thumb is: give just enough detail to keep the generations and time in perspective.

Besides writing about people, you will be writing about places in your history. Readers want to know what that "somewhere" was like. They want to feel the mood. They want detail BUT NOT OBVIOUS DETAIL. They know the sea had waves, but were there other significant details? Was the land completely submerged during storms? Were graves washed away until nothing remained but an endless shifting coastline? Report the unusual and interesting things you noticed during your research?

9

Conclusion. Knowing when to end is also very important. The last sentence or thought can turn your history from one of enjoyment to one of failure. A perfect ending should take the readers slightly by surprise and yet seem exactly right. They didn't expect the story to end so soon, but they know the ending when they see it.

Here's a rule: "When you feel like you've stated all the facts and made your point, look for the nearest exit." Often an ending will include one of the following:

1. What you now feel about the individual.

2. What characteristics you admire in the family.

3. What family traditions have carried on.

4. What research you would like to see done next.

5. How you built a case through the preponderance of evidence.

You might summarize these statements using a surprising fact, an interesting quotation, a twist of humor, or simply your delight at having gotten to know the people in your family history.

Locating Background Materials

Background information for your family history may come from other sources than published, filmed, or printed sources. Oral stories which have been transcribed help put the heart into your life histories. These are called *oral histories*. Techniques for executing oral histories will be given in Chapter Six.

Germany

Perhaps you do not know what the homeland, county church or courthouse, looked like. Some *on-site research* would be in order here if you have the money and time to actually travel to the home sites. Another way to locate homeland pictures is in bookstores selling used books and postcards; in public or county libraries; in state or county archives and repositories, or through the eyes of a *hired researcher*.

On-site research (using the Family History Library as a sample) will be covered in Chapter Four and techniques for hiring a researcher for doing this type of work will be covered in Chapter Five.

Selected Bibliography

Barnes, Donald R. and Richard S. Lackey. *Write it Right: A Manual for Writing Family Histories and Genealogies.* Ocala, FL: Lyon Press, 1983.

Gouldrup, Lawrence P. *Writing the Family Narrative.* Salt Lake City: Ancestry Incorporated, 1987.

Hartley, William G. "Family History Writing and Publishing." Pgs. 51-66, *BYU Annual Genealogy and Family History Seminar*, 1988.

Mills, Elizabeth Shown. "The Preponderance of the Evidence Principle: How to Build a Case When No Document Solves Your Problem" Session S-92, *Syllabus*, The Federation of Genealogical Societies, 1992.

Nurse, Howard L. "Do-It-Yourself Publishing with a Personal Computer and Software." Session S147, *Syllabus*, National Genealogical Society Conference, 1991.

Zinsser, William. *On Writing Well: An Informal Guide to Writing Nonfiction*. 3rd ed. New York: Harper & Row Publishers, 1985. (Correct writing principals with a chapter on word processing.)

Chapter One
Assignments: Defining Your Family History Objectives

1. Compare the works of several family historians. Examine family histories that have been published in either your public library or local FHC, or on fiche or film.

    Select three which you feel are good examples of family histories and state why you feel they are good examples.

    Consider whether they have: a flowing story line that keeps you interested, good illustrations to help you understand their travels, a pleasing layout, a legible print size, and an extensive index referring to clearly numbered pages. Have they analyzed the questions that you'd like answered about the family, and have they tried to answer them logically?

2. Compare several family histories that are published in periodicals. Are any **not** good examples of well-done family histories? Explain how you feel they could be improved.

3. Decide who the audience will be for your own family history.

4. Decide your time perspective: present to past, past to present, etc.

5. Pick a setting.

6. State a goal or problem you will solved.

7. What tense will you use?

8.   What tone will you try to achieve: casual, chatty, formal, historical, involved, detached, judgmental, ironic, or amused?

Will your style be one of a reporter providing information or that of a friend or relative?

How will you achieve this mood? Perhaps cite examples from family histories you have studied.

LAB ASSIGNMENT 1 Becoming Familiar with Your Computer Programs

1. Although you may be used to using a word processing program at
    home, it may be different in a college classroom because it
    may be set up or formatted to serve a number of people at
    once, or be part of a network system. In this book you will
    become familiar with the *WordPerfect*® program as your word
    processor as well as move in and out of your *PAF* and *GEN-BOOK*
    programs.   For this assignment:

    a.   locate the genealogy program(s) on your computer's
         menu.
    b.   locate the word processing program(s) on your
         computer's menu.
    c.   determine how many drives the computer has.
    e.   determine the "default" drive used by the computer
         program (usually drive a)
    f.   determine the "default" drive for the word
         processing program.

2. While in *WordPerfect*® determine if the **F1** key is a HELP key
    or a CANCEL key. If F1 is a CANCEL key, determine if F3 is
    the HELP key. Strike the HELP key twice and them hold down
    the **Shift** key with your left hand as you press the **print
    screen** button with your right hand to print a copy of the
    template. Then strike the **space bar** to exit that screen.
    Use the HELP screen again to determine the steps necessary to
    exit the program by striking the HELP key then the letter **e**
    until the word EXIT shows up in the alphabetical listing. If
    you want more explanation actually strike the key it states
    for you to strike...in this case F7 and more instruction will
    be forthcoming. Strike the space bar to exit the Help Screen.

3. Strike the **F7** key to exit and do not save the document.
    Follow the instructions on the screen and find the logout
    procedures on your computer menu if your computer has a menu.

CHAPTER TWO

Using *WordPerfect*® to Accomplish Your Objectives

This Chapter will cover these *WordPerfect*® features:

- Moving files from PAF to word processing
- Switching between two documents
- Retrieving your documents
- Typing text or word wrap
- Setting margins
- Centering
- Indenting
- Numbering pages
- Copying, moving, or deleting blocks of text
- Finding a word
- Replacing words
- Changing font sizes
- Changing font appearance
- Forcing to new page to allow for graphics
- Combining files or chapters
- Saving your documents
- Exiting *WordPerfect*® without saving a file

There are many word processing programs, and a few very powerful ones. Of these, I selected *WordPerfect*®, because of its popularity, and because it was available on a network system at the colleges where I teach. Also most of the accessory programs to the *PAF* program use *WordPerfect*® as well (this textbook will cover version 2.2 as over 300,000 copies of that program have been sold, but the appendix covers new features of version 2.3). Several other word processing programs are just as likely to work as well, but for our book this will be the word processor I will use to provide examples. If you are using a different word processor, or a newer version of *WordPerfect®*, please check your manual for instructions on how to access the features listed above.

Although *WordPerfect® 5.1* is a massive word processing program that can perform hundreds of functions that will not be taught in this book, there will be enough instruction to enable you to produce a fine report of the family you are working on. If you have *WordPerfect® for Windows,* the instructions in your own *WordPerfect®* Instruction Books should be consulted.

If you are preparing a short report for yourself and a friend, or doing a complete report for a client, it is advantageous to know that you can copy your notes from the *PAF* program to *WordPerfect®* by printing to file. (Follow the step-by-step instructions under Lab Assignment 2). This would serve the duel purpose of allowing you to have several pages of notes to practice *WordPerfect®* features (without having to type something in) as well as to practice the print file feature of *PAF.* If you do not have notes to transfer and learn from, just continue the lesson below.

Note: when you print to file from your *PAF* program, *WordPerfect®* leaves a hard carriage return marker at the end of each line. You will need to delete those markers if you want to manipulate your manuscript freely. The **Alt** plus **F3** command reveals these returns as **[HRt]** so you can quickly remove those which are unwanted. More on revealing codes below.

Getting Started

Let us begin our study of this program by bringing up the *WordPerfect®* program in whatever manner your menu indicates. Once into the program the bottom right hand corner of the screen will read **Doc 1 Pg 1 Ln 1" Pos 1**. When you work in *WordPerfect®*, you may work on two documents at once. To experiment with this feature hold down the **Shift** key and strike **F3**. Now the screen indicates you are in the second document by giving this notation at the bottom of the screen: **Doc 2 Pg 1 Ln 1" Pos 1.**

Go back to document one by holding down the **Shift** key and striking **F3**.

Typing Text or Word Wrap

As with the documentation portion of the PAF program, typing information into *WordPerfect®* is easily accomplished. If you type an incorrect letter or word you could press the backspace key, until the mistake is erased, then begin typing again.

It is not necessary to press the enter key when you reach the end of the line. The automatic return at the end of each line is referred to as word wrapping. At the bottom of the screen the status line lets you not only know what document you are editing, but it indicates the page, abbreviated **Pg,** you are on, and how far down the page the cursor is located by **Ln, or line.** The current position of the cursor across the page is indicated by **Pos,** or position.

The best way to learn is to practice doing. Type the next three paragraphs below into document 1, and then you can practice modifying them. (As a genealogist you'll also be interested in the content of these three paragraphs.)

The Bureau of Land Management recently announced that the General Land Office (GLO) Automated Record Retrieval System has been implemented. The new system can quickly access land title data. The BLM's Eastern States office in Springfield, Virginia, holds more than five million land documents for homesteads, cash sales, and military warrants dated from the late 1700s for the thirteen public land sales states. For some counties which suffered lost of records due to fires, etc., these are the only extant records.

Prior to the incorporation of the new system, researchers had to furnish a complete legal description of the property with each request. The new computerized data base can now be accessed through six fields: land description, patentee name, patent authority, land office, certificate number, or county. To date only data for six states are available; these are Arkansas, Florida, Louisiana, Michigan, Minnesota, and Wisconsin. The next three states to be included in the near future are Alabama, Mississippi, and Ohio; these will be followed by Illinois, Indiana, Iowa, and Missouri. It is projected that the entire collection will be completed within four years.

Remote retrieval from the new GLO system through your personal modem attached to a DOS system will soon be available through a terminal emulation software package. You may open an account with BLM using a major credit card and your own password. For more information, write BLM, Eastern States, 7450 Boston Blvd., Springfield, VA 22153.

Now we will work on changing or setting margins.

Setting Margins

To set a margin you should be at the top of your page. Press "Home" then press the "up arrow" key to move the cursor to the very beginning of the text.

Hold down the **Shift** key and press the **F8** function key which will take you to **Format** which will display a main menu of all the formats available. From this **format** menu you can select to change the: 1 -line format, 2 - page format, 3 - document format, or 4 - other.

We are going to change the left and right margins therefore select **1 - Line** by pressing **1**.

Select at the **Format: Line** menu number **7 - Margins Left Right** by typing **7**. It is probably already set at a 1" margin, so we will change it to 2" margins so you can see how this changes the text.

Type **2** and press **Enter** for the Left Margin. Then type **2** and press **Enter** for the Right Margin. Press the Exit[1] key which is **F7** to indicate you are finished and return to the document screen. Press the "Down Arrow" to reformat all the text to 2 inch margins.

Reveal Codes

Each time you change the format in a document, a code or instruction will be imbedded in the document. While the effects of these codes are usually evident, you do not see the codes themselves on the screen. But you can look at the codes if you want to. In fact, it is a good idea to review the codes to be sure you don't end up with multiple codes in a document that will cause the printed version to come out rather strange.

To reveal these imbedded codes hold down the **Alt** key and strike the **F3** function key. You will see a wide line splitting the screen into two areas. The upper portion of the screen displays your text and the lower screen revealing the text **and codes** which the *WordPerfect®* program uses. These codes will be in **bold** print. If you hold down the **Alt** key and strike **F3** again, the Reveal Codes screen will be removed.

Centering

To center a line in *WordPerfect®*, hold down the **Shift** key and press the **F6** function key. The cursor will move to the center position and you may then type what you would like. When you hit the **Enter** key it takes you out of the centering position.

Using this function, type and center **Automated Record Retrieval System** at the top of the paragraph you just typed.

---

[1]Anytime you are told to "Exit" strike the **F7** function key.

Indenting

Hold down the **Shift** key and strike the **F8** function key. Once again you are at the **Format** menu. Select **1** then select **8** – Tab set. The computer may already have been set for .5 tab setting which is 1/2 inch. If they have not, or you wish to change the setting, press the command to "delete to end of line" which is done by holding down the **Ctrl** key and pressing the **end** key to clear tabs from the tab ruler.

Now enter the number of spaces that you desire for the tab setting. When finished, press the **F7** exit key twice to return to the normal editing screen. Move to the first letter of each paragraph and press the **Tab** key to indent each paragraph.

Numbering Pages

When finished with a document, page numbers may be added. Before doing this, you should again move the cursor to the beginning of your document.

Move to the top of your document by pressing **Home** <u>twice</u> and then pressing the up arrow.

Hold down the **Shift** key and press the **F8** function key. Once again you are at the **Format** menu. Select **2** for page format, then select **6** – Page numbering. Now select **4** - Page number position.

A menu of page numbering options will be displayed. The **1** position indicates a page number in the upper left hand corner, **2** indicates upper center, **3** indicates upper right hand corner, **4** even and odd indicates that the number changes positions on odd and even numbered pages but the number is at the top, **5** indicates lower left hand corner, **6** middle bottom, **7** bottom right hand corner, **8** lower right or left corner depending on odd or even numbered pages, and **9** indicates no page number.

We will set the page number for the bottom center position so type the number **6** then you would strike the **F7** key which is the exit key to return back to your menu.

Copying, Moving or Deleting Blocks of Text

It is often necessary to mark a text and then move it, delete it or copy it to another place in your document. Mark the text by having the cursor at the front of the line or word you wish to move.

Start the block command by holding down the **Alt** key and pressing the **F4** function key.

Use the arrow key to move the cursor to the opposite end of the text which you wish to have moved, copied or deleted. This will highlight the information which is to be moved, copied or deleted. A **Block on** message will flash at the bottom left hand corner of the screen indicating the block feature is on.

Hold down the **Ctrl** key and press the **F4** function key, then select the block by pressing 1 - Block.

Now select the option you want: **1** Move **2** Copy **3** Delete or **4** Append.

To copy, select **2**. The highlighted, or blocked area, will turn off but the blocked section will remain unchanged. Now move your cursor to the position to which you wish the item to be copied. The bottom left corner will say, "Move cursor; press **Enter** to retrieve." to remind you that there is an item waiting to be moved somewhere. Once the **enter** key is struck, this message disappears, and a copy of the previously highlighted information appears where the cursor was flashing..

Copy the bottom paragraph of the Automated Record Retrieval System and place it below the first paragraph leaving a blank line. It should look like this:

The Bureau of Land Management recently announced that the General Land Office (GLO) Automated Record Retrieval System has been implemented. The new system can quickly access land title data. The BLM's Eastern States office in Springfield, Virginia, holds more than five million land documents for homesteads, cash sales, and military warrants dated from the late 1700s for the thirteen public land sales states. For some counties which suffered lost of records due to fires, etc., these are the only extant records.

Remote retrieval from the new GLO system through your personal modem attached to a DOS system will soon be available through a terminal emulation software package. You may open an account with BLM using a major credit card and your own password. For more data write BLM, Eastern States, 7450 Boston Blvd., Springfield, VA 22153.

Prior to the incorporation of the new system, researchers had to furnish a complete legal description of the property with each request. The new computerized data base can now be accessed through six fields: land description, patentee name, patent authority, land office, certificate number, or county. To date only data for six states is available; these are Arkansas, Florida, Louisiana, Michigan, Minnesota, and Wisconsin. The next three states to be included in the near future are Alabama, Mississippi, and Ohio; these will be followed by Illinois, Indiana, Iowa, and Missouri and it is projected that the entire collection will be completed within four years.

Remote retrieval from the new GLO system through your personal modem attached to a DOS system will soon be available through a terminal emulation software package. You may open an account with BLM using a major credit card and your own password. For more data write BLM, Eastern States, 7450 Boston Blvd., Springfield, VA 22153.

Deleting Text. If you wish to delete several words, you could either do a backspace over them, or you could use block delete. Beginning at a list of words, paragraph or sentence you wish to delete, hold down the **Alt** key and strike the **F4** key. Move the cursor to the end of the text you wish to delete, then hold down the **Ctrl** key and strike the **F4** key. Now select **1** to Block and then **3** to Delete. The information will be deleted.

Block delete the last paragraph, (the one you just copied) in the previous exercise.

Moving Text. Moving text is like copying except the text is deleted from its original position. Move the cursor to the front of the line you wish to move, hold down the **Alt** key and strike the **F4** key. Move the cursor to the end of the text you wish to delete, then hold down the **Ctrl** key and strike the **F4** key. Now select **1** to Block and **1** to Move. Now move the cursor to where you want the information moved, hit **Enter** and the information will be deleted from its original position and inserted in the new position.

Block move the first paragraph to the bottom of the page in the exercise presently in your computer. It would look like this:

Remote retrieval from the new GLO system through your personal modem attached to a DOS system will soon be available through a terminal emulation software package. You may open an account with BLM using a major credit card and your own password. For more data write BLM, Eastern States, 7450 Boston Blvd., Springfield, VA 22153.

Prior to the incorporation of the new system, researchers had to furnish a complete legal description of the property with each request. The new computerized data base can now be accessed through six fields: land description, patentee name, patent authority, land office, certificate number, or county. To date only data for six states is available; these are Arkansas, Florida, Louisiana, Michigan, Minnesota, and Wisconsin. The next three states to be included in the near future are Alabama, Mississippi, and Ohio; these will be followed by Illinois, Indiana, Iowa, and Missouri and it is projected that the entire collection will be completed within four years.

Bureau of Land Management recently announced that the General Land Office (GLO) Automated Record Retrieval System has been implemented. The new system can quickly access land title data. The BLM's Eastern States office in Springfield, Virginia, holds more than five million land documents for homesteads, cash sales, and military warrants dated from the late 1700s for the thirteen public land sales states. For some counties which suffered lost of records due to fires, etc., these are the only extant records.

As you can see, the nice thing about *WordPerfect®* is that it does so much automatically, which is a great advantage over typing and simpler programs such as the PAF notes editor. As you continue to work with *WordPerfect®*, you will find that there are shortcuts that let you copy, move, and delete text with even fewer key strokes.

Finding a Word

Finding a word in a document is easy with the "search" function. This can be especially helpful when you want to replace one word with another. For instance you just found out that the address on the document above was not 7450 but 7451. A fast method to move to the number 7450 from the beginning of the document is to strike the **F2** key. Now type **7450**. Then strike **F2** again. The cursor will move directly to that number. If the cursor is BELOW the number on the page, you will need to search "backwards" in the text. In that case hold down the **Shift** key and then strike the **F2** key. That takes the cursor to a word above the cursor.

Try to find 7450 and change it to 7451.

Replacing Words

Throughout your document you may have typed a surname incorrectly. Rather than having to reread twenty pages and correct that mistyped surname every time it appears, the program can find that word and replace it automatically.

Go to the top of the document by hitting **Home Home** then the **up arrow key**. Hold down the **Alt** key and press **F2**. The program will ask you if you wish to confirm what is done. This means the program will stop at every instance of the word and wait for you to say whether to change that occurrence of the word by typing **Y** for yes or **N** for no.

We will strike **Y** for yes. Now you can type in the word that needs to be replaced. For practice lets replace the acronym GLO. Since it is capitalized, capitalize each letter. Press **Alt** and **F2** again and type in the words to replace it with EXACTLY AS YOU WISH IT TO BE REPLACED. In this case type: General Land Office. Press **F2** again and it will begin its search. When the **Not found** message is displayed you can press "Home, Home, Up Arrow" to return to the beginning of the document.

For some more practice, change every word "can" to "will" by using search and replace. Continue typing **y** for "yes" until all occurrences of the word in the document have been changed.

Changing Font Sizes

To print the title, the first line, or a graph with different sizes of print, or to include italicized footnotes, or underline several lines of pretyped text, you will need to change font sizes or appearance.

Make the title of your project a larger font by holding down the **Alt** key plus striking the **F4** function key and moving the right or left, up or down arrow keys, which will define the area to be changed. Highlight the part of word, words, paragraphs or pages you desire to change.

Now hold down the **Ctrl** key and tap the **F8** (font) function key and then the **1** (size) key and then the **6** (very large size) key.

More font size changes: Alt+F4+arrow keys again defines an area to be changed by highlighting the part of word, words, paragraphs or pages you desire to change. **Ctrl+F8+1** (size) and then the addition of the following options allows for: +1 (Super-Script=above the line), **2 (**Sub-Script=below the line), **+3** fine, **+4** small, **+5** large, **+6** very large, or **7** extra large. Select various words on your screen and do each option.

      Preview your document: It's a good idea to hold down the **Shift** key plus striking the **F7** key and at the **Print** menu pressing **v** to view your changes. To exit the print menu and return to the document press **F7**.

      Making Large Title Text. To temporarily change the font hold down the **Ctrl** key and strike the **F8** key. Select **3** - Temporary Font. Select the type font and the font size option by moving the up and down arrow key to the correct font then striking the **enter** key and typing in the font size desired if fonts are not predetermined.

      In the document you are typing, change the font size using one of the various options mentioned above, to a larger size and type This Is A Title Line. On the screen the letters will ·be highlighted, and when printed they will look like this.

This Is A Title Line.

      To get a preview of what the printed page will look like hold down the **Shift** key and press **F7**. This will bring up the print menu. You could print the page if you wanted to, but there is no need to waste the paper. Just press the letter **v** for view, and you will see a "picture " of the page on the screen. To exit the print menu and return to the document press **F7**.

      To return the font to normal size, hold down the **Ctrl** key and strike the **F8** key and then **6** for normal.

      Other options once you have held down the **Ctrl** key and **F8** are to change the size in the existing font such as Super-Script (above the line), Sub-Script (below the line), fine, small, large, very large, or extra large. If you select "Large" for another line, your printer may only be able to print one size for both selections because there is only one larger font for the particular printer that you have. So although *WordPerfect®* has options for doing font sizes it is also determined by the particular printer you own.

Changing Font Appearance

You may also change the font appearance by either holding down the **Alt** key plus typing the **F4,** highlight the part of word, words, paragraphs or pages your desire to change, and then striking **Ctrl** plus **F8** key and the **2** (appearance) key to either make the letters: +1 (Bold), 2 (underline), + 4 italics, + 6 shadow. Select various words on your screen and do each option.

As you probably noted when you held down the **Ctrl** key and **F8** there is also a 2 - Appearance option. Characters may be changed to bold, underline, double underline, or italics. You can select any of these appearance attributes but what actually happens on the printed page depends on the capabilities of your printer. Press **F7** to "Exit" to exit the appearance attributes menu without making any changes.

By blocking a word and then changing its appearance, you can BOLD or italicize a word that was normal before. Select the word "Title" in the "This Is A Title Line." Block it and then italicize it. The word is now highlighted on the screen and will appear as:

This Is A *Title* Line

when printed.

There is a default font that is set up for normal typing. If you want to see what your base font is, hold down the **Ctrl** key and strike the **F8** key. Select **4** - Base Font. A highlighted bar will designate which font is active and a display of other fonts available will be shown. The **F7** key would return you to the editing screen.

To reveal codes hold down the **Alt** key and strike the **F3** function key. You will see below the screen split all the embedded codes for the changes you have made in your original document. Press the up and down arrow keys to look for indications of changes to your font size or appearance.

Forcing A New Page

Sometimes you would like to leave a whole page blank for maps or you want what you are going to type next to be on a new page.

If you wish to leave a blank page that will be numbered but not have any typing on it, hold down the **Ctrl** key and strike the **enter** key. A double line will appear on the screen indicating that the program has forced a new page to begin on. Hold down the **Ctrl** key and press **enter** a second time. You have now left page 2 blank and are ready to start typing on page 3.

Changing Your Mind

At any time if you think you have made a mistake, such as pressing the wrong key sequence, strike the **F1** key to cancel your last request. Try this out by typing "This is page three". Now Press **F1** and you'll be given a chance to "undelete" or restore the words.

Saving Your Documents

When you have finished entering your materials, strike the **F7** key. At the bottom of the screen *WordPerfect®* will question: **Save document?** Yes (**No**). Of course we wish to save what we have done. If it is erased we will have to start over when we want to add more information, so strike **y** for yes.

WordPerfect® will then ask **Document to be saved:** and wait for you to type in a name for your document. If you are saving it to a floppy disk as you would in a class, type **a:**, indicating you want

it saved to the "A" drive, and give the file a name such as **jones**.
The total name would then be **a:jones**. If you are saving it on the
computer's internal disk, just type the names **jones**.

If you are going to have several chapters you might want to
call it Chapter 1.   Or if it is on the Cooper family, you might
put cooper1. Put any name that is easy for you to remember, but
the name can only have a total of 8 letters and numbers with no
spaces between them.

Once the name has been entered, strike the **Enter** key and
WordPerfect® will save the document. Put a disk in drive A of your
computer and save the document you have been working on to a file
a:assn3.

WordPerfect® will then ask if you wish to exit the program.
If you hit the "Enter" key, it will automatically take the default
answer "No" and you will be left with another blank screen to type
the next chapter.

Check to see if the file was really saved by striking the **F5**
List File key. Then type **a:** at the bottom of the screen when it
asks what file to search for. Strike the **Enter** key and it will
list all the files that are on the "A" disk. See if you can see
your **assn3** file.

Combining Files or Chapters

It is wiser when typing a book or lengthy report to make
several smaller documents that can then be combined once the
finished product is ready to be printed. For example, if you have
a separate chapter for every surname you are working on, or for
each generation, then save as an individual file.

This is accomplished by giving each chapter its own title as
the text is saved. The file, or chapter, is later retrieved into
the larger document. The individual chapters will remain on the
disk to be edited later if necessary.

Retrieving your documents

To retrieve files that were previously worked on and saved, use the **F5** option to list the files you have saved. Remember, to type A: if you want to list the files on drive A. Then use the arrow keys to highlight the file you desire to retrieve. Next strike **1 - Retrieve** (the bolding means you can strike 1 or R and it will do the same thing). It will be brought up on the screen for you.

Retrieve the **assn3** document you had worked on previously. Press the Page Down key twice, and then add the paragraph below to page three of the document:

An Arkansas newspaper project is being sponsored by the University of Arkansas. For the past four years, individuals for the U of A have travelled throughout Arkansas inventorying and cataloging newspapers held in Arkansas repositories. They are also searching for newspapers which have never been microfilmed. To date, over 2600 newspaper titles and 7000 plus records have been entered into the union list of newspapers. In addition, they have prepared comprehensive lists of all the newspapers ever published in each county that have not yet been found or microfilmed.

Save the file by striking the **F7** key. Answer **y** you do want to save it. This time the same name **a:assn3** would appear and pause so you could decide if you wanted to keep this same name. If you keep this same name, the new document with the added Arkansas message will erase the old file and replace it with this new one.

If you did not wish to replace it, you would have to give this version of the document a new name. Then, both the old file (which is still on the disk) and the new one (you have edited) can be saved on the disk.

Move the cursor to the end of the current name and change it to **a:assn3a**, then exit by striking the **enter** key.

Exiting *WordPerfect®* Without Saving a File

Often you may type a note or short memo, print it, and not wish to keep a copy. To exit without saving the file to a disk, strike **F7** and at **Save document** select **No**.

It will respond with **Exit *WordPerfect®?*** If you type **y** you will leave the *WordPerfect®* program. If you type **n**, it will bring you to a blank screen to start another document.

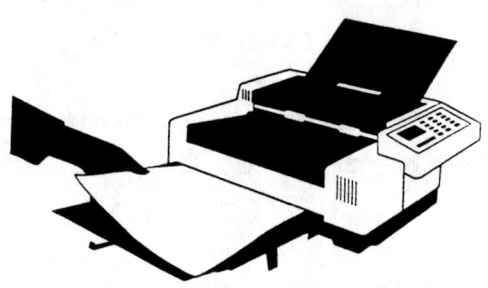

Selected Bibliography

Ames, Stanley Richard. *How to Write and Publish Your Family History Using Word Perfect*. Interlaken, NY: Heart of the Lakes Publishing, 1988.

Harvey, Greg and Kay Yarborough Nelson. *WordPerfect® 5.1 Instant Reference*. Alameda, CA: Sybex Inc., 1990.

Neibauer, Alan R. *WordPerfect® Tips and Tricks*. Alameda, CA: Sybex Inc., 1986.

_____. *WordPerfect® for IBM Personal Computers*. Orem, UT: WordPerfect Corporation, 1989, Version 5.1.

_____. *WordPerfect® Workbook for IBM Personal Computers*. Orem, UT: WordPerfect Corporation, 1989, Version 5.1.

Chapter Two
Assignments: Using *WordPerfect®* to Accomplish Your Objectives

1.   Do the assignments as they are given in the chapter.

2.   Type your name, class name, date and page number of the
      assignment in the upper right hand corner or the assignment.

3.   Print out the final results and submit.

LAB ASSIGNMENT 2: Using *WordPerfect®* (WP)

Moving files from PAF to word processing

      Put your PAF Disk in Drive B.
      Put your WP disk in drive A.
      Go into the Genealogy Program at your computer menu
      Select **#1** Family Records
      Select **A** Utilities, then **#4** to temporarily reconfig
      B:
      F1; F1; 0
      #4 Pedigree search to select a RIN; **x** to exit Pedigree search;
      #6 Print
      #1 Select Printing Option
      #2 Print to Disk File
      A Drive to print to
      File name **Assnt2**
      F1 to save
      0 to return to main menu
      #5 notes
      #1 Know RIN, **45** RIN Number
      y yes this is who you want
      3 Print Notes
      1 Print All Notes
      0 0 0 0 enter 0 to exit PAF.

WordPerfect®

      Find the Word Processing option on your computer menu
      Select WordPerfect®; enter;
      (follow instructions if in computer lab).
      After WordPerfect® has started, notice the bottom of the
      screen: **Doc 1 Pg 1 Ln 1" Pos 1**

Switching documents from screen to screen

      Shift + F3, switches you to a separate file: **Doc 2 Pg 1**
      Now shift back by **Shift+F3**, and notice **Doc 1 Pg 1**
      (This will allow you to work on two documents at once.)

Retrieving your documents

F5; use the arrow keys to highlight the file you desire to retrieve. Next strike **1 - Retrieve** (the bolding means you can strike **1** or **R** and it will do the same thing). Retrieve Assnt2.

Typing text or word wrap

Type your name, class name, date and lab assignment 2 in the upper right hand corner using **ALT+F6** for flush right. Remove paragraph markers at the end of the text where necessary.

Saving your document & exiting WordPerfect®

F7; At the bottom *WordPerfect®* will question: **Save document?** **Yes (No).** That word NOT IN PARENTHESIS is what the program will do if you do nothing but hit enter. Strike **y** for yes. *WordPerfect®* will ask **Document to be saved:** Type **a:assnt2a** and strike the **enter** key. Do you wish to exit? **Y** yes. **Esc** at Novelle menu and then to **Logout.**

CHAPTER THREE

Designing Your Book

This chapter will cover the main elements of text formatting:

- Margins
- Fonts
- Graphics
- Page Layout
- Paper
- Printing
- Binding
- Covers
- Costs

Most publishers request *camera-ready* copies of manuscripts for publication. These may be produced by a professional typesetter, on a computer or word processor, or on a very good electronic typewriter. This high quality final manuscript copy will be photographed for printing. If you are in doubt as to the quality of your final copy, check with the printer.

Margins

Most of us consider how much margin we should leave on an 8 1/2 by 11 inch piece of paper. If you are preparing a manuscript for a publisher or a periodical, you must consider their margin requirements. What is critical to them is the "typing area".

The typing area is defined by the width of the typing line and the distance from the first to the last line of type. This needs to be standard on all pages. It may be allowable to use a different area for charts or an index, for example, but the text area for each section should be consistent for all pages. Many publishers provide typing area charts to help you.

Publishers also provide stylistic suggestions to improve the appearance of your page and to alert you to any problems that might come up regarding reproduction.

Dealing with margins involves leaving enough space to bind the book or article, determining if the right and left margins should be flush, as well as deciding if printing will be done on the back and front of a page.

Justification

This is a sample paragraph in which *full justification* has been added so that both the right and left margins are exactly even. This makes a very nice finish to your book but sometimes you will find either large gaps between words or words almost overlapping. The paragraph above this has *left justifications* and the paragraph below has *center justification*.

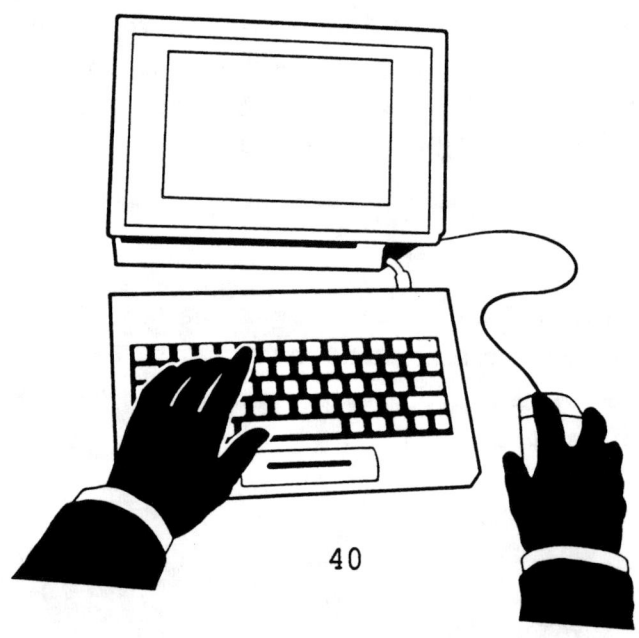

Center justification allows the writer to make beautiful poetical scripts which are centered on the middle of the page but not even on either the right or left margin. Sometimes the ending of a book looks very nice using this technique as shown in the example below.

YOUR FAMILY TREE
*

2 PARENTS

4 GRANDPARENTS

8 GREAT GRANDPARENTS

16 GREAT GREAT GRANDPARENTS

32 GREAT GREAT GREAT GRANDPARENTS

64 GREAT GREAT GREAT GREAT GRANDPARENTS

128 GREAT GREAT GREAT GREAT GREAT GRANDPARENTS

256 GREAT GREAT GREAT GREAT GREAT GREAT GRANDPARENTS

512 GREAT GREAT GREAT GREAT GREAT GREAT GREAT GRANDPARENTS

1024 GREAT GREAT GREAT GREAT GREAT GREAT GREAT GREAT GRANDPARENTS

Just 10 Generations
and You Have
1,024 Surnames
to Search

Thank goodness for a computer!

I will end this with an example of *right justification* which by
now you have discovered leaves
the right margin even and
allows the left margin
to go where it wants.
I have used this when
I have a picture I
wish to place in
the left margin. It
is an easy way to see
in advance what will
be left.

In a word processing program, you may also change the right or
left margin setting in the middle of your text which allows you to
fully justify text keeping both margins equally centered. That
technique has also been used throughout this book.

Font Sizes and Types

Some computer software programs measure type like a typewriter
using "characters per inch" or *cpi*. The width of each letter is
uniform in the cpi system. *Pica* type measures to 10 letters to the
inch while *elite* measures 12 letters to the inch. Some systems
also offer a smaller 17 cpi type. With cpi type, printers normally
plan a typing area that allows for some reduction afterwards.

Today's word processing desktop publishing for the computer
have a much wider choice to print sizes and thus can be worked
without reduction. Programs such as *WordPerfect® Microsoft Word®
Ventura®*, *PageMaker®*, and *Publish It!®* all have these options
available to you. When you use these programs, however, you will
probably not use the cpi type of calculations, but proportional
fonts (where an "m" takes more space on the line than an "i") and
point sizes.

A *point size* describes the size of your print by height rather than by width. These fonts emulate typesetting where letter **widths** vary. For example, 72 points measure 1" in height; half of that, or 36 points, measures 1/2 "; with one fourth of that equalling 18 points. Most text fonts under this system are set at 10 or 11 point. Chapter headings are 18 point. Footnotes and indices are 8 points.

This is a sample of a 10 point font.

This is a sample of an 11 point font.

This is a sample of an 18 point font.

This is a sample of an 8 point font.

In addition to font sizes, font types should be considered. Various software programs provide a variety of font types. The samples printed above were done using a font package called *PowerPack* which was purchased to use with *WordPerfect®* and the font type was called *Cobb (Normal)*. All the fonts used below are part of that package. Notice the variety.

This is a sample of a 10 point Hancock (Normal) font.

This is a sample of an 11 point Hancock (Normal) font.

This is a sample of an 18 point Hancock (Normal) font.

This is a sample of an 8 point Hancock (Normal) font.

While some fonts are very artistic, they are difficult for the eye to read when used for extended text. *This is a sample of AtchBrush (Normal) font at 12 points. Do you find it harder to read than the previous text?* Although

I like the artistic quality of Hancock font, printed in the following Salvation Army announcement, it actually looks better on a certificate than for extended reading. Some individuals use this font for italicized items in their text rather than the actual italicized font within the current font package.

SALVATION ARMY FINDS LOST PERSONS

More than 100 years after the founding of the Salvation Army, the missing-person program remains one of the least-known services. For a $10 filing fee (soon to be raised to $25) the Salvation Army will try to trace missing family members 18 years of age and older.

To utilize the tracing services, applicants must provide the missing person's full name, date and place of birth, names of parents, Social Security number (if known) occupation, last known address, and any other information that might aid in their search.

The Salvation Army make it clear up front that anyone not wanting to be found will be left undisturbed. No one's whereabouts is divulged without his or her consent.

You can get more information or a missing person inquiry form by getting in touch with the Salvation Army Territorial Headquarters at 30840 Hawthorne Blvd., Rancho Palos Verdes, Ca 90274.[2]

SALVATION ARMY FINDS LOST PERSONS

More than 100 years after the founding of the Salvation Army, the missing-person program remains one of the least-known services. For a $10 filing fee (soon to be raised to $25) the Salvation Army will try to trace missing family members 18 years of age and older.

To utilize the tracing services, applicants must provide the missing person's full name, date and place of birth, names of parents, Social Security number (if known) occupation, last known address, and any other information that might aid in their search.

The Salvation Army make it clear up front that anyone not wanting to be *found* will be left undisturbed. No one's whereabouts is divulged without his or her consent.

You can get more information or a missing person inquiry form by getting in touch with the Salvation Army Territorial Headquarters at 30840 Hawthorne Blvd., Rancho Palos Verdes, Ca.

---

[2]From the *California State Genealogical Alliance Newsletter* July, 1994.

I want to give a couple more examples in order to prove the point that mixing too many font types and sizes on a page also give a restless, troubled disorder to a page. This particular font is called Quincy (Normal). I am now changing to ProvLite (Normal) which has the advantage of being a proportional type font. That means some letters are much wider or thinner than others so more words can be placed on a page than in non-proportional type fonts as the Cobb- Normal Font which is used in this book.

A feature of Cobb is to make the font thinner as in this sentence being printed using Cobb Thin (Normal). One advantage to a non-proportional font is that items lined up on the screen as you type are usually lined up on the page. Going in and out of these fonts is as easy as two key strokes.

If you are using the services of a publisher, check with them before setting up your typing area to make sure your sizing is correct and your fonts pleasing after being reduced.

Gateway Press, Inc. specializes in helping people self-publish their books. They will send you a free *Guide for Authors* and they also sell a video entitled *Prepare to Publish* which sells for about $30.[3]

Graphics

There are several ways to add visual interest to your family history without adding the extra cost of hiring an artist. One is to use copyright free woodcuts or line illustrations. As long as these illustrations fit within the text area, no extra charge is passed on to you. Over the years I have used many of the clip art and line illustrations of *Dover Publications*.[4]

Many old documents, drawings, and maps also consist only of black lines on a white background. These reproduce well. Ones to

---

[3]Contact Gateway Press, Inc., 1001 N. Calvert Street, Baltimore, MD 21202.

[4]To receive their free catalog write to Dover Publications, 31 E. 2nd Avenue, Mineola, New York 11501.

avoid are those with multiple shades of gray. Such drawings and photographs require special half-tone processing before they will print well.

If original prints are used, they must be given to the publisher with all cropping indicated. Negatives are not acceptable. Photocopies of originals may be very difficult to reproduce, but in some rare instances they come out better.

All photographs should be identified by a number and caption on the back at the top using a soft tip marker or pencil. Marker will someday bleed through the picture, so if you are taking your only original, write the information on an acid-free, self-sticking photo strip and place the identifying strip on the back of the picture.

For a fee, publishers will reduce or enlarge the photograph as needed to fit the space left for it. You are responsible for typing the correct caption within the text and leaving the space for the photograph. If it does not require special sizing or cropping, most publishers then ask you to fix the photograph to the correct page, by either clipping the photo on the page it applies to or by using rubber cement adhesive (NEVER use scotch tape).

Extra long photographs may be reproduced as fold outs for an additional charge, fitted on a page sideways, or split down the middle to appear as a two-page spread.

Many people own clip art computer software programs today which add nice detail to their histories. Others scan photographs directly into their text. More information on scanning photographs into your histories will be covered later in this book.

Old newspaper clippings that contain photos and documents having a gray background will be treated as photographs. Again, if no special sizing is needed, do identify the items with the appropriate caption and type the caption in place on your manuscript allowing space for the document. Rubber cement any non-original documents in place yourself.

Page Layout

The bottom of this text includes the title of the book and a page number. This is called a *footer*. If the same information were given at the top of the page it would be called a *header or a running head*. Page numbers can be typed either in the bottom center or at the top left and right. Most word processing programs automatically do this for you.

Various indexing schemes will be covered under the computer software programs offered for converting family records to manuscript formats in Chapter Nine.

Paper

Quality books are made with high-quality, acid-free paper so the print will not fade over time. Acid free paper is available in a variety of colors but the white and natural (or off-white) are the most popular.

Any smooth-surfaced white paper is good for your paper. Most publishers do NOT suggest bond paper because of its irregular surface which will cause spotty reproductions.

Printing

If you are using a computer, a laser printer gives the nicest copies. If you have a letter-quality printer with a one-time carbon ribbon, it will give a nice look as well. An electronic or electric typewriter with a carbon ribbon is also satisfactory for putting together your book, but this approach means much more work on the part of the author.

Corrections can be made on your original as long as they are not visible after the correction is made. A very light shadow may not appear after the item is photographed, but smudges or smears will be very evident.

Since larger books use more film, paper and cloth, they cost more to produce. The most popular size with authors is the 6" x 9" size but they also come in a 5 1/2" x 8 1/2" size. Special formats such as that required by *Gen-Book* needs an 8 1/2" x 11" size.

There is a charge for "screening" any photographs included in your book. This allows photographs to be reproduced in books and there is a per picture charge since every photograph is treated individually because of the light and dark hues in the picture. The cost per photo will depend on the book size selected.

Most publishers require a minimum order for publication of about 100 copies. Gateway Press suggested ordering at least 300 copies since there was only an insignificant cost reduction for orders of fewer than that.

When calculating the number of pages in your book count ALL pages including the front materials (title, copyright, contents, acknowledgements, etc.), index pages, and any unnumbered and blank pages.

Binding

Case-bound books (or hard-back) are well constructed by having the pages first stitched, then cased-in with library quality cloth pasted over the binders boards.

Paperback titles are either "saddle-stitched" (stapled) or "perfect bound" (glued) and they can be printed in either glossy or non-glossy papers.

Cloth binding is much more durable than paper binding and increases the resale value of your book. Cloth binding must be used on books over 300 pages and paper binding is more appropriate for books with fewer than 96 pages.

Covers

Covers may be made of cloth, leather or a variety of artificial materials. The title and author's name may be stamped in gold on the spine.

Costs

Costs will vary all around the country, but I felt it was helpful to give you a "ballpark figure" so that you could decide on which option to pursue.

Let's talk about the mid to top-of-the line quality product in which you provide a camera-ready copy of approximately 950 pages to be printed on 50 pound, acid-free paper, Smythe-sewn and casebound

with nice linen-like cloth and the spine stamped in gold including 50 photographs. Approximate costs might be as indicated on the following page.

No. of Copies	8 1/2 x 11 Size	Price per Copy	7 x 10 Size	Price per copy
100	$9560.00	$95.60	$9005.00	$90.95
200	$10,500.00	$52.50	$9586.00	$47.93
300	$11,435.00	$38.11	$10,398.00	$34.66
500	$13,171.00	$26.34	$12,062.00	$24.12

Freight would be between $200-$400 and would be over and above the costs given here but most publishers would also do a limited amount of advertising if you print a large number of books.

Let us now compare this to a standard do-it-yourself printshop variety.

No. of Copies	8 1/2 x 11 Size	Price per Copy	7 x 10 Size	Price per copy
100	$			
200				
300				
500				

May I caution you not to base your final judgment on lowest cost alone. Consider the quality of the workmanship and the long-range potential. For class projects, of course, the less expensive method would be very appropriate. While you are doing your comparison shopping, ask if your local printer provides a service to print out your materials from a computer program to a laser copier and can they scan documents into your family history.

Selected Bibliography

Beach, Mark, Steve Shepro and Ken Russon. *Getting it Printed: How to Work with Printers and Graphic Arts Services to Assure Quality, Stay on Schedule and Control Costs*. Portland, OR: Coast to coast Books, 1986.

Hatten, Ruth Land. "Desktop Publishing." Session S-96. *Syllabus*. National Genealogical Society Conference in the States, 1988.

Hughes, Ann Hege. "How to Prepare Your Manuscript for Publication." Session F-65, *Syllabus*, National Genealogical Society Conference, 1989.

Norton, Don E. "Family History--Writing and Publishing." Pgs 104-116, *BYU Annual Genealogy and Family History Seminar*, Conferences and Workshops, 1989.

Chapter Three
Assignments: Designing Your Book

1.   Compare costs in your local community for producing a family
      history project the size you are contemplating. Include:
            cost of printing using archival quality paper,
                  cost per page,
                  front and back printed
            various types of binding,
            various coverings,
            the use of photographs,
            time involved to do the project, and
            printing on the spine and front.

2.   Does your local printing company produce your material onto a
      laser copier from a computer disk using your word processing
      program? Extra charges for this?

3.   Does your local company provide or scan clip art into your
      production for a fee? What is that fee?

4.   What format have you selected for your history?

      Margins
      Justification
      Font type and size
      Graphics
      Page layout
      Paper
      Printing method
      Binding
      Covers
      Estimated cost

LAB ASSIGNMENT 3:   Continuing to Use *WordPerfect*®

Go to WordPerfect®

Retrieving your document
F5; highlight **assnt2a; 1** OR Retrieve

Top of page
"Home" (twice) + "up arrow".

Changing margins
Shift + F8; 1 Line; **7** Margins left & right; change both right and left margin to 2" by typing **2** and **Enter** for the Left Margin. Type **2** and press **Enter** for the Right Margin.
Press the Exit[5] key **F7**.   Press "Down Arrow" to see what you've done

Reveal imbedded codes
Hold **Alt** key and strike **F3** function key. The upper portion of the screen displays your text and the lower screen revealing the text **and codes** in **bold** print.   **Alt + F3** removes reveal code option.

Centering
Shift key and **F6** - Center a title on your materials

Print
Shift key and striking **F7** and selecting **2-Page**.

Saving your document
F10 and at **Document to be Saved** type **a:assnt3** and **enter** and it will save to disk but leave you on the screen.

---

[5]Anytime you are told to "Exit" strike the **F7** function key.

Exit without saving

F7; at Save Document? Yes (No) select **N**o. Exit Doc 1? **Y** for yes you wish to exit Doc 1 and/or WordPerfect®.

CHAPTER FOUR

Picking Up Background Materials through Field Research

This Chapter will cover:

• The need for background information
• Setting goals in advance of your trip
• Locating the best repositories for information
• Learning about the locality you'll be visiting
• Organizing materials from your on-site visit
• Inter-Library Loan System (ILL)

Once you have laid out the design of your book, you will discover that information is missing in one or more areas. You will need to make at least one research trip, to either Salt Lake City or to the actual locality of an historical event being included in your family history in order to pick up some additional background materials.

Both *Genealogy and Computers for the Complete Beginner* and *Genealogy & Computers for the Determined Researcher* dealt with various research strategies for extending your pedigree. These beginning and intermediate texts covered in depth the use of the Research Calendar. The consistent and wise use of the Research Calendar is your greatest tool for outlining missing information and for solving difficult genealogy problems. If you still find

yourself stumbling over how to use a research calendar, review the chapters in those books and create a research calendar that reflects the current status of your research.

I have students who have been out of my classes for four or five years come up to me and indicate that they finally solved their research problem by using the research calendar. Before this time, they thought they knew what they wanted and where they wanted to go but found out that it didn't take long before they forgot what their goal had been and what steps they had already covered. Not only does the calendar give you a plan of attack, but it keeps track of your negative and positive findings. Finally, it can become an index to all previous articles, photographs and items you have researched. (A blank research calendar is included in the appendix of this book for you to copy. Don't forget to add your name and address to it in case it is misplaced.)

If you are preparing to visit a new locality for the first time remember these steps:

Setting Goals in Advance

Set goals and organize in advance of your journey to a new library or locality. This includes preparation of research calendars. Limit your research objectives by looking at your draft family history layout, and writing down specifically what it is you are seeking.

56

Locating the Best Repositories

Take your research calendars with you as you try to locate a guide to the particular library or location you plan to visit. Try to determine what people, books, films or fiche provide answers to your questions. Then try to determine the exact location of the records you need.

If you are visiting a library or research facility that is totally new to you, write several months in advance requesting information on services, holdings or where you might obtain a catalog of their holdings, special privileges, hours of operation, etc. Also inquire about nearby hotels in case you need to stay overnight.

Once you know something about their holdings, call or write requesting other specifics such as whether indexes exist for their specialized collections, are there other nearby repositories of similar records, or do they know of people who might be able to help.

Learn About the On-Site Locality

Applying the above techniques to a visit to the famous Family History Library in Salt Lake City, we would want to search the *Family History Library Catalog* at a local Family History Center, (look in the phone book under Church of Jesus Christ of Latter-day Saints), before we left our home town. We would put all the likely sources on Research Calendars, and learn as much about the Salt Lake facility as possible. The Family History Library has much to offer.

1. All the census records and nearly all the census indexes are available

2. Free classes are offered and specialists are available on various days of the week to aid in research.

3. Computer files (which may also be searched at local Family History Centers before going to save time for other things when in Salt Lake) can save a lot of searching time.

4. Rest rooms are on all floors. Elevators connect all floors. Photocopies run from $.05 to $.20 each depending on size and kind of machine and change is always available. Change machines are on all floors.

5. All U.S. fiche and microfilm are on the first floor up and this area is often less used than other areas. There are plenty of fiche and film readers. You can also take up to 5 rolls of film, plus books down to the main or first floor, where there is hardly ever a long line at the copy machines.

6. A snack bar is on the main floor.

7. Lockers to lock your items are on the U.S. floor.

8. Restaurants are all around the area.

9. On the same block as the Library but directly behind it, is a parking lot for $3.00 a day. Actually there is parking all around at various prices.

10. A City Information Center is on the same street as the Library. It will provide you with some great recreation ideas to keep the kids and spouse busy if they are not "INTO" genealogy like you are.

11. The heating and cooling system is designed to preserve books and films. Taking a light-weight sweater or jacket into any library is advisable. Depending on if you are doing a lot of sitting quietly (at which time the air conditioning might make you cold) or running around making copies (at which time you could take off the sweater), it is always advisable to have an extra layer of clothing along.

12. There are so many opportunities for research that you'll want to pack lightly to leave room to bring back photocopies of all you found. One medium size suitcase per two-week trip is adequate provided you can wash clothes once a week. Women: 1 silk-like wrinkle-resistant dress in the spring, summer, or early fall (there are marvelous free concerts and events in many cities, especially Salt Lake City), 1 skirt with 4 blouses, along with a sweater or jacket that goes with everything, and three pair of slacks. Tennis shoes or low shoes for all the running and heels for evening or with the skirt to dress up one day. The major criteria for sweaters or lightweight jackets is: they MUST HAVE POCKETS to carry change, pencils, etc.

13. Attire is informal. It's not necessary to dress up in the library. Shorts may be too informal (and too cool) in an air-conditioned library, however. Opportunities for nearby diversions. Men usually need a suit or sport jacket and tie for an evening activity, but it's not necessary to dress up in most libraries.

14. Staplers, paper cutters, and hole punchers are located near the photocopiers on each floor.

15. Be prepared to take back a lot of material. It is wise to take manila file folders (blank) to bring your research home in an orderly fashion. A bag of rubber bands are helpful when dealing with large stacks of slippery copies. Bring a spiral notebook for notes. (Use a separate page for each family surname and don't tear out any pages until you get home so you don't loose them). Don't waste time hand copying any items of substantial length. I either type them into my computer or photocopy them.

16. Bring 3 or 4 different colored high-lighters. (Different colors accent different surnames or areas as needed.)

17. You should also bring pens with erasers, paper clips, and address book with names and addresses of people you may need to contact while away.

18. Bring extra Research Calendars and forms you are used to using. Other forms can be purchased at the FHL.

As you can see, knowing some things in advance can make an on-site research trip much more enjoyable.

Organizing Materials From Your On-Site Visit

You will return from your on-site experience with a great deal of data. Pull it all together before you enter it into the computer by following these steps:

1. Place the documents copied with a copy of the family group record to which they belong into separate folders. You will probably have written notes on the family group record which also need to be entered into the computer.

Don't discard information until a new printout has been made and you verify that all the new information has been entered.

2. Pick up one item at a time and enter it into the PAF program under the person to whom it applies. Enter events in chronological order. Write the MRIN in pencil in the upper right hand corner of each document once it has been entered.

3. When finished with one folder, make a new printout of the family group record.

4. File the numbered documents behind the family group record (MRIN) it applies to.

5. File items which pertain to an entire surname under the surname section of your notebook.

6. Study the information in the notes and summarize briefly what new information you now know.
(a) Does this information lead you to new sources? If so, write these new research goals on a fresh research calendar before you forget.
(b) Has this information answered your goals? If so, state the conclusions you arrived at and why.

7. Continue this process until all information has been entered.

Inter-Library Loan System (ILL)

There are times when it will be impossible to travel to all the places you need to obtain information. If you have more time than money, consider borrowing books, films, etc. from other libraries. You can borrow any book on any topic but you need to work through your local librarian, and that can be the problem.

I've had the good fortune to have a ILL librarian working for me for several years. She is well versed in how to obtain materials but in many libraries that is not the case. The librarian may not be aware that such a service is possible and say that the particular book you are seeking is not available for loan at their library. However, while a California library might keep a California item in a special non-circulating collection, they might allow an Illinois book from their collection be part of the circulating stacks.

Any library is able to borrow books/materials from any other library that is willing to lend its materials by using either the **ILL** form or by an on-line computer service. The standard on-line services are networks that link member libraries.

Thousands of libraries around the world are linked by the *OCLC* and *RLIN* databases. These in effect serve as 2 giant card catalogs of library holdings. In the usual **ILL** request a library will look up the book on *OCLC*, find all of the libraries that own it and request it to be sent to the requesting library for your use. The key here is the experience of the librarian. The experienced librarian knows which libraries are likely to lend a book.

Genealogical and local history titles are most often lent by smaller college libraries that do not regard them as "special" items and keep them in their circulating stacks.

The Library of Congress has a policy that if a local library can demonstrate that it has tried and failed to borrow a book from other sources then it will lend its own copy of the item to the local library.

The Mid-Continent Public Library located at 15616 East 24 Highway, Independence, MO 64050 under the direction of Martha L. Meyers routinely issues a directory of genealogical titles that she loans titled "Genealogy from the Heartland". Many state libraries maintain special **ILL** collections of Local historical materials just to assist libraries in tracking down the items that their patrons need.

The Family History Centers of the Church of Jesus Christ of Latter-day Saints exists to loan microfilm/fiche copies of items held at the central library in Salt Lake City. It is an easy way to borrow items not widely held by public or college libraries such as copies of original vital records, probates, land and property and tax records.

There are also a number of commercial and non-profit groups that offer an **ILL** service as part of their membership. The New England Historic & Genealogy Society (NEHGS) is an example of one of these. Other groups advertise in the Everton's Genealogical Helper. AGLL (Bountiful, UT) is an example of a large commercial lending network.

Persistence and patience should enable you to obtain the items that you are looking for and you will get 99% of the items that you are looking for.

Selected Bibliography

_____. *Family History Library and Family History Centers*. Salt Lake City, UT: Church of Jesus Christ of Latter-day Saints, 1992.

_____. *News of the Family History Library*. Salt Lake City, UT: Church of Jesus Christ of Latter-day Saints, 1993-4.

Sperry, Kip. "An Overview of New England Records at the Family History Library, Salt Lake City, Utah" Pgs 139-155, *BYU Annual Genealogy and Family History Seminar*, Conferences and Workshops, 1989.

Chapter Four
Assignments: Picking Up Background Materials through Field
Research

1.   Using reference materials such as the Family History Library
      Catalog, add to your research calendars items you might wish
      to include in your draft family history to bring out the his-
      torical background and a better understanding of the family or
      to extend your ancestral lines.

2.   Using information gathered from a visit to any repository, use
      the 7 steps outlined to enter information into your computer
      data base.

3.   Show your Family History Notebook including a copy of your
      latest family group record with the accompanying documents to
      your teacher.

LAB ASSIGNMENT 4: Continuing to use *WordPerfect*®

Go to WordPerfect®; retrieve your document **F5**; highlight **assnt3**;
1 OR **Retrieve**.

Copy the entire contents of assnt3 twice by...

Coping, Moving or Deleting Blocks of Text
      At beginning, Mark text by **Alt+F4**
      Move the cursor to end of text
      Ctrl+F4 and **1** OR B for Block.
      Select** **2** Copy; move cursor to where item is to be placed
at the end of the first document and strike **Enter**

      (**Select either **1** Move **2** Copy **3** Delete or **4** Append.)

Indenting
      F4 at the beginning of the paragraph. Indent one paragraph
      in this manner.

Numbering Pages
      Move to the top of document by **Home** <u>twice</u>+up arrow.
      Shift+F8 for **Format** menu
      Select **2** = page format
      Select **6** = Page numbering
      Select **4** = Page number position
      Bottom center position = **6** + **F7** to exit

Finding a Word
      F2 plus type the word you want to find then **F2** again

Replacing Words
      Alt+ F2 and **Y** for confirm; **F2** each time comes up
      Change a word from lower case to upper case such as "Census"
to "CENSUS" with search and replace

Print, save your document & exit
      Shift+F7; 1-Document; **F7** and at Save Document? **y** then type
      a:assnt4

CHAPTER FIVE

Contracting Out Some of the Research

This Chapter will cover:

- When to hire professional services
- How to find a researcher
- What to do in advance
- How to contact a researcher
- What you should expect to pay
- What you can expect from a researcher
- What to expect to have sent to you
- Suggestions to help the researcher
- How to evaluate a research report
- What to do if you are unhappy with a researcher

Do you wish to add historical background, humorous stories or true-life adventures, pictures, or other interesting tidbits to your family history but cannot get to the locality on your own. Perhaps this is the time to look into the services of a professional genealogist.

When to Hire Professional Services

There are times in anyone's genealogy when they may find it advantageous to hire a researcher. Even professional researchers hire other researchers. There are several reasons for doing this:

1.   When on-site research needs to be conducted.

2.   When a record repository does not do research for others, so you must send someone there.

3.   When a repository reports that it did not find a record that should be there.

4.   When it is cheaper to have a researcher do the work than to have staff in the repository do the work.

5.   When it is faster to have a professional researcher do the work.

6.   To receive expert advice on how to continue research in an area that you are unfamiliar with or to receive help with a foreign language problem.

7.   When an expert is more familiar with the sources available than you may be.

How to Find a Researcher

An excellent source for finding a researcher is the free list of *accredited* genealogists available from your local Family History Center or by writing to the Family History Library, 35 North West Temple Street, Salt Lake City, Utah 84150. These individuals have passed an eight-hour written exam, oral exam, and have submitted a four-generation family history prior to 1870 in their area of specialty. If researchers have passed this accreditation test, you can be relatively assured they know at least the basic, fundamental information necessary to do research in their area of specialty.

Another source is the list of *Certified* researchers approved by The Board for Certification of Genealogists. To obtain this list, write to The Board for Certification of Genealogists, P.O. Box 19165, Washington, D. C. 20036-0165 and send $3.50.

One way to find a record searcher in a particular locality is to check with area libraries, societies or archives. The *FHL Research Outlines* for each of the United States, as well as the *Handy Book for Genealogists*, will give you names and addresses of major repositories in those states. You can then correspond to those societies or libraries and request a list of researchers whom they might recommend.

A fourth reference source is the *Directory of Professional Genealogists* put out by the Association of Professional Genealogists, 3421 M Street, N. W., Suite 236, Washington, D. C. 20007. The cost is $15.

You can also ask other genealogists for recommendations or check ads in the *Genealogical Helper* periodical. Be aware, however, that there is no guarantee of the qualifications of a researcher who advertises in this magazine or in other periodicals.

What To Do In Advance

First, organize all your records and then analyze your problem thoroughly. You should have written down all records that you have already searched and what records you would like to research. Then send your genealogist everything you know about the problem you want solved. This background information should include:

1. A pedigree chart and family group records that include the names of spouses, brothers and sisters, names of known children; birth, marriage and death certificates, or abstracts that you have typed into your notes; and abstracts of all obituaries and funeral cards.

2. A photo copy of foreign documents if you are not sure of what they say.

3. Any family histories or traditions, occupations, military records, and any known residences of the ancestor. Also send any copies of research calendars and reports that you or others have already done.

How to Contact a Researcher

One of the easiest ways to make initial contact is to use a form letter addressed to several researchers. Ask them about their fees by the hour, by the day, or by the project, and ask if there are additional charges.

Some of the charges for services that a genealogist may provide (and for which the client may be billed) include: Consultation time; writing letters, reports and family histories or biographies; instructing other agents to do special research; long distance telephone calls; responding to correspondence; analyzing the research; search fees that may be required at libraries, court houses, archives, cemeteries, and churches; fees for copying military or pension records; field research and travel expenses; photography; postage; supplies; photocopies; and clerical expenses for such secretarial, typing, and bookkeeping services.

Ask if a retainer is necessary. Tell the researcher specifically what you wish them to do and be sure to place in writing what you expect to pay for each project. Remember, that in paying for photocopying you will be paying for two copies. One that will be sent to you and one that the researcher will keep in order to continue the research.

Many researchers do require a retainer in advance. This enables them to cover fees and costs that are necessary to begin research.

What Should I Expect To Pay?

Fees vary considerably. They range anywhere from $10 to $75 per hour. The average fee currently is between $10 and $40 per hour for United States researchers. Many researchers prefer to charge a flat daily fee such as $100 to $300. This is for an eight-hour work day so the per hour costs are usually comparable to hourly rates.

What You Can Expect From A Researcher

Some people feel that the genealogists they hired did not deal honestly with them when they didn't find anything new. No one can honestly predict how many generations he or she will be able to find. Every genealogical problem is unique. Some are easy to solve because the records are readily available, while others are more difficult because some records may have been destroyed or are in a large city which often makes record hunting tedious and time consuming. Some surnames such as Johnson, Baker and Smith require much more research time. Researching common names is not impossible, but it is very time consuming and may cost more money.

73

In all cases, you should expect professional researchers to be qualified, knowledgeable and experienced in the particular area

where your ancestor lived. They should know how to locate and search the needed records and be able to do the research efficiently in a reasonable amount of time.

What To Expect To Have Sent To You

You should receive a research report explaining all the searches that were made and the results of those searches. This report should include not only the new findings, but also a list of sources he or she searched that were unproductive. Also there should be suggestions for continued research. You should also receive a research calendar showing a complete list of all searches that were made.

You should also receive copies of all the researched documents, either as a photocopy or an extract. The researcher will need to retain a duplicate copy of everything for future reference. An abstract may be very appropriate when the original is faded or otherwise illegible. Finally, the researcher should send you an updated family group record or pedigree chart based on the new information which was found.

Suggestions To Help The Researcher

If you have a set time by which you want this information received, be sure to notify the researcher. Often researchers are working on many clients at a time. They schedule their time in order to save you money by going to repositories in which several research topics can be done at once for many clients. This is especially true if you are only paying for an hour's worth of work in a library that is many miles away. If you are in a hurry, the researcher may be able to accommodate your schedule, but will have to charge more.

Because of economics of scale, it is less expensive to pay a researcher in larger payments that allow the researcher to do a larger block of investigation rather than small $50 portions in which the researcher must repeatedly stop and report to you before proceeding.

How To Evaluate A Research Report

There are at least seven areas that should be analyzed in order to evaluate a report.

1. The time devoted to producing it.

2. Adequate coverage of the sources available.

3. Thorough analysis of the problem.

4. Setting a defined research goal and following the directions of the client.

5. Excellent citations and very few typographical errors, properly put together; in other words, the clerical aspects.

6. The quality of the report itself. (Is the report well organized and clear? Is it creative and innovative in style? Is it skillfully written?

7. Did the researcher give you good direction on the next steps to continue your research?

A poor research report indicates a likely lack of acceptable knowledge of sources and methods which could invalidate most of the researcher's work. An unsatisfactory researcher may work on lines that were not specified by the client, may have poor writing skills with no creativity, may not demonstrate any original research ideas, or give no indication of what to do next. A very unsatisfactory project may need to be redone.

In contrast, an excellent report will use a broad range of sources, including obscure sources not known to hobbyists, and good use of other researchers and correspondence. The researcher should write skillfully, use good sentence structure, be well organized and clear; and use a creative, innovative approach in responding to the goals set by the client. It should be clear that the researcher read the client's correspondence, determined exactly what the client desired, and then addressed all the questions that were asked. No corrections should be needed, citations should be complete, copies should be legible, and there should be no duplication of prior research unless an important reason for doing so is stated. Lastly the report should be turned in on time and the fee charged should be acceptable.

What To Do If You Are Unhappy With a Researcher

First of all, tell the researcher why you are dissatisfied. The problem may be the result of a simple misunderstanding or an inadvertent omission. If the researcher is not willing to address your concerns, tell the library or society which sent you the name. And please don't condemn all researchers because of one unhappy experience. Haven't we all, at one time or another, been dissatisfied with the medical advice of a doctor we visited?

Chapter Five
Assignments: Contracting Out Some of the Research

1. Using the steps outlined in this chapter, write a general form letter as though you were considering hiring a genealogy professional.

2. Write a second letter as though you had selected a specific researcher and were asking him/her to do your research. Attach copies of all information you would send with this letter.

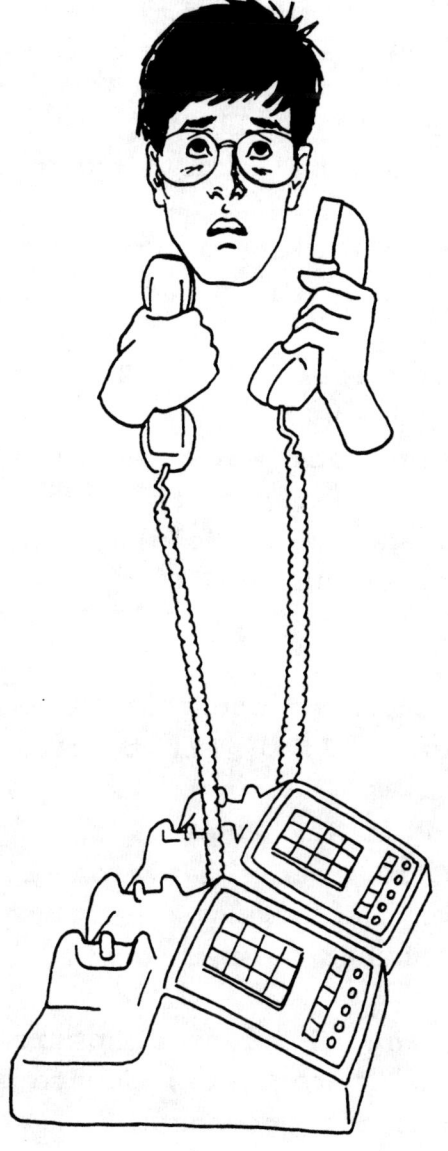

LAB ASSIGNMENT 5: Continuing to use *WordPerfect*®

Go into WordPerfect®; retrieve **F5**; highlight **assnt4**; **1** OR
Retrieve; center **Shift+F6** this title: LAB ASSIGNMENT 5.

Changing Font Sizes Make the title in large print
    Alt+F4, highlight the part of word, words, paragraphs or pages
    you desire to change
    Ctrl+F8 (font) + **1** (size) + **6** (very large))
    More font size changes: Alt+F4, highlight the part of word,
words, paragraphs or pages your desire to change, **Ctrl+F8+1** (size)
+**1** (Super-Script=above the line), **2** (Sub-Script=below the line),
+**3** fine, +**4** small, +**5** large, +**6** very large, or **7** extra large.
Select various words on your screen and do each option.

Preview your document: Shift+F7 and at menu press **v** for view
    To exit the print menu and return to the document press **F7**.

Changing Your Mind - Esc key

Changing Font Appearance: Alt+F4, highlight the part of word,
words, paragraphs or pages your desire to change, **Ctrl+F8+2**
(appearance) +**1** (Bold), **2** (underline), + **4** italics, + **6** shadow.
Select various words on your screen and do each option.

Default font
    At top of document **Ctrl+F8**. Select **4** - Base Font; change or
    exit **F7; OR F10** to save format

Forcing A New Page
    Ctrl+enter Leave one blank page in the middle of four pages
    on the screen. Put cursor on that blank page and retrieve
    another page into it.

Combining Files or Chapters
    F5 to retrieve; locate **assn2**; **1** OR Retrieve; Retrieve into
    current document? **Y**.

Print, save your document & exit; **Shift**+F7; **1**-Document; **F7** and at Save Document? **y** then type **a:assnt5**.

CHAPTER SIX

Collecting Background Information
Through Oral Histories

This Chapter will cover:

- Advantages of Oral Histories
- Whom to interview
- The order of events
- Sample topics
- The unwilling informer
- Physical arrangements
- Length of time
- Recording techniques
- Equipment
- Effective questioning
- Conducting the Interview
- Sample interview plan
- Transcribing an Oral History
- Editing an Oral History

Other valuable information might be added to your family history through simple conversations with individuals. The product of such interviews is called an "oral history".

You have probably dealt with numerous examples of written or published sources, but have you ever considered the advantages of oral histories? Oral histories not only jog the mind of interviewees so that they may remember clues about the past that help extend the research, but they also put life and substance onto the skeleton pedigree charts that are the framework of the family history.

Advantages of Oral Histories

The main advantage of oral histories is that things are captured that might not otherwise be recorded down. There is marvelous detail, joy, and enthusiasm all recorded in the actual words of the individual who lived the history you are recording. Even if you don't return the actual recording as part of the family history, it is nice to have their own phraseology captured on notes or a transcription..

Whom Should You Interview

Who is to be interviewed depends on what you want to know. If you want to learn more about yourself try interviewing your parents. Ask them what you were like as a child. Ask your older brothers and sisters what you were like as a child or adolescent.

If you want to find out about your spouse interview his or her parents or siblings. If you want to find out about your relatives contact their parents, grandparents, aunts, uncles, or any other relatives old enough to have known them.

If you are trying to learn more about the history of the town your ancestors came from, the business they owned or worked in, the college they attended, the church they supported, etc., interview current or past leaders, co-workers, alumni, or clergy.

If you cannot personally do this, look for related oral histories in local and regional libraries.

The Order of Events

Many people worry about how to start their history. Sequence is not critical because the transcriber can easily reorganize items later. An agenda, however, is good. By giving the interviewee an agenda ahead of time he/she has time to recall details. It should not hamper a free flow of recollection, however. Successful interviewing requires preparation <u>and</u> a willingness to deviate from your plans.

Sample Topics

If a complete life story is conducted, a general overall plan is very helpful. Sometimes a chronology of events is perhaps the easiest.

Sometimes it is helpful to have a few ideas to start with before embarking on a new project. Here are some topics you might wish to consider:

A.   Earliest remembrances
     Childhood activities and playtime
     Elementary school experiences
     Family activities

B.   Teenage years
     High school
     First job
     Learning to drive
     Meeting spouse
     Wedding plans, honeymoon, adjusting to in-laws

C.   First home
     Arrival of children
     Further education, training, or job skills
     Job advancements
     Memorable experiences with the family

D.   Church service, community service
     Life experiences [tragedy, wars, hope, despair, joy]
     Advice to posterity

Background research is very helpful. Use pictures from the family scrapbook, maps, or memorabilia to get the conversation started and then practice interactive listening.

Ideas for Children. There are also ways to interest children in doing oral histories. Let the children ask the grandparents about who is who in the old family album with the tape recorder already set up in the background. Don't be formal. Record discussions right after the Thanks-giving dinner or at a Christmas gathering. Use the kind of tape recorder with a built-in microphone so that people will not be intimidated. Don't forget to use a pencil to write names and the date on the back or sides of any pictures discussed, as to who is who. Finally, follow the lead of the

discussion. If they mention a song they used to sing get everyone to sing it. This involvement will get everyone involved and elicit more memories.

The Unwilling Informer

Most people will come around if you are patient after approaching them. Give them a few days, if necessary, to get used to the idea. They will probably not be sure you really want to hear what they have to say. Be sure to express your eagerness to hear what is to be said.

When the day arrives to set up, proceed confidently to set up and start the tape recorder. Awkwardness is common in doing something new, so practice ahead of time and this step will hardly be noticed. Soon you will both be quite at ease and forget a tape recorder is even running.

Physical Arrangements

The most important considerations are that you are comfortable and that the informant is in familiar surroundings. Then, there are just a couple of other details to plan for. Place the microphone or tape recorder on a soft or padded surface as close to the informant's mouth as possible without creating awkwardness (this is usually about 2-3 feet away). The interviewer will want to have the on-off switch close to him to keep track of the tape, etc. without too much trouble. You might place a card table or TV tray, with a towel under the recorder, slightly to the side, between you and the informant.

Length of Time

A comfortable friendly visit can last up to two hours, but after that it can get rather tiring. Be sure you've set aside at least that much time, so you don't feel rushed, but be considerate and don't stay too long.

Recording Techniques

Use high-quality, 60-minute cassette tapes with 30 minutes on a side. Longer tapes are very thin and not as durable. Thin tapes are more likely to stretch, garbling the recording and to tangle in the recorder, making them unusable.

Practice so you know that the recording volume (and the recorder) is sensitive enough to capture what is said in the configuration you plan to use. Label the tape with the date, place, and who was interviewed. Interview one-on-one or in small groups clustered around a table.

Obtain a good quality recording by avoiding interfering noises such as fans, heaters, clocks, TV's, children, telephones, and closing doors.

Equipment

Tape. The kind of tape you use depends on what you want to do with the tapes. Do you intend to store them for a permanent historical record, transcribe the contents and reuse the tapes, reproduce the tape for others, or play them frequently or periodically. Determine about the time limit you have so you don't run out of tape and have enough tapes to record the whole interview.

86

Recorders. There are many sufficient and inexpensive recorders usually under $125. These are used for tapes which will not be reproduced, only shared with a few individuals in small groups at most.

Mid-range recorders (for the serious amateur historian) cost anywhere between $150-$250. These tapes may be reproduced, shared with family members, or preserved.

High-quality recorders can cost $225 and up. They are used to provide tapes that will be professionally reproduced and shared with others, be repeatedly played, moved to large groups where excellent sound quality is required, or stored for a permanent history.

The extra features found on a recorder includes a pause switch, battery-operated for unusual settings only, normal use of electric current, a good microphone (either built in or on a separate cord...nice to have both), and a ten foot extension cord. Expensive machines also have foot controls, headsets, tone, and speed controls to slow down the recording when transcribing difficult to understand phrases.

Tape Storage. Store tapes in a cool, dry area with relatively even temperatures. Stand tapes on their edge. Tapes can be kept flexible by fast-running them through a machine yearly. Shelf life is about ten years.

Effective questioning

There are several ways to ask questions, and the way you ask has an impact on how it will be answered. The simplest questions to ask and answer are yes/no questions. Yes/no questions have one principle use and one major disadvantage. If the informant is very reticent to begin talking a yes/no question is usually a good way to get a response.

The major disadvantage of these questions is that they do nothing to keep the interview going. If you ask a yes/no question, always be prepared to follow it with a "wh—" or "how" question that will require a longer answer. Remember, a few yes/no questions may get things started, but a series of yes/no questions without follow up will not start a conversation. Instead, too many of these questions will make your friendly interview feel like a survey or, even worse, an inquisition.

"Choice" questions, like yes/no questions, are easy to answer. They present a limited set of options, but they are better conversation starters. A choice question such as, "In school, were you more of a serious student or a goof off? is more likely to generate a lengthy response than the yes/no question, "Were you a serious student?"

The best questions to elicit extended responses are "open-ended" questions. These questions are easy to create if you simply remember to start each with a "wh—" question word (who, what, where, when, why) or with "how." "How did you feel about school?" is probably going to be a better interview question than either of the two version above.

Conducting the interview

A good interview has three phases: the warm up, the body, and the conclusion.

The purpose of the warm up is to establish rapport with the informant and to build momentum that will carry you into and through the more substantive questions that will follow. As mentioned above, yes/no and choice questions may work well to get things started or to change topics.

As you move into the body of the interview it is important to follow the informant's lead and ask questions related to things he or she is interested in rather than strictly following the questions you planned in advance. A critical skill in keeping the conversation going is "interactive listening."

We all feel more like talking when we know that someone is listening. Interactive listening is the skill of showing through your interactions with the informant that you are listening and interested in what is being said. You can do this through head nodding and short utterances ranging from "Uh huh, and then ..." to short summaries of what was just said like "So you walked to school everyday?" What you should not do is take over the conversation and do most of the talking.

Another skill that requires some sensitivity is knowing how to probe for additional information. Usually, interactive listening with genuine interest will be all that is needed. Be careful not to give the impression that the informant is under pressure to give the right answer. Questions like "How did you feel about ...?" or "What do you think of ...?" are generally non-threatening, because a there is no single correct answer. If informants avoid answering questions, it may be because they don't know the answer or because they don't want to answer. In either case, remember how you'd feel in the same situation and don't force the issue. Maybe someone else will be more willing to discuss this topic.

The third phase of the interview should not be omitted. Although the conclusion phase is not likely to add any new information, it is an essential part of the interview. Use it to confirm points you weren't sure about, express your thanks, make the informant feel good, bring the discussion to closure, and get permission to call back with additional questions if necessary.

Don't hesitate to interrupt AT NATURAL PAUSES to check on a spelling of a name or clarify a point, but keep your own comments to a minimum.

Allow time for pauses as the informant thinks. Respond naturally to your informant's remarks or the conversation becomes awkward. Non-verbal responses and comments show interest and enthusiasm, give guidance and draw out necessary details.

(Sample Interview)

An Immigrant's Child

GOAL: What do you know about your immigrant ancestors?

After filling out a pedigree chart starting first with the informant, the informant's parents, grandparents, etc., until the immigrant ancestors are listed, set up an agenda of items to discuss such as these:

"Did you ever personally know any of your immigrant ancestors?"

IF YES...

"Did they speak English?"
"Did they think it was important to speak English?"
"Did they come to America with a group, with family members or by themselves?"
"Do you know the first city they settled in?"
"Why did they come to America?"
"When did they arrive in America?"
"How did they get here?"

IF NO...

"Do you know what country they came from?"
"Have you heard any interesting stories about them?"
"Have you ever attended family reunions or picnics with your relatives?"
"Do you know if any of them changed their names to make them sound more American?"
"Do you know who in the family has records about the original immigrant ancestor?"
"Do you have any words in your vocabulary that have been used by your
        ancestors...any special meanings to them?"

"Do you eat any special ethnic foods, because of family or holiday traditions?"
"What countries do these foods come from?"
"What different ingredients are in these foods that make them traditionally part
               of the recipe?"
"Are there any special ethnic crafts you have learned?"
"Who taught you how to do them?"
"Have you ever heard folk songs from your immigrant ancestor's home? When and
               where did you hear it/them?"
"Have you ever seen anyone dance folk dances from your immigrant ancestor's area?"
"Does your family have any ethnic celebrations? When do they take place?"
"Have you ever visited your ancestors' homelands? Where did they come from?"
"Would you like to visit a special place sometime? Where?"
"What would you like to see?"
"Do you know anyone who lives in your ancestral homelands?"

Transcribing an Oral History

There are only eight steps to transcription of the oral
history tape:

1. Typing the information off the tape.
2. Editing the script.
3. Proofing the edit with the tape.
4. Reviewing with the informant the final transcription.
5. Preparing the final copy.
6. Adding pictures, maps, family history charts, etc. with
    the aid of the informant.
7. Producing a printed or video mini-history or putting it
    together with other materials for a complete family
    history.
8. Making the history available to others.

Transcribing Equipment

Ideally a computer word processor should be used when
transcribing the oral history. If one is not available, a
typewriter is sufficient. If you are not so fortunate as to have
playback equipment that allows the transcription to be done with
the aid of a foot pedal, use the "pause" button on your tape
recorder. A tape counter is also helpful so you can mark and

return to places of interest on the tape.

Step One. 1. Transcribe the document verbatim at first. Once the interview is transcribed, edit the text to eliminate "false starts" and stammerings. Then use the text to ask clarifying questions. 2. Listen to a short segment, as much as you can remember accurately, then write it down. Sometimes you may need to listen ahead several sentences to figure out what was said and then return. 3. It is helpful to double space so you have room to make corrections. 4. The editor may combine, rearrange, emphasize, delete and otherwise rework what another has spoken or written so that the intended meaning emerges, in the language as close as possible to that of the informant.

Step Two. A skilled editor will enhance the informant's statements by making them clear, connected, and carefully put together as the informant would have done had he not been speedily going through many disjointed situations at a time.

Two important points to keep in mind are: what was the informant's meaning and what was his intent.

Step Three. Review your transcription once more to insure the retention of all essential words and phrases. Keep most sentences intact, but combine all essential wording into simple, direct sentences of various lengths and construction. Remove run-on's or sentences that go on and on with "and's" and "then's". Divide the script into logical paragraphs and chronology.

Draw together under a clear heading all information on one event or time period. Drawing arrows may be sufficient for moving paragraphs on some transcriptions, but using scissors and scotch tape can be even better. Here is where a word processor works wonderfully.

Begin by scanning your text and jotting in the left-hand margin each separate topic taken up. Write on a separate sheet all the topics in a rough out-line manner. Cut into pieces those that are not continuous and put them in order with scotch tape or a stapler. Finally rearrange the text on your word processor.

Step Four. Give the tape and the transcription to the informant and advise him to keep in mind two questions: 1) Does the written text "sound" like the informant? and 2) Does the writing say what the informant meant?

Step Five. Prepare the final copy by printing out or typing onto acid-free paper. Acid free paper for the creation and storing of important documents is available at stationary stores. Make several copies.

Step Six. Decide if you are going beyond the transcript to include this in your other histories, in a video history or adding pictures, charts or maps.

Step Seven. Let others know of your plans. Announce it in your holiday letters. Include an order form with name and address and how many copies are desired. State the cost, including the postage and handling. If you plan to recover your printing costs, request that readers pre-pay their orders. Shop around for the best quality and prices.

Editing an Oral History

Edit your oral history as soon as possible after the interview so your memory can fill in the blanks. If necessary, change the text to make it coherent but retain as much of the original as possible. You could change the questions to be part of a statement and a flowing narrative. For example:

Interviewer:	Where were you born?
Informant:	In Guernsey County, Ohio.
Edited version:	I was born in Guernsey County, Ohio.

Omit "uh's", excessive "and's", or "you know's", etc. Do short segments at a time. Listen then transcribe it. Use complete sentences in logical sequence. Use simple transitional words and phrases to create a logical flow. Headings will help to point out important transitions.

Transcribe the final copy on acid free paper. Don't put off printing and distributing the transcript. Living relatives can make corrections and enjoy your work, and dead relatives can't.

Adding Interest to Your Transcribed History

Family pictures, postcards, county histories, and maps from public and private libraries, family history centers, and correspondence with county historical societies can add interest to your transcribed history.

Selected Bibliography

Embry, Jessie L.   "Oral History and Historical Research."   Pgs. 170-175, *Annual Family History and Genealogical Research Conference*, Brigham Young University Conferences and Workshops, 1984.

_____ "Guidelines for Conducting an Oral History Interview,"   Pgs.   175-181, *Annual Family History and Genealogical Research Conference*, Brigham Young University Conferences and Workshops, 1984.

_____ "Transcribing,   Editing   and   Publishing   Oral History,"   Pgs.   182-187, *Annual Family History and Genealogical Research Conference*, Brigham Young University Conferences and Workshops, 1984.

Chapter Six
Assignments: Collecting Background Information Through Oral
Histories

1.   Do your own oral mini-interview. Sample topics might include:

    WHY I CHOOSE TO WRITE A FAMILY HISTORY
    MY DAILY LIFESTYLE: a typical Sunday, vacation, or
        weekday
    FAVORITE FAMILY FOODS: childhood foods, holiday foods,
        philosophy of nutrition
    INVENTIONS/ADVANCES: medicine, dentistry, video, TV

2.   Conduct an oral interview to include in your family history.

Include the following items:

    1.   Write an agenda of questions you could ask.
        (a) (Make sure that most are not yes/no questions)
        (b) Add follow up "Wh--" or "How" questions for all
            yes/no questions.
    2.   Set up and conduct the interview.
    3.   Play back the tape. Keep the tape.
    4.   Transcribe it using *WordPerfect* or another word
        processing program able to be used by the computer
        program you will be using to do your family history.
    5.   Edit the interview.

THOSE OLD PICTURES

"Distinguished" is how I'd describe his military suit,
Could the baby be a boy or girl in a gown so very cute?
Here is someone's granny, with the prim and proper hat;
And this must be a man in pain by the very way he sat.

No names to tell us who they are, or from whence they came.
I know they must be relatives, because somehow
we're the same.
No dates, no scenes I recognize, it's a down-right mystery,
These branches needing grafting to my growing family
tree.

LAB ASSIGNMENT 6: Continuing to use *WordPerfect®*

Go into WordPerfect®; retrieve **F5**; highlight **assnt5**; **1** OR Retrieve
Assnt5. Flush right your name, assignment 6, and date.

Deleting blocks of text
>   Mark text by **Alt+F4**; move the cursor to end of text
>   **Ctrl+F4** and **1** OR B for Block.
>   Select **3** Delete

Headers
>   **Move to the top of document** by Home <u>twice</u>+up arrow.
>   **Shift+F8** for **Format** menu
>   Select **2** = page format
>   Select **3** = headers
>   Select **1** = header 1
>   Select **2** = every page
>   Center **Shift + F6** and give a title to your work; **F7** exits.

Start with new page number
>   **Move to the top of the page 2**
>   **Shift+F8** for **Format** menu
>   Select **2** = page format
>   Select **6** = page numbering
>   Select **1** = new page number
>   Type **10**; **enter** and **F7** to exit

Print, save your document & exit
>   **Shift+F7**; 1-Document; **F7** and at Save Document? **y** then type
>   **a:assnt6**

CHAPTER SEVEN

Making International Connections

This Chapter will cover:

- Clues in American Sources
- Research Strategies
- Evaluation of Information

Because most people publish their first family history at that point in their research where their ancestor arrived in the country, introductory techniques for making an international connection possible will be covered in the next two chapters.

It is also one of the most common requests of a United States genealogist to help a client trace a line back to its origins outside of the United States. Once that is accomplished, the client next requests information on the exact foreign town their ancestor came from so that they might go to that place and hopefully visit relatives who have remained there.

Clues in America

It is usually through United States resources that overseas linkages are substantiated. Finding the exact town or parish of an immigrant ancestor requires a basic knowledge of:

1. **The ancestor's complete name.** Often names are changed when the immigrant enters this country. Middle names may not be used on every record so a combination of records may need to be checked to find all the given names as well as the correct spelling of the surname. It is sometimes necessary to learn name variations that might also be used in the country of origin.

Names Changed to Sound the Same
(Finnish)
Kamsula to Kampsula
(German)
Hätig to Hettich

Patronymic Changes
(Danish)
Svenby (farm name used as a surname)
to Davidson (because grandson of David)

Some German Surname suffixes contain clues to regional origin: "bach" from southwest Germany; "burg" throughout Germany; "haus" from Westphalia; "ecke" from Hesse and Thuringia; "ingen" from Bavaria; and "ski/zke" from East Pomerania.

2. **A date to associate with an ancestor.** This might be a birth, christening, marriage, confirmation, military release, or some other date. If the immigrant was alive in 1900 and living in the United States, the 1900 census will even give the month and year of birth. If the person was naturalized,  the naturalization application may give the date of birth. If the individual was an indentured servant, his indenture papers

might give his age. Many types of documents provide this information.[6]

3. **The ancestor's general geographic area.** Although finding the country of origin is helpful, a region, state, or province is even better. This may come from the 1880-1920 census records, obituaries, death records, cemetery records, newspapers, or family records, or numerous other sources.

   Often family records contain the name of the country in its native spelling such as: Deutschland (Germany), Eire (Republic of Ireland), Sverige (Sweden), Bystrou Moravia (Czechoslovakia), or Cechy (Bohemia). You may need to ask someone to help you find the correct locality or look at samples in this book. Be careful - sometimes locality definers are mistaken for localities themselves such as the German word for district (Kreis), the Swedish word for parish (Socken) or the Hungarian word for county (Megye).

4. **Other relatives or friends of the ancestor.** The records of those who came with your ancestor from that same area might provide more exact clues than you can find about your own ancestor (see also Table 7.1). This is why it is necessary to trace entire families as you prepare your family history.[7]

---

[6]Karen Clifford, *Genealogy and Computers for the Determined Researcher* (Baltimore: Clearfield Company, Inc., 1993).

[7]Ibid.,

Table 7.1 Foreign Group Connections

BLACK DUTCH: A term I have heard and explained numerous ways in the past few years is "Black Dutch." Many people believe they are of "Black Dutch" ancestry, but they do not agree whether the term refers to Spanish-Dutch ancestry, Black Forest origin, connections to Scots-Irish or French ancestors, or intermingling with Indian background. An in-depth study of families claiming Black Dutch descent is being undertaken to further clarify these traditions. If you believe you have Black Dutch ancestry, please contact Datarace Systems, P.O. Box 1587, Stephenville, TX 76401 or call (817) 965-6979.

HESSIANS: German troops used by the British during the Revolutionary War. Many deserted and remained in America.

HUGUENOTS: French Protestants that fled persecution from 1685 onward. They went to Prussia, the German Palatinate, England, Ireland and then to America. Some also went from the French West Indies to the southeastern coast of America.

MENNONITES: A Swiss Protestant sect founded in 1525 who migrated by way of Alsace, England and Russia to America to settle in Pennsylvania, Minnesota, and Kansas.

MORAVIANS: Protestant group (United Brethren) formed in Bohemia about 1415. Spread to Poland, Prussia, Germany and England. They later went to Pennsylvania, North Carolina, and other American states.

QUAKERS: The Society of Friends was founded in England in 1648. Persecution brought them to New Jersey in 1675. Some 230 English Quakers founded Burlington, New Jersey in 1678. William Penn was granted Pennsylvania in 1681. Within two years about 3000 Quakers were in Pennsylvania.

SCOTCH-IRISH: Descendants of Presbyterian Scots placed in the northern counties of Ireland by British rulers early in the 17th century. Most came to America about 1718 until the Revolution. They settled in Pennsylvania, then to the south and west with the moving frontier.

WALLOONS: From southern Belgium. Their language was a French dialect. Cornelis May of Flanders, with about 40 families, came to America and settled Fort Orange. It is now known as Albany, New York.

5. **The neighborhoods the ancestor lived in here in the United States.** There are likely unrelated families who have traveled, intermarried, or worked with your ancestor and left more clues about the family's homeland.[8] For example, *Prussian Netzelanders and Other German Immigrants in Green Lake, Marquette & Waushara Counties, Wisconsin*[9] by Brian Podoll offers an alphabetical listing of those Prussian and German immigrants, and who gives their homeland birthplaces. They are broken down into the Prussian county or other German state from which they came.

6. **Religious affiliation of the ancestor.** This is important because in foreign countries most of the vital records were kept by the churches. Find clues from death records, burial places, marriage certificates, *Bible* entries, family and holiday traditions as to the ancestor's religious affiliation.

---

[8] Ibid.,

[9] Available from Heritage Books.

7. **Family traditions.** Even though many of these traditions may prove to be erroneous, they may also be based on some particles of truth that could lead to other clues. It is important to keep facts and traditions separated, but never totally disregard traditions until they are proven false.[10]

The exact town of birth for an immigrant is usually found more easily in the U.S. than searching in a shot-gun manner in the land of departure. Untrained genealogists often switch too quickly to records of the country of origin which lead to discouragement, expense, and erroneous conclusions. It is best to find clues or the actual place of birth in records in the country of arrival before switching to records of the homeland.

Several types of records give such clues: ship passenger lists, arrival lists, departure lists, dates of immigration, naturalization records and applications, probate records, church records such as arrival records for new parishioners, the 1920 census for Germanic countries, the 1820 and 1840 census records for new immigrants to this country, the tombstone, and obituaries.[11]

Research Strategies

It is assumed, since this is the third in a series of beginning, intermediate and advanced texts, that the same research strategies learned in the beginning will be applied to this problem, i.e.:

---

[10]Karen Clifford, *Genealogy and Computers for the Complete Beginner: A Step-by-Step Guide to the PAF Computer Program, Automated Data Bases, Family History Centers, and Local Sources*, (Baltimore: Clearfield Company, Inc., 1992)

[11]Ibid.,

104

1. **Preliminary Survey:** A search of compiled records has been undertaken to see if others have already located the place of origin. This includes researching printed family histories, local histories, large database collections such as *FamilySearch*, family newsletters and research documents, hereditary and lineage society materials biographies, and manuscript collections of family materials.[12] If you already know the country of origin, search biographies and genealogies published for that particular country or region. Germany and Sweden are two countries that have many of these lineage books.

2. **Original Research:** Conduct research in census records[13] for each locality where the individual lived during the time periods the individual lived there. Research vital, property, church, probate, and military records for the same locations and times.

3. **Evaluation:** Comb all documents for clues about the immigrant such as occupation, religion, friends (from names of witnesses, godparents, guardians, trustees and neighbors), regional locations of birth from census and vital records, and the same records for the female lines on a family[14].

    A Record Evaluation Form (See Table 5.1) might help you extract the crucial data you need. But remember, whenever possible, try to photocopy the record. An original copy is always preferable to a transcribed copy.

4. **Background Information Obtained:** At one time or another, all of us find ourselves in a geographic area about which we know very little. Whether you decide to hire someone else, or do the research yourself, you should become familiar with the

---

[12] Such as those found in the National Union Catalog of Manuscript Collections.

[13] See *Genealogy & Computers for the Complete Beginner.*

[14] Ibid.,   ; *Genealogy and Computers for the Complete Beginner.*

topography, history, language and culture of the area in question.[15]

This scenario may occur: You've done your preliminary survey and no one that you have researched as been able to "cross the waters." Everyone states that the family was German. However, as you have accomplished United States research in the census records (especially the 1920 which gave a more definitive description for Germanic birth places, see Table 5.2), as well as obituaries, family customs, etc., you feel that the family came from an area with a more clearly defined name than "Germany".

Background information on the Germanic areas indicated that Austria was the given country of birth prior to 1918 for anyone born in the provinces of the Austrian Empire and later on, the Austro-Hungarian Monarchy. At the end of WWI, this entity disintegrated into a number of different countries, and a birthplace listed as being in Austria may actually be in any of these modern-day countries.

You also found out that in the past, the following organizations in some of these successor countries of the Austro-Hungarian Monarchy and the Austrian Empire have been helpful in matters of genealogical research:

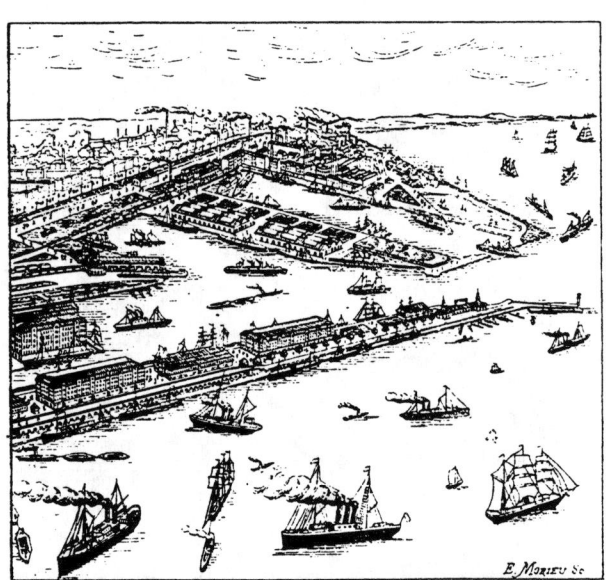

Archivni Sprava
Trida, Obrancy, Miru 133
Prague 6 CZECHOSLOVAKIA

Magyar Leveltar Orszagos
Becsi kapu ter 4
Budapest HUNGARY

Naczena Dyrekcja Archivwow
Panstwowych ul. Wilcza 9a
Warsaw 10 POLAND

---

[15]Ibid., ; *Genealogy & Computers for the Determined Researcher.*

106

If there are nobility in your line no matter what degree, it is advisable to contact:

> Heraldisch-Genealogische Gesellschaft Adler
> Landstrasse Haupstrasse 140
> A-1030 Vienna AUSTRIA[16]

Once the above sources have been researched, use the information gleaned to lead to other sources. For example, United States Federal Census records give clues such as those in Table 7.2.

---

[16]Information from the Austrian National Tourist Office.

Table 7.2 RECORD EVALUATION FORM   TODAY'S DATE_____

1. NAME OF RECORD OR DOCUMENT:	SOURCE TYPE:_____
	P = PRIMARY or S = SECONDARY

2. OTHER NAMES BY WHICH THIS RECORD IS KNOWN:

3. TIME PERIOD COVERED	4. PHYSICAL LOCATION OF RECORD	5. REFERENCE NUMBER

6. JURISDICTION THAT CREATED ORIGINAL RECORD:

7. TYPE OF RECORD: __MANUSCRIPT; __TYPEWRITTEN; __PRINTED; __OTHER:_____

8. PERSONAL NAMES PROVIDED IN THE RECORD:

9. KINDS OF DATES PROVIDED IN THE RECORD:

10. GEOGRAPHIC LOCATIONS PROVIDED IN THE RECORD:

11. RELATIONSHIPS BOTH BIOLOGICAL AND SOCIAL INDICATED:

12. EVENTS LISTED IN RECORD:

13. ABSTRACT OF INFORMATION, USE BACK IF NECESSARY:

EVALUATION PERFORMED BY:

Table 7.2 Description

1.   Identify the document: Directly on the document write a

description, the jurisdiction responsible for creating the document, and a reference to go back to for more information. Example: 1850 CENSUS: Greene Co., PA, FHL #345678, page 23. This information can be written on the top or bottom of the actual photocopy or it can be written on an attached note.

2. Fill out a Record Evaluation Form which includes the name of the record or document; other names by which the record might be known; time period covered; location of the record; call numbers, volume letters, page numbers; jurisdiction creating the record; type of record; all personal names on the record; kinds of dates on the record by type as well as date, e.g. date of death of so-and-so on a probate record; any geographical locations provided in the record, i.e. location of death of a person, location of residence, names of streams and rivers; relationships giving either biological or social relationships; and any events that were listed.

3. Analyze if the information listed is primary or secondary source information.

Primary or Secondary Source Information

a. Names: Primary if associated with the event for which the record was created, otherwise, mark secondary.

b. Dates: Primary if recorded immediately after the event occurred. Any other recording is secondary.

c. Geographical Locations: Primary if recorded immediately after the event and directly related to the location of the event.

d. Relationships: Primary if based upon the personal testimony of an informant who was living and whose name also appears in the record or whose signature was affixed to a record of an event.

e. Event: Primary if recorded at or near the time of an event by a responsible person and generally witnessed by two or more individuals.

Some types of records may be considered as primary on one occasion and secondary on another. The time elapsed between the event and the creation of the record is the major determining factor.

Table 5.2

U. S. CENSUS TERMS PLACES OF ORIGIN	FOREIGN EQUIVALENTS OF PLACES OF ORIGIN
Upper Canada	Ontario
Lower Canada	Quebec
Canada West	Ontario
Alsace-Lorraine (German speaking family)	That part of Germany now in France
Russia (Finnish speaking family)	Finland which was governed by Russia during time period in question
Russia (German Speaking family)	Could be German colonizers who lived in Russia

By now you may find yourself struggling with a foreign word or two. Word lists containing the basic geographic features and most commonly used genealogical terms are available for many of these foreign counties at local Family History Centers. Research outlines on foreign countries may be ordered for $.75-$2.00. Request form 34083, Family History Publications List, from the Salt Lake Distribution Center, 1999 West 1700 South, Salt Lake City, UT 84104-4233. Also request an order form, #33360.

Looking at a gazetteer could indicate several towns or parishes

with the same name. This is why it is important to watch for regional clues at the same time you are watching for the parish or town name. Many places changed their names as they were conquered by another people. French names became German, German names became Polish, Finnish names became Swedish, etc. Other names have evolved over time. History books covering regional areas will often clear up the mystery for you.

Once a word or term is identified, try to locate that place in a good gazetteer of that country. Find the closest large city as the immigrant may have indicated he was from that large city rather than a smaller parish or town nearby. Clues from the person's occupation could indicate that he was not from a city at all. For example a farmer would more likely be from a rural area. Occupation clues are found in family sources, census records, passenger lists, city directories and death records.

Again, be cautious. Sometimes the immigrant would indicate as his place of origin the port town he left from rather than his birth place. The most common port cities included Amsterdam, Antwerp, Bremen, Copenhagen, Gothenberg, Hamburg, Le Havre, Lisbon, Liverpool, London, Naples, Oslo, Rotterdam, Stockholm, and Trieste[17]. This information could lead to records of departure in that country.

---

[17]Family History Library, *Research Outline Tracing Immigrant Origins*, (Salt Lake City: Family History Department, 1992), 5.

As learned in United States research, spelling was not an exact science among our ancestors. Names might be phonetically spelled, misread and mistranslated by others, or contain special characters or letters of the alphabet that do not exist in English. Some very common variations are the German *ä* which often is made *ae* in English, the Czech *š* which may become *sh* or *sch*, and the Dutch *ij* which is usually written as *y*.[18]

I remember a student who was one of the first Americans to return to his ancestor's homeland of Lithuania. He was so excited and had already made several successful on-site research tours to American localities. He was surprised to learn that some documents involving his ancestors were written in 5 different languages on the same document. There might be Latin, Russian, or Polish with a Lithuanian dialect and written in an alphabet totally foreign to you. Thanks to the kindnesses of the archival leaders, he was guided through a maze of repositories to locate his family back to the 1600's.

There are many repositories available to assist you in locating the origin of your ancestor. Many of those were covered in the beginning and intermediate textbooks of this series. Also check archives and libraries such as the Immigration History Research Center at the University of Minnesota, the Swenson Swedish Immigration Center at Augustana College in Rock Island, Illinois, and the Ellis Island Family History Center. Other sources are mentioned in Elizabeth Petty Bentley's book, *The Genealogist's Address Book*.[19]

---

[18]Ibid., 6.

[19]Elizabeth Petty Bentley, *The Genealogist's Address Book*, (Baltimore: Genealogical Publishing Co., Inc., 1991).

There are also major book collections and indexes such as P. William Filby's *Passenger and Immigration Lists Index* which indexes over 3,000 published lists of immigrants from the earliest dates of United States history. Other major collections such as *German's to America*, *Italians to America*, and *The Famine Immigrants* focus on specific ethnic groups.

As mentioned briefly above, the 1920 census is very helpful for locating some areas of birth because the province or city of birth was recorded for those people born in Austria-Hungary, Germany, Russia or Turkey. The 1925 New York state census lists more information than the federal census does.

Tombstone inscriptions and records of the cemetery sexton sometimes give the birthplace. If you are fortunate enough, the village or parish will also be given. I have found birth towns given in Catholic cemeteries for Irish immigrants.

I have found marriage and death records to be the most helpful for clues or outright statements on the location of birth. Some religious denominations were very helpful in listing birth places, while others were not. Some entire religious units moved together so that if any one of the congregation could be located, the rest could be found nearby.

Foreign language newspapers published in the United States often contained obituaries or articles covering the death of individuals that included their birth towns and parishes. In some cases newspapers published advertisements for ship arrivals, for runaways, or for missing persons that mentioned their place of birth.

While researching a family in France, I used a local directory to find someone of that name in the area. Upon writing to them, I was lead to an individual who was related and a wonderful correspondence ensued. Computerized phone directories are now available for Germany[20] on compact disk from Phone Disc USA, 20 Edenville Rd, Warwick, NY 10990 and in France through Minitel and Geopatronyme computer services. If the name you are searching is uncommon enough, you may search the entire country of origin and narrow your search to areas where the name appears. Sometimes contacting the people using the AT & T translating service[21] may lead to at least the origin of the name in Europe which these people know from their own family traditions.

I live twenty minutes from the home base of the AT & T Language Line. This profoundly helpful service, is based in Monterey, CA because of two language schools in the area: the Monterey Institute of International Studies and the Defense Language Institute which is under the Department of Defense. There are many people in our area who speak and read 100's of languages.

---

[20]1990 West German Telephone Directories are now available on CD's. This enables genealogical researchers to determine where in the former West Germany people with the surname they are now researching live. Unlike the majority of their American counterparts, they do not consist of a single alphabetical listing. Instead each volume contains separate alphabetical listings for every locality in the area which it covers. The current telephone directories for united Germany, issued by Telekom, fill 118 volumes. Now instead of the page by page search, there is an easier method to locate relatives in the 11 states that make up what was formerly West Germany. If you wish them to do a search for you, ask for a form to request the information by writing to the German Genealogical Society of America, P. O. Box 291818, Los Angeles, CA 90029. Costs range from $2.00 to $15 (for 101-125 listings.)

[21]Send a good copy (not the original) of the item you wish translated to Translation Department, Language Line, 1 Lower Ragsdale Drive, Monterey, CA 93940. Include your name, address, area code and phone number. Within 48 hours the document will be examined and you will receive a price quote either by phone or mail. The minimum charge is $80 for translation of 250 words. There-after the charge is from $.21 to $.25 per word. More difficult languages in non-Roman script, such as Chinese, can cost more. Each translation is then proof read by two different individuals to insure accuracy. An invoice will be mailed to you. The complete process takes about 5 or 7 days.

Another translating service is The Sophienburg Archives in New Braunfels, Texas. This is a repository for materials on German settlers in Texas, especially the German history of New Braunfels, Comal County and the German settlement area of the 1840's. The Sophienburg Archives staff will answer mailed research questions and translate documents for a fee of $10.00 per hour (minimum one hour). They will also encapsulate documents for $10.00 plus the cost of materials. Copies of photographs may also be ordered. Write to: Sophienburg Archives, 200 N. Sequin Street, New Braunfels, TX 78139. Phone: (512) 629-1900.

More and more emigration lists are being indexed and made available in either book or computerized formats. Many of these can be identified at Family History Centers through a computer search of the Family History Library Catalog. Just type the name of the country and the words EMIGRATION AND IMMIGRATION.

Many young men served in the military before emigrating. Military service was required of most of them, and those records were kept by their country of origin. Military records often contain excellent information on the origin of birth. For instance, many British soldiers moved to Canada after their discharge, and their records are in British sources.

Thousands of records have been microfilmed of individuals who served the Austrian Empire, but you usually need to know the soldier's regiment to search these records. This information may be in records already in the possession of the family.

During the Nazi regime, each citizen of Germany was required to carry an *Ahnenpass* (or pedigree identification) with six generations of ancestry for government officials and military personnel, and three generations for all others. This requirement was also imposed on some of the countries that were controlled by Germany during WW II, such as Holland and Belgium. The German pedigrees were published as *Stamm-und-Ahnentafel* (pedigree and ancestor tables). Volumes for Italians of Aryan descent were also published. The Genealogical Society of Utah (the Family History Library repository) has microfilmed the Ahnenpass for the area of

Mitgtel-franker in the Brenner Collection (671 reels) with supporting documents.

After traveling through Europe several years ago, I realized the enormous paper trail I was leaving through the hotel registers that the police required of citizens and foreigners in most of the countries I traveled through. You can write to the city or regional archives to see if these records are available. For example, if you knew your ancestor was in Hamburg during certain years, you could inquire about the police register of citizens and transients for those years. In Antwerp, Belgium, hotel registers were kept from 1834-1898 (with some gaps), and they are located at the Municipal Archives in Antwerp.[22]

Census records or tax records in foreign countries may also lead to the place of origin. When neither a census nor tax list exists, try Tithe Applotment Books (Ireland), Valuation Books (Ireland), Clerical Surveys (Sweden and Finland), or any other types of records which listed families in complete units with their residences, for clues to their places of birth.

---

[22]Ibid., 27.

Shown below are the years the first census was taken for European regions or countries:

Austria	1815
Bavaria	1818
France	1801
Great Britain	1851
Greece	1836
Norway	1815
Prussia	1810
Russia	1897
Saxony	1815
Spain	1789
Sweden	1759
Switzerland	1860

Sometimes searching ancient records can be very time consuming. For example, searching for ancestors in unindexed British Isles census returns is frustrating unless you know the street address. The returns were recorded on a house by house, street by street basis. Just as in the United States, directories are frequently the best way of discovering the address and then use that address to lead you to other records.

The British Isles Directories Projects make a search of these directories possible. For a fee of £7.50 (US$15) a search will be made of three directories for any given name, a report provided of all entries found, plus up to 3 photocopies of original pages. More extensive searches will be made on request for which the fee will be £10 per hour plus the cost of any photocopies specifically requested. Send your request to:

GWEN KINGSLEY, LYDON, QUEEN ST.,
KINSWINFORD, WEST MIDLANDS,
ENGLAND, DY67AQ

Checks should be made payable to "Gwen Kingsley." US dollar checks accepted. For inquires only please send 2 International Reply Coupons. All prices include Airmail postage.

The directories themselves are available for libraries and societies at a cost of $6-$60 on microfiche depending on the area. For example, Bedfordshire 1850 (Slater) 1 fiche is $5.00 while Hampshire 1895 (Kelly) on 12 fiche is $60.

Customers placing a standing order will receive a discount of 25% and will be notified automatically of all future releases. Past customers qualify for a 10% discount.

Evaluation of Information

Once an individual has been located who matches all the criteria provided for the person being sought for, evaluate carefully the information. Does it match with all that has been found in country of arrival records? Is the name so common it might be found in many families? Do all the brothers and sisters match?

At this point some genealogists test the information received by trying to disprove the relationship to the individual they have located. Thus, they make sure they are on the correct track before undertaking a long research project in a foreign country. For example, if the individual you found died in the old country before coming to the new country, he couldn't be the one who came to the U. S.. Once you are sure of the relationship, it is time to locate ancestors in the foreign country.

Areas that seemed closed to genealogical research just a few years ago are open today. The Federation of Eastern European Family History Societies (FEEFHS) is an example of a new society which serves to assist researchers of all ethnic and religious groups in Albania, Austria, Belarus, Bosnia and Herzegovina, Bulgaria, Croatia, Czechoslovakia, Estonia, Germany (particularly the area that was formerly part of East Germany), Greece, Hungary, Latvia, Lithuania, Macedonia, Moldovan, Poland, Romania, Russia, Siberia, Slovenia, Ukraine, and Yugoslavia.

As of 1994 information on FEEFHS could be obtained by writing to Charles Hall, 7612 South 2700 East, Salt Lake City, UT 84121. Goals of the organization are to publish a newsletter, develop a data base of genealogical data and resources, maintain liaison with societies in other nations, promote genealogical, and to publish resource material pertinent to Eastern Europe. We will be looking forward to their publications.

The Genealogical-Heraldic Society in Poznan, is the first organization of this kind in Poland. It was founded in 1987 by scholars and amateurs interested in genealogy and heraldry. *The Society does NOT offer any research services.* Poland has no tradition of amateur genealogy and therefore their is considerable work to be done.

Donations from private persons have made it possible to publish four issues of their quarterly *GENS* but more is needed for the work to continue, and they are looking for sponsors who could help raise funds to continue publication. They would also be grateful for any donations of genealogical or heraldic books and periodicals from other countries, so that their library collection might form a nucleus for a future center of research in the country.

Each member can enter any number of surnames to be included in the Genealogical Data Bank, which is published semi-annually to establish contacts between people researching the same families or areas. Members may also subscribe to the quarterly magazine *GENS* and contribute articles which are published in Polish with short

English summaries. The quarterly is available for members only, or through publication exchange. Annual membership fee is $15 and subscription to *GENS* is $10 (for 4 issues).

For the first time they can now accept foreign members. Their publications may also be issued in English versions when there are enough foreign members to justify it.

The money can be sent either directly to their account at PKO BP I/O Poznan, Nr 63513-4356-132 or by sending a postal money order, or a bank draft, payable to Towarzystwo Genealogiczno-Heraldycznew Poznaniu to Towarzystwo Genealogiczno-Heraldyczne Societas Genealogica Ac Heraldica, Wodna 27 Palac Gorkow 61 -781 Poznan, POLSKA. Personal checks are not accepted.

More sources are becoming available all the time. These will make your research easier, but it is still up to you to verify any relationship and birth place data before you invest the time and money to take up further research overseas.

With all the excitement over finally getting into the eastern European countries, we must not forget the thrill of working in a country where everyone speaks and writes English. Right! Well, that is debateable. It doesn't take long to discover that the alphabet is the same and the words look the same, but how they are pronounced and sometimes used may be completely different.

Again it is important to become familiar with the customs of the area through a bit of background investigation. A familiarity with the record repositories is also important. For example, if you were doing research in Bedfordshire, England, it would be most helpful to find out what records are available in the United States on some sort of interlibrary loan or through local Family History Centers.

Using the search terms ARCHIVES & LIBRARIES while using the *Family History Library Catalog* along with the locality, i.e.: ENGLAND, BEDFORDSHIRE, ARCHIVES & LIBRARIES, will lead you to film calendars which are like an inventory of the County Record Office holdings. Sometimes the calendars even index the records by name. These calendars are available for all shires. The Bedford calendars are on fifteen rolls of film.

The Family History Library cataloging system breaks down the records into different categories for ease in locating records. If the County Record Office does not have a particular record, the local county library or Family History Library might. For example, Bedfordshire had a card index to all marriages NOT on the IGI in Bedford and it was on their microfilm list.

What types of records should you watch for?

1. Land records so you can see where people moved. They are available between 1780-1830's in the shires.
2. Marriage bonds and applications to determine relationships.
3. Parish registers to locate birth, marriage and death information and relationships.
4. Parish Chest materials which included the church warden accounts and the poor rolls so that you might locate those who did not leave estates or property and determine what caused them to leave their homeland for another. Here might also be found bastardy papers and some early census records.
5. Poor Law Unions in the Quarter Sessions (Court records) where you may determine settlements in your parish, who worked for who, licenses, and small taxes such as hair powder taxes will list people. This become a locality finding aid for individuals.
6. Other records that act as finding aids are Registers of Electors and School Records.
7. In Bristol City there are lists of servants to plantations. Many of these have been published but here are the originals of those who left Bristol for America.
8. Monumental inscriptions are the cemetery records

Poor law documents are really underused and underestimated by American researchers. Prior to 1834 the parish was responsible for the poor. After 1834 the poor were sent to a Poor House or a Work House. One poor law document was the *Settlement Certificate* which a person had to bring from his parish so the new parish could send him back if they had a problem with the person. It is quite apparent what a boost this would be as a locality finding aid.

Another document you might find is the *Church Warden Account* where the warden would list the amount he paid to cover such and so individual. There were also *Examination Papers*. If an individual belonged to a different parish, they were examined by a written statement. Many questions were asked to determine where you belonged. *Removal Orders* were written forcing an impoverished individual to return to his original place of residence rather than becoming a burden on the new place.

Quarter Session Rulings determined where a child went if no one could take care of him/her. Some poor law papers are absolutely full of gossip. The *Bastardy Bond* papers indicate individuals going to great lengths to determine the father of a child in order to cover that child's expenses. In 1830 this bonds were used to help people immigrate to the colonies to get rid of the poor in their parishes.

There are many more records to watch for but these should whet the appetite. Today the 1881 British Census Index is available on microfiche at most Family History Centers to help individuals locate their English ancestry. A few other good tips on English research involved the Federation of Family History Societies. Every county in the British Isles has at least one society and sometimes more. Almost all have a quarterly report. They provide the researcher with a contact in an area who can help, a helpful periodical, and they may sell published materials on your particular area.

A good book to study if you are doing English research is *Tracing Your Ancestors in the Public Record Office*[23] Another good resource is *British & Irish Biographies 1840-1940* available in the Family History Library. There are many biographical dictionaries

---

[23]ISBN 0-11-440222-1 or write to HMSO Publications Centre, PO Box 276, London SW85DT; General inquires may call 071-873-0011; telephone orders 071-873-9090.

in the British Isles on microfiche such as Baptist's Who's Who; Crockford's Clerical Directory, Who's Who is Kent (and all the other shires), etc. This sources indexes 200 titles and if a person is listed it may tell in the index when he dies.

Finally, Chadwick Healey's *National Inventory of Documentary Sources in the United Kingdom and Ireland*[24] publishes archival calendars, private repositories, etc. It is a finding list for archives and is available on microfiche which can be circulated to the Family History Centers. His also gives the Family History Library fiche numbers. The Family History Library research finding aids will give you the register number to the genealogy library's microfiche number for this publication.

The National Inventory also lists many places researchers might be interested in that have not been filmed. Therefore, it helps researchers plan a trip or prepare research calendars for their research. Since it costs about $8000/year to subscribe only large University libraries have the inventory. Chadwick Healey has a Virginia office.

Sending Money Overseas

Ruesch International Financial Services makes sending overseas payments simple:

1. Phone their Los Angeles office, (800) 696-7900 or (310) 277-7800, or their Washington DC office, (800) 424-2933.
2. Ask for the International Division.
3. Tell the representative which country you want to send a check to.
4. The Ruesch agent will tell you the cost of the check (the dollar equivalent based on the exchange rate of the day, plus a $2 service fee per check.)
5. If you called the Washington DC office, you will then be given a transaction number <u>which must be written on your</u>

---

[24]Locate FHL fiche number 6341118 for the index.

<u>payment check</u>.

6. The same day you make the call, send a check for the quoted amount, payable to Ruesch International, to the office you called:

> Ruesch International
> 1350 Eye Street NW
> Washington, DC 20005

> Ruesch International
> 1875 Century Park East
> Suite 1450
> Los Angeles, CA 90067

7. Ruesch will send you a draft which your foreign correspondent can cash at his/her bank.

Ruesch offers additional services including wire transfers ($15), conversion of foreign checks to U.S. currency ($2), commission-free travelers checks in 10 foreign currencies or U.S. dollars ($2 per currency per person) conversion of U.S. dollars to foreign currency for overseas travel (1% of order, with $2 minimum and $10 maximum fee.)

JUST FOR FUN

Did you know this about Ireland?

Volume I, No. 2 (Fall 1993) of *The Irish At Home and Abroad* includes several valuable articles for the Irish researcher and others. David E. Rencher's lead article "All the Irish Records Were Destroyed," will give renewed hope to those of you with research in Ireland. Other valuable articles include "The British Parliamentary Papers," "McClung Historical Collection," "County Mayo," "Transportation Registers, Ireland to Australia," "The McCormick Family," "The Irish in New Orleans," and "The Irish in Montreal."

The Master Book of Irish Surnames: has over 60,000 listings - the largest collection of variant spellings, locations, ethnic origins, and source listings ever compiled on Irish Surnames. The complete IGF subject and topic index is included in this book as a bonus.   ISBN 0 94013432 2. 320 pages, hardbound.   From the publishers of *Keatings History* and *The Book of Irish Families*, great & small, comes this #1 collection of Irish surnames. $21.95 complete.

Did you know this about Russia?

The newspaper *Neues Leben* must be read all over Russia and by all those interested in locating relatives. Arlene Rolfs of Genesco, KS says, "While traveling with a group to the Volga area in May 1993, we visited the offices of the newspaper Neues Leben in Moscow. While there, several of them put notices in the paper, at a cost of $30 American stating our names and addresses and the names and villages of the relatives for whom they were searching. Within four weeks, she began to receive answers from several parts of the old Soviet Union." If you are interested in advertising for relatives use the following address: Neues Leben, 101461 GSP-4 Moscow, Bumashny Projesd 14.

Did you know this about Sweden?

In 1686, a law was passed in Sweden, stating that detailed records had to be kept of all the people living in the country. As all Swedes belonged to the Lutheran Church, the task of record keeping was assigned to the Lutheran State Church. These records are unique and extend back to the 17th century. You can find names and dates and places of birth and death and movements of families as they grew and changed. For information about obtaining copies of these records, write to The Swenson Center, Box 175, Augustana College, Rock Island, IL 61201-2296 or visit your local Family History Center.

Did you know this about Canada?

The National Archives of Canada in Ottawa has a collection of early Ontario news-papers and will search and copy obituaries. You must supply the name, locality, and date of death. They will do a two-week search. The minimum charge is $2.00 per order or 50 cents per copy. Write to: Service Section, National Archives of Canada, 395 Wellington St., Ottawa K1A ON3 CND.

If you find the abbreviations "L.C." AND "U.C." and are stumped - L.C. is a common abbreviation for Lower Canada or Quebec. U.C. refers to Upper Canada, an area roughly equivalent to the southern part of the modern province of Ontario. These two designations are often found in enumerations of states on or near the Canadian border.

A research outline for all of Canada is published by the Family History Library for a minimal fee. It describes the content, use and availability of major regional and nationwide genealogical records. By using the general Canada outline with the outlines of the Provinces, a researcher is able to set research goals and select the records that will help achieve results.

Generally you must know the town in Canada where your ancestor was born or resided before beginning research. Indexes to censuses, church records and other genealogical sources may provide this information. If your ancestor came to the U.S., study U.S. sources before starting research in Canada.

More genealogical records are available for Quebec than for other provinces. French law and custom required that Quebec keep detailed Catholic church records of christenings, marriages and burials beginning in the 1620's. In English-speaking regions of eastern Canada, land records and probate records began in the late 1700's, but other detailed records were not kept until about 1867.

This outline covers "Canadian Search Strategies", a "Records Selection Table", a super map, information on provincial archives and libraries and their addresses, Canadian biographies, business and commerce records, cemeteries, census, church records, court records, directories, emigration & immigration, gazetteers, genealogy, historical geography, general history, land and property, languages, maps, military records, minorities, variant name spellings, native races of Canada, naturalization & citizenship, newspapers, notarial records, obituaries, periodicals, probate records, societies and vital records. You may purchase a copy at your local Family History Center or by writing to: Publications Coordination, Family History Library, 35 North West Temple St., Salt Lake City, UT 84150.

There seems to be a great deal of confusion about Canadian censuses even among the Canadian researchers. There were some early censuses done in the Maritimes and Quebec and some isolated areas in Ontario. These were Head-of-Household only. The first *Nominal Census* was in 1851.

For Nova Scotia, New Brunswick, Quebec and Ontario complete censuses were taken and are available for 1851, 1861, 1871, 1881, and 1891.

The Western Provinces were later being settled and full Nominal Censuses for Manitoba, Saskatchewan, Alberta and British Columbia only began in 1881. The 1891 Census was released in approximately 1989.

If you are looking for a Canadian place name on a map and cannot find it, write: Ministry of Energy, Mines & Resources, Geographic Names, Ottawa, Ontario, K1ADE9, Canada.

If you find yourself doing research in Quebec, be sure to read the article in the March 1994 issue of the *National Genealogical Society Quarterly* on Notarial Acts and their genealogical value. As is pointed out at the beginning of the article, French notaries do not simply witness signatures, they drafted the legal documents that the parties signed. They were there when a person started his first job, married, bought a farm, built a house, donated property, made and will and even deserters used a notary.

Canadian Homestead Records for Alberta, Canada are in the custody of the Provincial Archives, 12845-102 Avenue, Edmonton, Alberta, T5N OM6, Canada.

French-Canadian Abbreviations

"Feu" = deceased; *"maj-Major"* = having attained majority; *"min-mineur"* = under age; *"Vf-veuf"* = widower; (San Mateo Co GS, Vol 11 No.9, November 1993)

Do you know this about Chinese genealogy?

Although, I've only been asked to help about 5 people in this area in my entire 25 years in research, I feel this will be a great area of research in our area (California) in the near future. I have learned that surnames are very limited in Chinese genealogy but there is no limit to the variety of given names in this language. The Chinese language is also a wealth of dialects so the very same surname may be spelled in a variety of ways (sounds like southern states research). For example, the name Cheng could be spelled Chang, Chung, Djang, Jang, Jeong, Jung, Tee, Thai, Trunh, Ty, Zheng depending on the dialect.

It was thought that the surnames were originally tribe names. A book entitled *Your Chinese Roots* available from Heian International Inc., PO Box 1013, Union City, CA 94587 ISBN 0-89346-285-3 will help you.

Also, once the person arrived in the United States, the name could be spelled however the person heard it pronounced. Some individuals had what were called, "paper names". This means that during the 1880's when the Exclusion Act permitted entrance of U.S. citizens and offsprings of U.S. citizens, efforts were made to enter this country by these means.

People would claim to be offsprings of those already in the country. With such a limited number of surnames, this was relatively easy to accomplish. Therefore, a family name which was used in this country, may not be the ancestral name.

Also in the 1906 earthquake and resultant fire, many records were destroyed so dating from the fire, many Chinese claimed that they were born in San Francisco. With his citizenship intact, the father would then claim citizenship for his offspring born in China and on subsequent trips there, the father would report the birth of a son when in reality there wasn't any. This would then make available a "slot" which could be sold to boys who had no family relationships in the U.S, to enable them to enter this country as "paper sons".

As in any other foreign research, it is important to find the village name in this country. Talk to relatives and older people who might know of the origins in China. Even today there is no one book to all the villages. Even the officials do not know. We need to talk to older people for help. It is critical to find the real surname and given name as well as the village.

Chinatown had its own districts where immigrants would go to speak or live near people with their own dialects and customs. Various business associations were set up in this country according to the Pearl River Delta Region basic areas where the people were coming from.

Another unique item involving Chinese genealogy is the dating systems. There are genealogy charts available to help you translate the dates. There are also relationship charts available. Each relationship in Chinese has a different and unique term. So that your mother's oldest brother is not just an uncle but a name for someone who is your mother's oldest brother. There are word lists of Chinese Kinship terms in Cantonese, for example. This included words for father, mother, older brother, younger brother, older sister, older brother's wife, younger brother's wife, sister's husband, brother's son older or younger, etc.

Ninety percent of the Chinese emigrants came from the area the size of the San Jose area which is part of the Pearl River Delta area. There are thousands of villages here and the main language is Cantonese. The only way to start is to start asking questions now. If you don't ask questions now, the information will be gone forever. If your people stopped in Hawaii on their way over there are cross indexes to births and ship passenger lists.

The Chinese Historical Society has a book department at 650 Commercial Street, San Francisco, CA 94111. I purchased a copy of *A History of the Chinese in California: A Syllabus* by Thomas Chinn and *Chinese American Family History and Genealogy*. Both books are very helpful and could give in much detail what I have only brushed on here. They informed me of many of their interesting workshops so I encourage you to write to them at the above address if you are interested in Chinese genealogy.

It is nice to have a little background information when I need to help those who call on me. Basically genealogy principles are the same in every country, but the techniques, language and sources change.

Selected Bibliography

Jensen, Larry O.   "Determining Places of Origin and Connecting Lineages in Germany." Session T-16, *Syllabus*, The Federation of Genealogical Societies, 1992.

Maness, Ruth Ellen.   "U.S. and European Emigration/Immigration Sources."   Session S-79, *Syllabus*, The Federation of Genealogical Societies, 1992.

Meyerink, Kory.   "Tracing Immigrant Origins."   Pgs. 194-200, *Genealogy and Family History Conference*, Brigham Young University Conferences and Workshops, 1993.

Chapter Seven
Assignments: Making International Connections

1. Complete the following information for an individual you are
   researching in a foreign country:

The ancestor's complete name.	
Date associated with that ancestor such as birth, christening, marriage, confirmation, or military release.	
The ancestor's general geographic area.	
Other relatives or friends of the ancestor.	
U.S. neighborhoods the ancestor lived in.	
Religious affiliation of the ancestor.	
Family traditions regarding the ancestor.	

2. Examine the research to see if the following has been
   undertaken:

   a. **A preliminary survey on the surname.**

   b. **Original research** in census records for each locality
      the individual lived during the time periods the
      individual lived there.

c.   **Original research** in vital, property, church, probate, and military records.

3.   Evaluate all documents for clues regarding occupation, religion, friends (from names of witnesses, godparents, guardians, trustees and neighbors), regional locations of birth from census and vital records, and the female ancestral lines of the family. Use the evaluation form included in this chapter.

4.   Obtain background information on the geographical area from which the ancestor came using Research Outlines, how-to books, historical books, etc.

LAB ASSIGNMENT 7: Using *WordPerfect®* to Begin Your Family History

1. Either start from scratch by stating your goal for writing this semester, or pull your data from one of the notes in *PAF*. Select an ancestor where you have stopped for the time being, and move those notes into your word processor as explained in the past few lab assignments.

2. Restate those items you mentioned as your goals in assignment one.

3. Indicate in order what items you wish to appear in your family history project this semester. For example:

    a. A table of contents
    b. A page of acknowledgements
    c. An index of every surname and...
    d. A title page
    e. A copyright page
    f. A photo section, etc.

4. Go into your word processing program and lay out these basic items leaving a blank page between them for retrieving information as you go along.

5. Save as **Assnt7**. You will need 5 formatted floppy disks to use in the next few assignments because each assignment will build on the rest and will require more storage space.

CHAPTER EIGHT

Research Aids for International Connections

This Chapter will cover:

- Geographical reference tools
- Language aids
- Handwriting Aids
- Naming conventions and customs

Starting family history research in a foreign country can be very intimidating. The purpose of this chapter is to help alleviate fears and provide an introduction to the abundance of resources available to help you every step of the way. From personal experience, I have been able to leap into Swedish, Finnish, Norwegian, Danish, English, Irish, German, Spanish, and Canadian research and have experienced great success using the fundamental genealogical techniques explained in my previous two textbooks.

This doesn't mean I would recommend you do all your own foreign research. Specialists who spend forty hours a week working in a specific geographic area and who also have the training, not only in the language, but the records available can save you time and money. They may aid you in getting started or getting over a hump in your research. Even if you are going to hire a researcher, however, you should learn the basic sources, research strategies, language aids, and historical background as this will aid you in selecting a professional researcher.

Research anywhere in the world will require a knowledge of the geography, language, handwriting, naming conventions and customs.

Geographical Reference Tools

You will need to know the **Civil Terms** used in registration, census, military and/or probate districts. They are often broken down into national or regional terms, county terms, and town or parish terms.

An example of national terms includes *Great Britain* which refers to England, Wales and Scotland. The term *United Kingdom* has been used since 1921 to refer to Great Britain and Northern Ireland. Between 1801-1921 it included Great Britain and all of Ireland. *Wales* consists of twelve counties which does not include Monmouthshire even though many Welsh people lived there, while *England* consists of forty counties, excluding Wales but including Monmouthshire. Each country will have differing civil geographical terms.

County terms would include the words *shire* which is the Anglo-Saxon word for county. Berkshire, Shropshire and Wiltshire are examples. The word *county* was borrowed from the French and is the equivalent of shire, but it is not used to form compound nouns. It would be appropriate to say "County of Cornwall," but not county of Berkshire.

Another term is the word *hundred* which is a division of an English county known to be about 100 hides. At the Domesday Survey a hide was approximately 120 acres, or enough to support a working farm which included family, laborers and slaves. This old English word *hide* is a unit of measurement for taxes on the land and later a measure of land varying from 80 to 120 acres. The 1841 English census uses the term *hundreds*.

Civil Parish units are non-ecclesiastical versions of the Church of England parishes. They often coincided with the ecclesiastical parish, but sometimes did not. Many records were kept in these parishes. A *chapelry, hamlet, township, tithing,* or *village* are sub-parish terms.

Ecclesiastical terms in Great Britain include *province* which referred to a jurisdiction headed by an archbishop. In England and Wales there were two: the province of York which included the eight northern counties of Cheshire, Cumberland, Durham, Lancashire, Northumberland, Nottinghamshire, Yorkshire, and Westmorland. The remaining thirty-two counties were in Canterbury including the twelve counties of Wales. A province would issue marriage licenses and probate records.

Each province was broken down into several *diocese* headed by a bishop. These dioceses covered all or parts of several counties and they produced bishop's transcripts, marriage licenses and probate records.

Each diocese was broken down into *archdeaconries*. They were headed by an archdeacon who produced marriage and probate records as well. There were several *rural deaneries* in the archdeaconry which produced few records of genealogical value but they sometimes filed records produced by others.

The basic ecclesiastical unit most familiar to English researchers is the *parish*. A Church of England parish was headed by a rector or vicar. A parish was usually located in a single church but some were wide-spread, or quite populous, in which case additional churches called *chapelries* were established and headed by curates. Parishes produced parish registers and occasionally other records that we use in our research. Those parishes assigned to keep other records were called *peculiar*, meaning they were assigned special privileges.

Sometimes people lived in such isolated areas that their records would be designated as *extra-parochial* or not included in the limits of any one ecclesiastical place. Their records might be in any of the neighboring parishes.

In England, the state church was the Church of England. Their local units usually took the name of the town or village in which they were located. Their name also included the name of the denomination. Local units could have belonged to larger jurisdictions called *circuits*, *conferences*, or *unions*. Because there was a state church most everyone's records can be found in church records. However, there have always been *non-conformists* whose religious views did not conform to the state church.

These, and other geographical and ecclesiastical terms are included in Research Outlines produced by the Family History Library (see chapter 1); on microfilm via interlibrary loan to local Family History Centers; and in genealogical how-to books produced by various companies. A sample of a loan films of this type would be:

Allgemeine Dorf-Geographie von Deutschland: Oder Alphabetische Beschreibung der Dörfer, Flecken, Stifter, Klöster, Schlösser, Festungen, Herrschaften, Ritter und

Landgüter, Vorwerke, Meyerhöfe, Eisen und Kupferhämmer, Salz- und Fardenwerke, Glashütten, Papiermühlen, auch einzeln liegenden Häusern und Schäfereyen etc.. (Salt Lake City: Filmed by the Genealogical Society of Utah, 1979.) FHL film #256330 item 2-3. Geographical dictionary of Germany.

Historical Background Affecting Genealogical Research in Germany and Austria. (Salt Lake City: Genealogical Society of the Church of Jesus Christ of Latter-day Saints, 1977.) Research papers (Church of Jesus Christ of Latter-day Saints. Genealogical Department). Series C ; no. 19 on microfiche 6000035.

Koch, Georg Aenotheus, (1802-1879). *Deutsch-Lateinisches Vergleichendes Wörterbuch der Alten, Mittleren und Neuen Geographie: eine Beigabe zu Jedem Deutsch-Lateinischen Wörterbuche.* (Leipzig: Hahn'sche Verlagsbuchhandlung, 1835.) Place names in German with Latin equivalents. FHL film # 0924810 item 4.

Kredel, Otto and Franz Thierfelder. *Deutsch-Fremdsprachiges (Fremdsprachig-Deutsches) Ortsnamenverzeichnis.* (Berlin: Deutsche Verlagsgesellschaft, 1931.) Place-name-change dictionary showing German place-names assigned following World War I to the following countries: France, Belgium, Denmark, Poland, Lithuania, Russia, Czechoslovakia, Hungary, Yugoslavia, Italy, Switzerland, Latvia, Estonia, Luxembourg, and Romania. FHL film #0583457

Samples of how-to books include:

Baxter, Angus. *In Search of Your British and Irish Roots: A Complete Guide to Tracing Your English, Welsh, Scottish & Irish Ancestors.* (Baltimore: Genealogical Publishing Co., Inc. 1991.)

Baxter, Angus. *In Search of Your German Roots: A Complete Guide to Tracing Your Ancestors in the Germanic Areas of Europe.* (Baltimore: Genealogical Publishing Co., Inc. 1991.)

Cory, Kathleen B. *Tracing Your Scottish Ancestry*. (Baltimore: Genealogical Publishing Co., Inc. 1990.)

Gardner, David E. and Frank Smith. *Genealogical Research in England and Wales*. (Salt Lake City: Bookcraft, 1956-1964).

Grenham, John. *Tracing Your Irish Ancestors*. (Baltimore: Genealogical Publishing Co., Inc. 1993.)

Pelling, George. *Beginning Your Family History in Great Britain*. (Baltimore: Genealogical Publishing Co., Inc. 1989.)

Brandt, Edward. *Contents and Addresses of Hungarian Archives with Supplementary Information for Research on German-Speaking Ancestors from Hungary*. (Baltimore: Clearfield Company,) A starting point for researching German-speaking ancestors living in Hungary during the first part of this century. It contains addresses of some 70 Hungarian archives, as well as a listing of holdings, various maps showing the changed county names and boundaries, a dateline of historic events in Hungary, and a selected bibliography.

Gazetteers are the next basic tool to use in a new area. They are invaluable for finding the records of your ancestor. Some are available in microform such as:

Deutsches Kirchliches Adressbuch: ein kirchlicher Führer durch die Evangelischen Landeskirchen Deutschlands. (Berlin: Evang. Pressverband, 1927.) Directory of Protestant Churches in Germany. Includes German Protestant Churches throughout the world. Film # 0584897

Bundesanstalt für Landeskunde. *Amtliches Gemeinde- und Ortsnamenverzeichnis der deutschen Ostgebiete unter fremder Verwaltung*. (Remagen : Bundesanstalt für Landeskunde, 1955.) Official gazetteer of place name changes of localities taken from Germany after World War 2 and incorporated into Poland and Russia. V. 1 includes folded maps. V. 2 shows German place names with new foreign names. V. 3 shows foreign place names with the former German names. FHL Film #0824243 or microfiche #6053256.

The National Gazetteer: A Topographical Dictionary of the British Isles. 3 Vol. (London: Virtue, 1868.) Contains a complete county atlas. Vol. 1. Abb-Eyw. FHL Film #0253079; Vol. 2. Fac-Myt. FHL Film #0253080; Vol. 3. Naas-Zou. FHL Film #0253081.

Meyers Orts- und Verkehrs-Lexikon des Deutschen Reichs: auf Grund amtlicher Unterlagen von Reichs-, Landes- und Gemeindebehörden. (Leipzig: Bibliographisches Institut, 1912-1913.) Meyers gazetteer and commercial directory of the German Empire. Shows information concerning each place name, including churches, civil offices and jurisdictions. Since not every village had a parish, use Meyers which is listed alphabetically. Family History Centers provide a helpful handout for using this very valuable gazetteer. Available on FHL microfiche #6000001-6000029.

Many gazetteers or place name guides are available only in printed form. A few examples are:

Mokotoff, Gary and Sallyann Amdur Sack. *Where Once We Walked: A Guide to the Jewish Communities Destroyed in the Holocaust.* (Teaneck, N.J.: Avotaynu, 1991.) Classified list of Jewish communities throughout Europe (with emphasis on Central and Eastern Europe. Names are based on the U. S. Board of Geographic names. Includes the Daitch-Mokotoff Soundex system so names may be located by variant spellings.

Smith, Frank. *A Genealogical Gazetteer of England: An Alphabetical Dictionary of Places with their Location, Ecclesiastical Jurisdiction, Population, and the Date of the Earliest Entry in the Registers of Every Ancient Parish in England.* (Baltimore: Genealogical Publishing Co., Inc., 1968.)

*General Alphabetical Index to the Townlands and Towns,
Parishes, and Baronies of Ireland*. (Baltimore: Genealogical
Publishing Co., Inc. 1984.)

Maps and Atlases are essential
for a visual picture of the juris-
dictional boundaries of the topographical barriers affecting the
record keeping jurisdictions, and
migration of your ancestors.[25]

Maps and atlases can be found on the *Family History Library
Catalog* by typing in the name of the country and the word MAP.
Some are available as separate publications, such as:

Suomi Kartasto Kartbok Över Finland 1897/1915 (Helsinki:
Suomen Matkailulitto r.y., 1984). ISBN 951-838-020-1. (A
Finnish atlas with farm names given.)

*A Series of Parish Outline Maps for the Counties of England
and Wales*. (Logan: Everton Publishers,   ).

Gardner, Harland, and Frank Smith. *Genealogical Atlas of
England and Wales*. (   )

Mitchell, Brian. *A New Genealogical Atlas of Ireland*.
(Baltimore: Genealogical Publishing Co., Inc., 1986).

Language Aids

Word Lists. Once you have established a place to search, the
next step is to obtain a list of genealogical words which you might
find in the records of the area under study. Some countries
require several word lists. For example, research in Finland

---

[25]Detailed maps of Great Britain that are useful for genealogical research
can be ordered from Olde World Maps. Send for a free catalog to RFD 5, Box 437C,
Gardiner, ME 04245.

requires a list in Finnish, Swedish and Latin depending on the time period and the records being used.

The Family History Library in Salt Lake City provides a very basic word list for the most commonly researched areas of the world. More complete sources are also available as complete dictionaries or glossaries. Two examples of this genre are:

Thode, Ernest. *German-English Genealogical Dictionary.* (Baltimore: Genealogical Publishing Co., Inc., 1992.)

Wright, Andrew. *Court Hand Restored with an Appendix Containing the Ancient Names of Places in Great Britain and Ireland: An Alphabetical Table of Ancient Surnames, and a Glossography of Latin Words Found in the Works of the Most Eminent Lawyers, and Other Ancient Writings.* (Salt Lake City: Filmed by the Genealogical Society of Utah, 1970. 0832246 item 1).

Naming Conventions and Customs

Record types, calendar systems, naming customs, terminology and place names varied considerably in each country. Therefore, it is necessary to obtain good resources on these variables before moving into original research. The following resource samples should be of help:

Brinkmann, Hermann. *Alte und Neue Zeitrechnung: Unterhaltsame Kalenderkunde Für Jedermann; Datumschlüssel für den Sippenforscher; mit einer Beilage, "Ewiger Kalender".* (Görlitz: C.A. Starke, 1939.) Old and new calendars. Date reckoning for genealogists. Calendar calculator. FHL film #1181644 item 7.

Burke, Sir John Bernard, (1814-1892). *A Genealogical and Heraldic History of the Colonial Gentry*. (Baltimore: Genealogical Publishing Co., Inc. 1970.) Also on FHL film # 1426151 item 3-4.

Jones, George F. *German-American Names*. (Baltimore: Genealogical Publishing Co., Inc., 1990).

Markwell, F. C. & Pauline Saul. *The A-Z Guide to Tracing Ancestors in Britain*. (Baltimore: Genealogical Publishing Co., Inc., 1989). Contains a glossary of terms relating to genealogical research in Britain.

Moody, David. *Scottish Family History*. (Baltimore: Genealogical Publishing Co., Inc., 1990).

Webb, Sidney. *The Parish and the County*. (London: Frank Cass, 1963.) Reprint of 1906 edition. Contains the history and function of the local parishes, indexed. FHL film #0962460.

Woulfe, Rev. Patrick. *Irish Names and Surnames: Sloinnte Gaedheal Is Gall*. (Baltimore: Genealogical Publishing Co., Inc., 1993).

Yonge, Charles Duke, (1812-1891). *The History of the British Navy from the Earliest Period to the Present*. (London: R. Bentley, 1863.) FHL film #0990318 items 1-2.

Yurdan, Marilyn. *Irish Family History*. (Baltimore: Genealogical Publishing Co., Inc., 1990).

Handwriting Aids

Paleography, or the study of old writing, is important to family history researchers. If they are to obtain the information from original records needed to compile a family history, they must be able to read the handwriting style of the scribe who made the record - including the letters AND numbers of the original document. Since about 1550 similar handwriting styles have existed across the English-speaking world. However, in the courts, specialized handwriting was often found. These writing styles may need to be studied in such sources as:

Cope, Emma Elizabeth Thoyts. *How to Decipher and Study Old Documents: Being a Guide to the Reading of Ancient Manuscripts.* (London: Elliot Stock, 1893.) FHL film #0990313 item 3.

Emmison, Frederick George. *How to Read Local Archives, 1550-1700.* (London: Historical Association, 1967.)

Grieve, Hilda Elizabeth Poole. *Examples of English handwriting, 1150-1750: With Transcripts and Translations.* (Essex: Essex Education Committee, 1954.) Transcripts from Essex parish and other archive records. FHL film #0897346 item 4.

Ison, Alf. *A Secretary Hand ABC Book.* (Reading, England: .A. Ison, 1982.) ISBN 0-9508366-0-5.

Stryker-Rodda, Harriet. *Understanding Colonial Handwriting.* (Baltimore: Genealogical Publishing Co., Inc., 1989).

As you begin working with foreign gazetteers, the foreign typescript might intimidate you, but it will give you good practice for the handwriting which is to come. You will also find that although handwriting used throughout even the English-speaking countries may have been similar, there are enough variations to require several practice sessions before you will feel comfortable with this. This will be covered in greater depth in the next chapter.

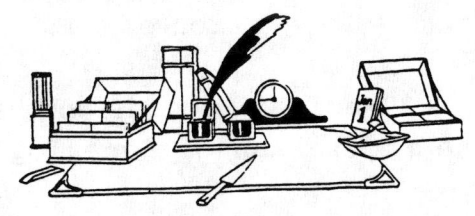

Selected Bibliography

Chapman, Colin R. "English Church Records, Other than Parish Registers." Session S-97, *Syllabus*, The Federation of Genealogical Societies, 1992.

Choquette, Margarita. "Swedish/Finnish Research." Pgs 93-96, *Genealogy and Family History Conference*, Brigham Young University Conferences and Workshops, 1993.

Gardiner, Duncan. "Slovak, Czech, and Moravian Research: New Developments." Session F-43, *Syllabus*, The Federation of Genealogical Societies, 1992.

Hunter, Dean J. "What's New in British Research, and the Current Growth of the British Collection at the Family History Library." Session F-46, *Syllabus*, The Federation of Genealogical Societies, 1992.

_____ "The Pot of Gold at the End of the Rainbow-Irish Holdings of the Family History Library." Session T-27, *Syllabus*, The Federation of Genealogical Societies, 1992.

Maness, Ruth Ellen. "Scandinavian Research Sources and Methodology." Session T-36, *Syllabus*, The Federation of Genealogical Societies, 1992.

Mokotoff, Gary. "Shtetl Geography--The Changing Face of Central and Eastern Europe." Session S-106, *Syllabus*, The Federation of Genealogical Societies, 1992.

Ryskamp, George R. "Tracing Your Hispanic Heritage." Session S-77, *Syllabus*, The Federation of Genealogical Societies, 1992.

_____ "Mexican Records and Research." Session S-108, *Syllabus*, The Federation of Genealogical Societies, 1992.

Schlyter, Daniel M. "Records and Research in the Former Russian Empire; Including Impact of Recent Events." Session F-64, *Syllabus*, The Federation of Genealogical Societies, 1992.

Wagner, Anthony Richard. *English Genealogy*. Rev. Ed., Oxford, 1982.

Warren, James W. "A New Spot on your Ancestral Map: Approaches for Researching an Unfamiliar Locality." Session S-85, *Syllabus*, The Federation of Genealogical Societies, 1992.

Wuehler, Anne. "First Steps in Scottish Research." Session F-40, *Syllabus*, The Federation of Genealogical Societies, 1992.

_____ "English Research for Beginners." Session T-13, *Syllabus*, The Federation of Genealogical Societies, 1992.

Chapter Eight
Assignments: Research Aids for International Connections

1.   Locate the English translation of civil, geographical and ecclesiastical terms for a country of interest by obtaining a word list of the most commonly used genealogical terms for the area under study.

2.   Locate and copy a page from a gazetteer which covers the time period of the country of interest.

3.   Locate and copy a map of the foreign area of research which is near the time period the individual lived and a current map of the same area.

4.   List several sources for obtaining instruction on naming customs, record sources, and jurisdictions for the particular area of interest you will be studying.

5.   List emigration and immigration sources for the area of interest and report what is available.

6.   Identify what foreign language newspapers involving the country of interest have been published in the United States.

7.   Identify what foreign directories are available for the area your ancestor moved from or for an area of interest.

8.   Identify library catalogs which would have census records, tax records, clerical surveys or similar large data bases of information which might be indexed or arranged in geographic areas in the foreign country under study. Record their numbers for later reference or make a computer copy of the information for use later.

LAB ASSIGNMENT 8: Using *WordPerfect*® to Write Your Introduction

1. Retrieve the file (the outline of your family history which you started last week). Go to a blank page near the front of the information. Keeping your time perspective in mind, write one sentence which includes some sort of an indication if this book is from present to past, past to present, etc. Also include something of the setting and the goal or problem you will discuss.

    Example: In the fall of 1705, John and Martha Cook left their homeland of Maine and headed southward toward Massachusetts and later into Pennsylvania. Famine and Indian uprising was the reason most settlers left. Where they originated before Maine is still a mystery?

2. Do the same sentence again but use either a different tense or a different tone (casual, chatty, formal, historical, involved, detached, judgmental, ironic, or amused).

    Example: As the cold wind blew across the jagged rocks and the grey-blue autumn sky seemed to mourn, John and Martha Cook left the home they had always known on Maine's northern coastline after a terrible year of famine and Indian assaults and headed south toward Massachusetts in 1705 and then westward into Pennsylvania.

3. Look at your paragraph again. Does it contain the important *who, what, when, where* and *how*? What can you add? Try elaborating upon family that you know? Bring the family forward (or take it back) one generation and indicate how you know for sure this is your family.

4. Print this page out and turn it in to your instructor.

5. Save your file as **Assnt8**.

150

CHAPTER NINE

Making Sense of the Documents You've Found

This Chapter will provide:

- A short historical background of handwriting techniques
- Basic techniques for studying any handwriting sample
- Samples of
  - German paleography
  - Scandinavian gothic script
  - British Isles court handwriting
- Calendaring challenges
- Historical background of the time period

Several handwriting exercises were presented in *Genealogy & Computers for the Determined Researcher* which were commonly found in the United States, but there are other styles of writing commonly found in foreign countries. These will be discussed in this chapter. More samples can be found in the Research Outlines for various nations prepared by the Family History Library as well as in several published sources. This chapter will deal with the most commonly requested foreign scripts: English, German, and Scandinavian. Latin is also found in all of these countries.

Historical Background

The older records are very intimidating to the new researcher. There are many causes for this. Before the 1800's quill pens were the instrument used for writing. The point was very hard and often skipped across the paper. Therefore, letters do not always look completed. The ink was not always a good grade or was made with iron compound that turned to rust and flaked off when very old. The minister or clerk sometimes watered down the ink giving it the character of disappearing ink after a few years. Finally, the storage of the records was not always the best and records may be blotchy, faded, moldy, or eaten away.

Basic Techniques

Reading original records in any country provides its own challenges ranging from knowing which records were damaged in wars and natural disasters to the national customs behind the records. Although the process may look daunting, each script can be studied and learned by following a few basic steps:

1. Start with the latest year and work back to earlier years to allow yourself time to practice the handwriting of the scribes, and learn customs of the record keepers, and the common names of the area (both locality names and surnames).

2. Read for logic rather than for word-by-word translation.

3. Find the letters you can't read in other words on the page that you do know, and see if they make more sense in familiar contexts.

4. Find the same word written again in another context.

5. In parish registers look for another entry involving the same person.

6. Read on a few pages (skipping what you cannot read) and then come back. With more context the words are often easier to comprehend.

7. Use reference materials such as surname books, gazetteers, place name books, etc.

8. When reading wills or long legal documents, quickly scan the entire document then go back and read word by word.

9. If a microfilm is hard to read, change machines and see if another reader makes it easier.

10. Become familiar with each scribe's own style of handwriting.

German Paleography

One of the greatest hurdles in reading older manuscripts is the use of abbreviations. Fortunately most scribes used standard forms that were developed during the Middle Ages. The simplest abbreviations are those in which the last few letters of the word are left off (truncation). Some familiar examples of this are *corp.*, *co.*, *fig.* In German documents one might find *num.* (nummer), *fol.* (folio), *geb.* (geboren), *gest.* (gestorben), *verh.* (verheiratet), *Eheschl.* (Eheschliessung).

A word could also be shortened by leaving out the middle letters (contraction). Examples of this form are *pg.* (page), *ltd.*

(limited), and *pt.* (part). In German documents you'll find *vgl.* (vergleiche), *Jhrg.* (Jahrgang), *Jhs.* (Johannes), and *Hmbg,* (Hamburg).

Sometimes initials were used to represent words: *a.m., p.m., p.p.d.* (postpaid), *a.D.* (ausser Dienst), *i.R* (im Ruhdestand), *DM* (Deutsche Mark), *zt.* (zurzeit).

A writer could also use symbols to indicate abbreviation of a word: ✝ (death), *oo* (marriage), # (birth), *&* (and), *8ber* (Oktober), *9ber* (November), *Xber* (Dezember), *H'zog* (Herzog), *Vat'* (Vater). Some symbols always indicated the same letters were left out, others had a variable meaning. A comma above a word (') meant an *-er, -ar,* or *-ur* had been omitted as in *d'* (der). An *ē* symbolized *-em* or *-en*. In latin *q;* symbolized *-que,* but *p* could be *per-, por-,* or *par-*. The foregoing examples demonstrate that words can also be abbreviated by replacing beginning letters with symbols. (underline P)

Still another method called for placing a missing letter, usually a vowel, above the abbreviation: w^eden (werden), st^ibt (stirbt), v^orwe (vrowe).

Dots (˙), lines (¯), and tent-like (ˆ) figures above letters served to alert the reader that something was left out. Often it was up to the reader to know what was missing as in p'est' (prester) or p^imus (primus).

German and Latin abbreviations which a researcher will encounter may be best found in a dictionary of abbreviations. For documents created in the Germanic areas of Europe the best dictionary is Paul Arnold Grun, *Schlüssel zu alten und neuen Abkürzungen* (Lumburg/Lahn: C. A. Starke Verlag, 1966).[26]

---

[26]**Sample Latin Abbreviations on Church Records**
d.s.p.   decessit sine prole = *died without issue*
d.s.p.l.   decessit sine prole legitima = *died without legitimate issue*

The following two pages contain the lower case and upper case letters of the German alphabet taken from *Schreiblesefibel für den Unterricht der Elemntarklassen* (a writing book for elementary school) which should help you recognize the letters you will see in the German documents.

Scandinavian Gothic Script

The old Gothic script is a great obstacle in Scandinavian genealogical research, but it is necessary to have some knowledge of it before attempting to do research. The best way to learn the script is simply to practice writing it, and to compare words that are more clearly written with other less legible entries.

There is a great value in having a basic understanding of the language, but only a minimum of words are actually required to be memorized since you are dealing with highly formatted records and not really reading the language. A small word list with most of the words that are used in the different genealogical records are provided by the Family History Library. If some more uncommon words appear, you can usually find an individual or a larger dictionary to translate them.

Anna

barn

Pigan

---

d.s.p.m.	decessit sine prole mascula = *died without male issue*
d.s.p.m.s.	decessit sine prole mascula supersitita = *died without surviving male issue*
d.s.p.s.	decessit sine prole supersita = *died without surviving issue*
d.unm	*died unmarried*
d.v.p.	decessit vita patris = *died in the lifetime of his father*
d.v.m.	decessit vita matris = *died in the lifetime of his mother*

Table 9.1

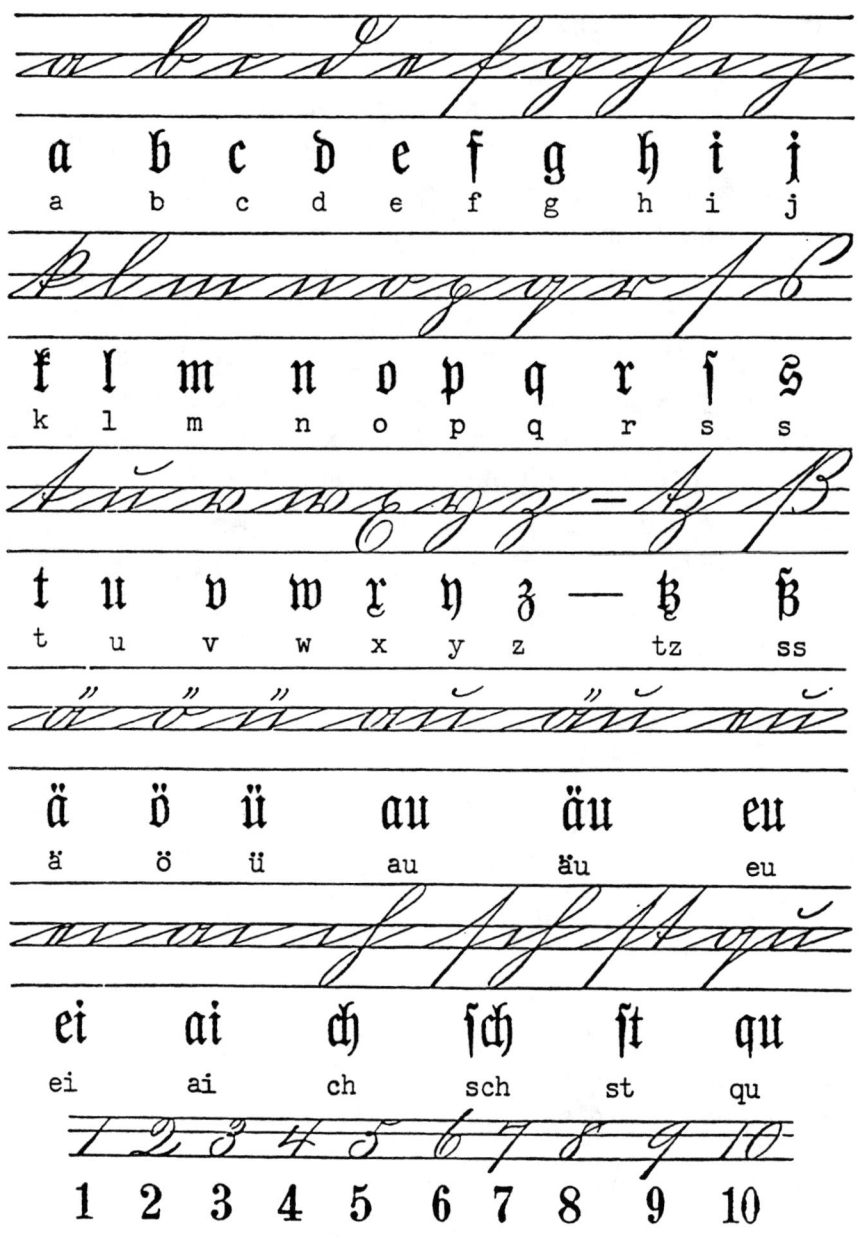

Das kleine Alphabet.

a	b	c	d	e	f	g	h	i	j
a	b	c	d	e	f	g	h	i	j

k	l	m	n	o	p	q	r	ſ	s
k	l	m	n	o	p	q	r	s	s

t	u	v	w	x	y	z	—	tz	ß
t	u	v	w	x	y	z		tz	ss

ä	ö	ü	au	äu	eu
ä	ö	ü	au	äu	eu

ei	ai	ch	ſch	ſt	qu
ei	ai	ch	sch	st	qu

1 2 3 4 5 6 7 8 9 10

156

Table 9.2

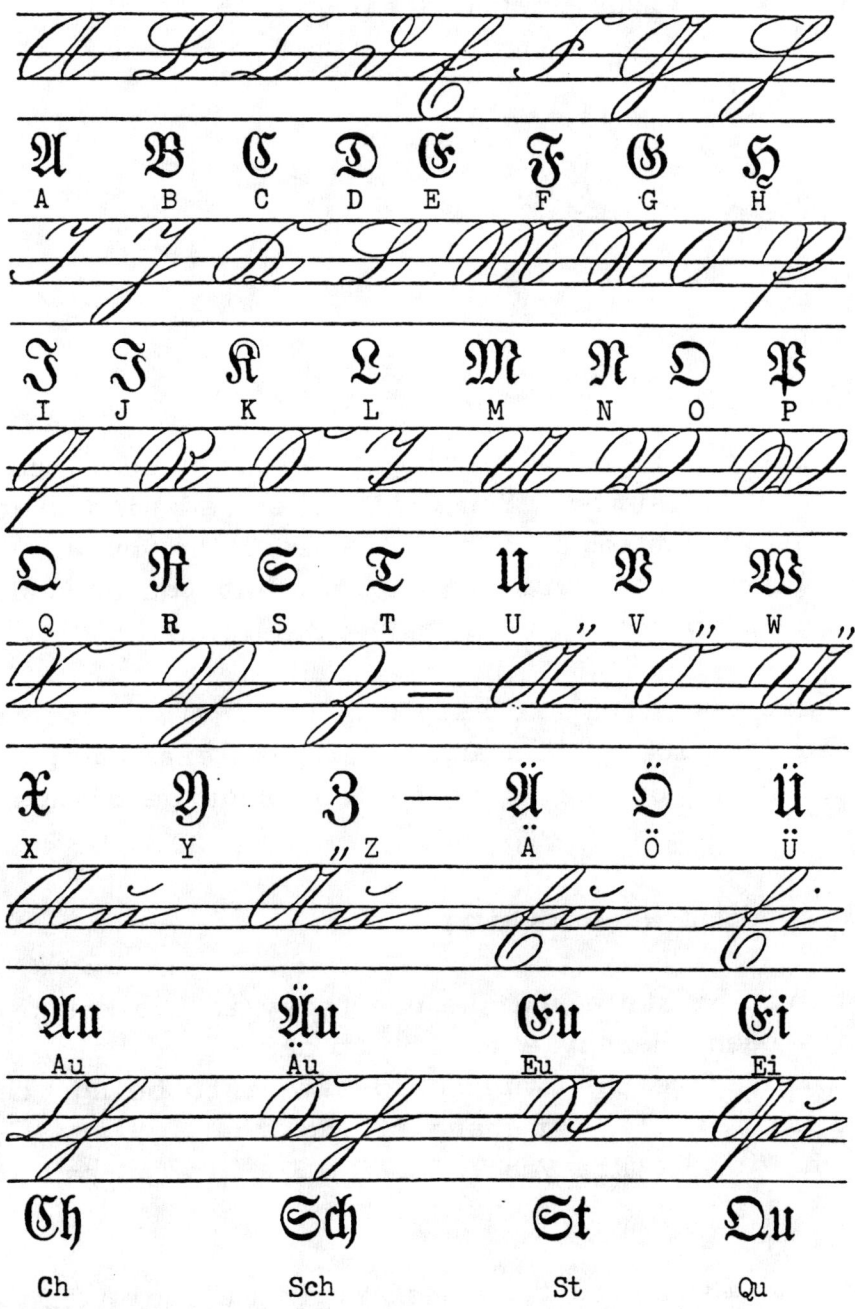

Das große Alphabet.

A	B	C	D	E	F	G	H
A	B	C	D	E	F	G	H

I	J	K	L	M	N	O	P
I	J	K	L	M	N	O	P

Q	R	S	T	U	V	W
Q	R	S	T	„U	„V	„W

X	Y	Z	—	Ä	Ö	Ü
X	Y	„Z	Ä	Ö	Ü

Au	Äu	Eu	Ei
Au	Äu	Eu	Ei

Ch	Sch	St	Qu
Ch	Sch	St	Qu

157

The best way to learn is to take a few letters at a time and repeat writing them several times. Continuously writing them helps you to memorize them without much difficulty. Start with the lower case letters, then focus on the capital or uppercase letters, finally put the letters together into words. Try writing the name Anderson, for example, using the Gothic script.

Repeat this practice by writing your own name 10 to 20 times following the Gothic style. You will be amazed with what you are able to do. As you attempt to read old records you will run into hundreds of different handwriting styles. As you encounter a new style this type of practice will be very helpful.

On the next few pages are sample Scandinavian scripts for you to practice in both lower case and upper case examples. See Table 9.3 for a comparison of the Scandinavian language groups.

British Isles Court Handwriting

The handwriting style that we use today is the *round hand*. It has not always been the style used. It came into being about the middle 1700's. Before the round hand came into being, there were several different styles of handwriting that existed over the centuries such as the *Court Hand*, *Italic*, *Secretary Hand*, *Legal* and *Chancery*.

It is not necessary to know each alphabet thoroughly or to be able to tell which letters belong to which alphabet. It is necessary to become familiar enough with the letters to be able to read the early documents. Many records before 1730 are written in Latin. Letters of the Latin alphabet that are difficult for us to read today are: *c, e, d, h, p, r, s, f, t, y, v,* and *w.*

Capital letters are difficult as they are normally written in a very fancy style. Abbreviations appear often in the records and are indicated by raised letters; by a colon, semi-colon, or a period; by a straight line drawn above the word; by a curvy line above the word or at the end of the word; or by a line through a letter

After the initial shock of trying to read a document that is written in Latin, rather than English, you'll find that the Latin in parish registers is not difficult once you learn a few of the basic words. There is a list of common Latin terms found in the book *Genealogical Research in England and Wales* by David Gardner and Frank Smith, volume 3 as well as several of the research outlines of the Family History Library. Most wills are not completely in Latin after about 1500. Every word in Latin has an ending on it according to how it is used in the sentence. This includes names, so they appear in modified forms such as Mariae, Henricus.

Summary:

Now that you've been introduced to several styles of old handwriting, you'll need some practice to develop your ability. Several practice opportunities are provided at the end of the chapter. A key is included at the back of the book so you can check your transcription <u>when you have finished</u>.

Comparative Word List

Table 9.3

English	Danish	Norwegian	Swedish	Latin
age	alder	alder	alder	aetas
baptized	døbt	døpt	döpt	bapti-satus
born	født	født	född	natus, nata
brother	Broder, Bror	bror	broder	frater
buried	begravet	begravet	begravd	sepultus sepulta
child	Barn	barn	barn	filia, filius
city, town	By	by	stad	urbs
daughter	Datter	datter	dotter	filia
day	Dag	dag	dag	die, dies
grand-child	Barnebarn	barne-barn	barn	nepos, nept
husband	Husbonde	Mann	man	is maritus
married	copuler-ede,gift, viet	gift	gift	nuptus, nupta
month	Maaned	maned	manad	mensis
parents	Foraeldre		föral-drar	parentes
wife	Hustru, Kone	hustru	hustru	conjunx, conjux
year	Aar	ar	ar	annus

160

Table 9.4   Lower Case Scandinavian Script

Lower Case Letter Comparisons

Table 9.5   Lower Case Scandinavian Script (Cont.)

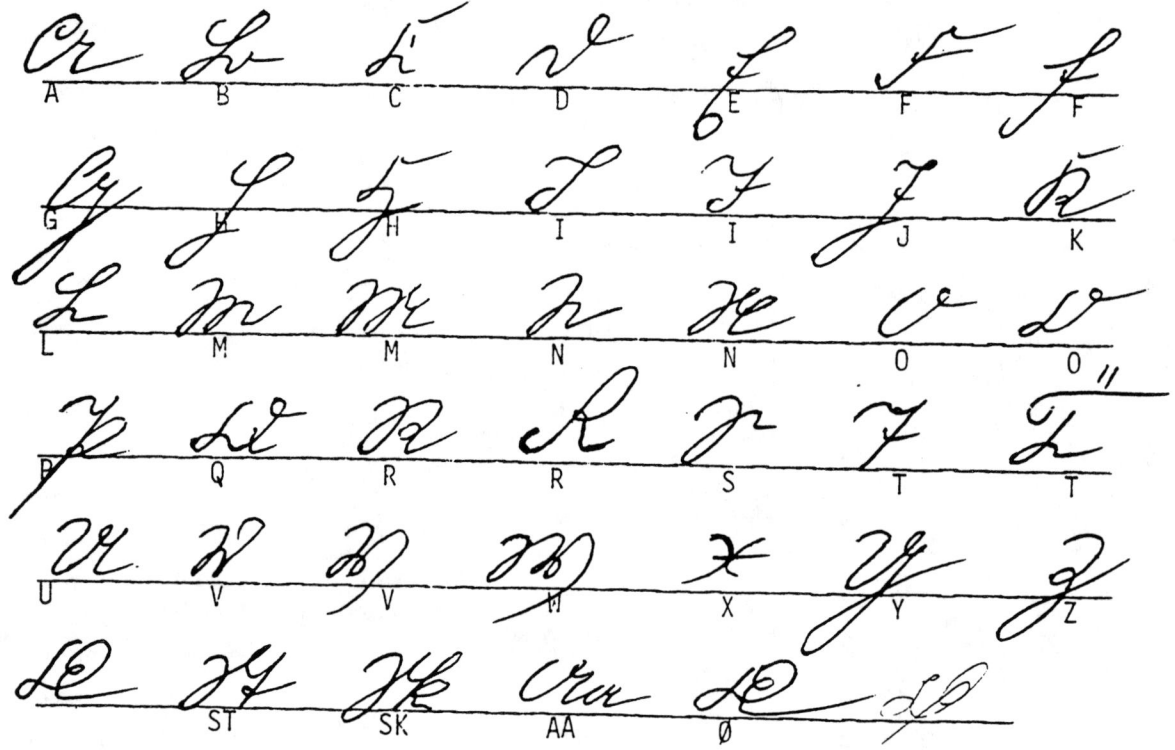

Upper Case Scandinavian Script

Table 9.6 Upper Case Letter Scandinavian Comparisons

The table shows handwritten cursive variations of upper case letters for Scandinavian comparison. Each letter of the alphabet is presented in the left margin followed by several handwritten examples.

A (six handwritten variations)
B (six handwritten variations)
C (six handwritten variations)
D (six handwritten variations)
E (six handwritten variations)
F (six handwritten variations)
G (six handwritten variations)
H (six handwritten variations)
I (six handwritten variations)
J (six handwritten variations)
K (six handwritten variations)
L (six handwritten variations)
M (six handwritten variations)
N (six handwritten variations)
O (six handwritten variations)
P (six handwritten variations)

Q (five handwritten variations)
R (six handwritten variations)
S (six handwritten variations)
T (six handwritten variations)
U (six handwritten variations)
V (six handwritten variations)
W (six handwritten variations)
X (four handwritten variations)
Y (three handwritten variations)
Z (four handwritten variations)
Å (six handwritten variations)
Ä (three handwritten variations)
Æ (six handwritten variations)
Ö (five handwritten variations)
Ø (six handwritten variations)

Calendaring challenges

There are calendaring problems in all the countries. Before 1752 the calendar year was from March 25th to March 24th. In 1752 the beginning of the year was changed to January 1st. Sometimes you will find dates written as follows: 7 ber, 8 ber, 9 ber, 10 ber. This indicates the month and the months are September, October, November, December.

The dates are often written in Roman Numerals: I, II, V, VI, X, L, C, D, M. Often, the *I* will be written with its stem going below the line making it look more like a *J*. At times the day will be written out such as Michaelmus. These dates can be converted to give the date on our current calendar.

Early English records, including English Colonies, often have the date expressed as, "In the seventh year of the reign of...". Unless the readers know the reigning period of the various rulers, they haven't a clue as to when the document was written. Table 9.7 indicates the various reigning years that affect American History.

164

Table 9.7

```
                    Guide to the Reigning Years


ELIZABETH I:                            17 Nov 1558 - 24 Mar 1603
JAMES I:                                24 Mar 1603 - 27 Mar 1625
CHARLES I:                              27 Mar 1625 - 30 Jan 1649
INTERREGUM (Cromwellian period)         30 Jan 1649 - 29 May 1660
CHARLES II:                             29 May 1660 - 06 Feb 1685
 (Royalist refused to recognize the Cromwell period and consider the reign of
 Charles II to begin 30 Jan 1649)
JAMES II:                               06 Feb 1685 - 11 Dec 1688
WILLIAM III:                            13 Feb 1689 - 08 Mar 1702
   (William III ruled jointly with Queen Mary from 13 Feb 1689 - 27 Dec 1694)
ANNE:                                   08 Mar 1702 - 01 Aug 1714
GEORGE I:                               01 Aug 1714 - 11 Jun 1727
GEORGE II:                              11 Jun 1727 - 25 Oct 1760
GEORGE III:                             25 Oct 1760 - 20 Jan 1820
```

Historical Background

Once you have found your area of study, understand the customs and naming patterns, know what jurisdiction might have the records, and you feel comfortable enough to tackle the language, it is necessary to study the historical and migrational history of the people under study. Watch for sources that will aid you in this research. They are found on the Family History Library Catalog under the name of the country and the subtopics *History* or *Emigration and Immigration*.

Green, John Richard, (1837-1883). *England.* (Salt Lake City: Filmed by the Genealogical Society of Utah, 1985.) A general history of England from 449 to 1898, indexed. FHL film #0994069 items 1-5.

History of the Counties of England. (Salt Lake City: Filmed by the Genealogical Society of Utah, 1959.) FHL film #0182308. Microfilm of manuscript (typescript). Written in old English.

Harris, Ruth-Ann Mellish. *The Nearest Place That Wasn't Ireland: A Study of Pre-famine Irish Circular Migration to Britain.* (Ann Arbor, MI: University Microfilms International, 1980.) FHL film #1368207. An original doctoral thesis Tufts University, Medford, MA.

Hotten, John Camden. *The Original Lists of Persons of Quality: Emigrants; Religious Exiles; Political Rebels; Serving Men Sold for a Term of Years; Apprentices; Children Stolen; Maidens Pressed; and Others Who Went from Great Britain to the American Plantations, 1600-1700, With Their Ages, the Localities Where They Formerly Lived.* (New York: G. A. Baker, 1931.) FHL Microfiche #6051412 (on 7 fiche).

State Street Trust Company. *Towns of New England and Old England, Ireland, and Scotland: Connecting Links between Cities and Towns of New England and Those of the Same Name in England, Ireland and Scotland; Containing Narratives,*

Descriptions, and Many Views, Some Done From Old Prints; Also Much Matter Pertaining to the Founders and Settlers of New England and to Their Memorials on Both Sides of the Atlantic. (Washington, D.C.: Filmed by the Library of Congress Photoduplication Service, 1988.) FHL film #1550240. Original copyright Boston: State Street Trust, 1920.

You will then find yourself learning about a variety of new sources which you have not tried to use before such as:

Allgemeine Deutsche Biographie. Compiled by the Historische Commission bei der Königl. Akademie der Wissenschaften. (Salt Lake City: Filmed by the Genealogical Society of Utah, 1967-1969.) Originally published in Leipzig: Dunchker & Humblot, 1875-1912 in 56 volumes. 29 Microfilms FHL film# Biographies of prominent Germans from the earliest period of the end to the 19th century. Indexed. 0599579 through 0599604, and 0483721.

Beckett, J. D., editor. *A Dictionary of Scottish emigrants into England and Wales.* (Manchester: Anglo-Scottish Family History Society, 1989). Three volume set contains information taken from such records as census returns, monumental inscriptions, and family records of individuals in England and Wales whose place of origin was Scotland.

Great Britain. Consulate (Chinkiang, China). *Consulate Register, 1865-1927.* (London : Public Record Office, 1987.) On microfilm #1494324 covering an alphabetical list of British subjects 1890-1916; as well as; probate records 1889-1924; marriages 1896-1918; notices of marriages 1897-1919; arrivals, departures, etc. 1909-1927; births 1865-1866; foreign births 1889-1926; deaths 1865-1866; 1889-1927; internments in the British cemetery 1865-1921.

Understanding the history, leads you to more sources. For example, if you knew a major war was taking place during years in which your ancestor would have been between 18 and 35, he may likely be found in military records. If a flood or natural disaster occurred in the village your ancestor came from, he may have moved to another locality along with others in the same village. Follow his neighbors and friends if you cannot trace your own ancestor and they may lead you to an area where you will find your own ancestor. Perhaps you will find an entire series of new sources such as the extracts of the 1938 German census concerning non-Germanic minorities where the emphasis is on the Jews.[27]

In any case, you can do much of your own foreign research and have a most enjoyable time while you are at it. There are so many interesting aspects of family history just waiting around the corner to be discovered.

---

[27]See for example FHL film #1742355-1742356.

Table 9.8

Roman Numerals

Abbreviations

So. (son) to   DA (DAUGHTER) To   DA (DAUGHTER) to

was bap(tized)

Table 9.9

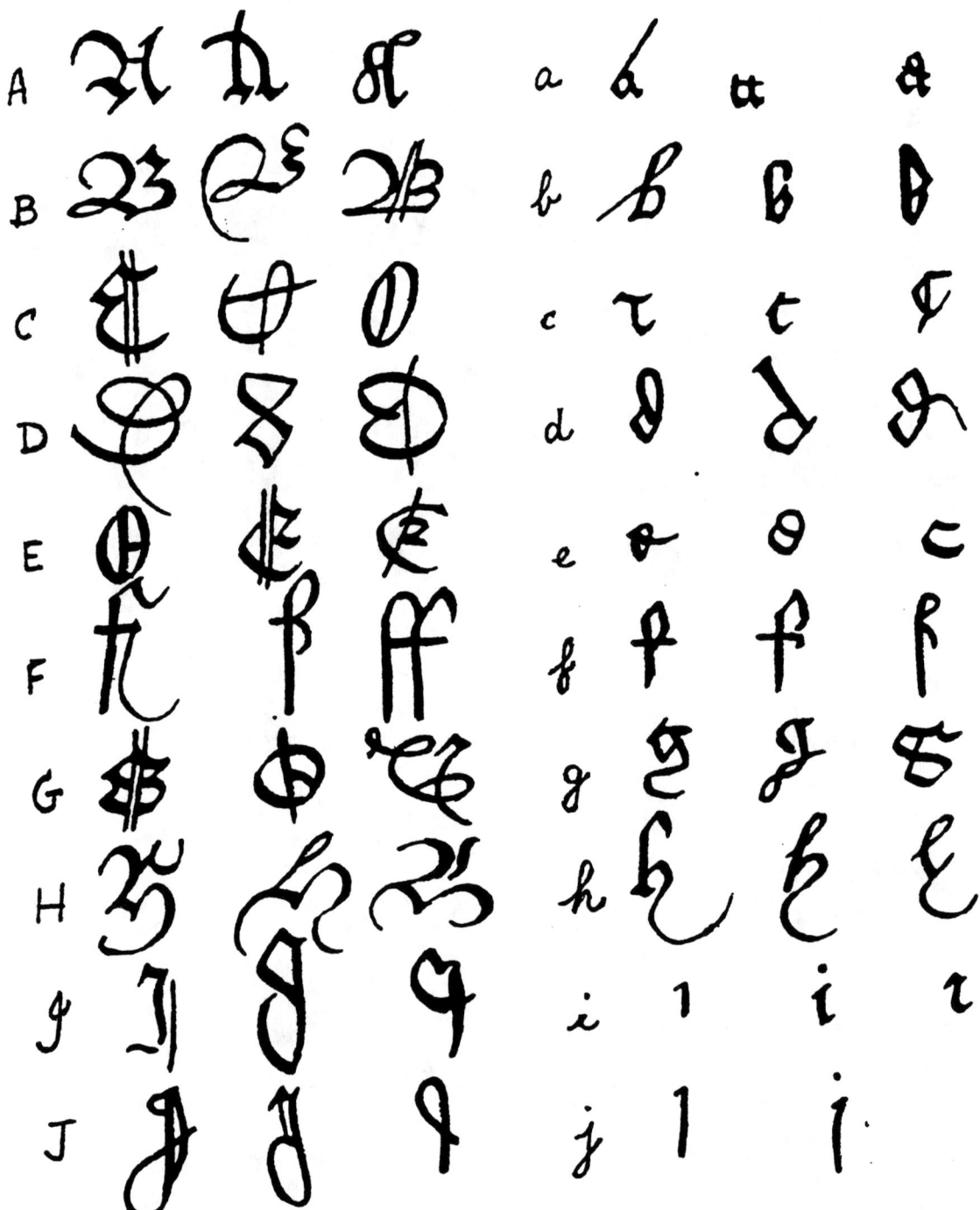

K

L

M

N

O

P

Q

ff

ss

s at
end of
word

171

Chapter Nine
Assignments: Making Sense of the Documents You've Found

1. List several sources for obtaining help on reading the paleography and the language of your area.

2. Select one of the following pages to transcribe.

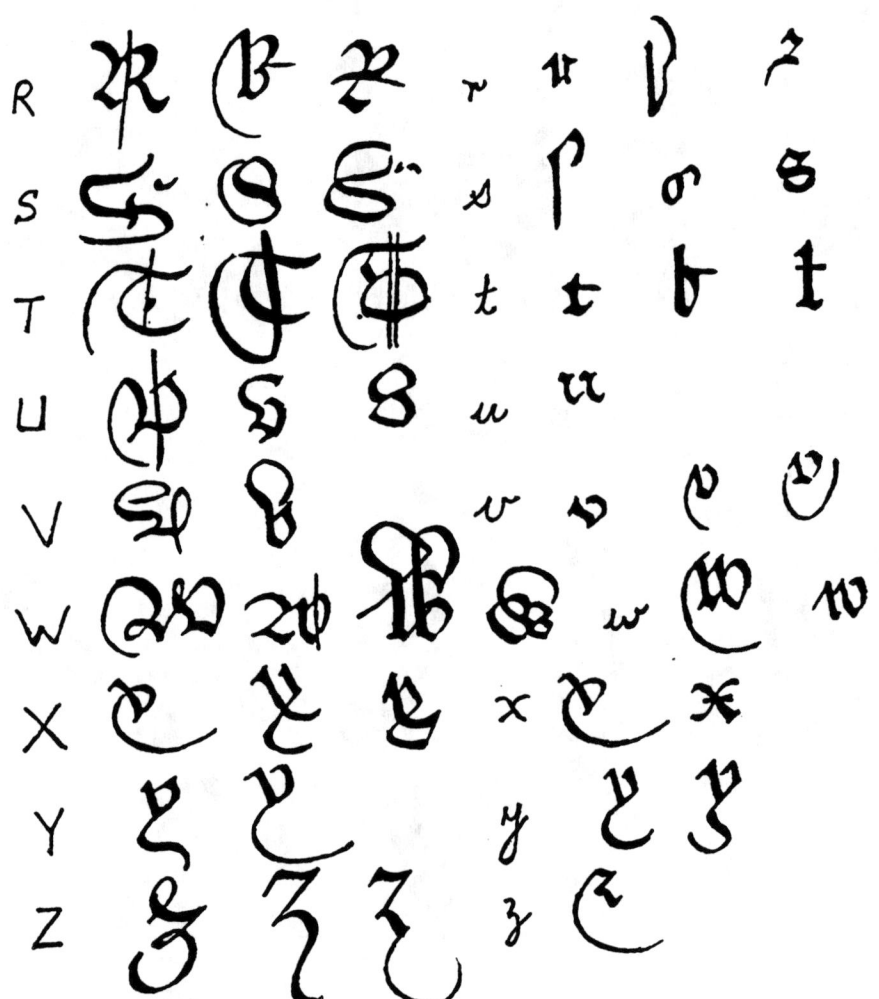

① Widow   ② Wm   ③ Eliza

④ the 26th of may   ⑤ the 19th of June   ⑥ his wife

⑦ The ninth daie of August

⑧ Potter   ⑨ sonnes   ⑩ So to

⑪ Mary daughter of william ffoster of wilton borne the fiate of October. 1686

⑫ Anne the Daughter of John Dunfon was baptyzed ye xxviijth of maye

⑬ 5 July was bap: Susanna daughter of John Brooke

⑭ John thur son sonne of Richard Harrison

Ellinor his wife in Grayes Inn

173

vigde

hon

Lysning

Född

ifrån

Piga

Johan

Döde

Döpte

på

Fader

Moder

med

dräng

Novemb:

Barn

Hustru

vet

Ålr

Månad

år

utbonn

ing

Namn

Anno

Select a foreign document of your choice and transcribe it into the computer so someone else can translate.

Selected Bibliography

Christensen, Gunnar C.. "Paleography (handwriting) - Scandinavian Gothic Script." Pgs. 100-104, *Annual Family History and Genealogical Research Conference*, Brigham Young University Conferences and Workshops, 1984.

Jensen, Larry O. "German Handwriting and Terminology." Pgs. 110-129, *Genealogy and Family History Conference*, Brigham Young University Conferences and Workshops, 1993.

Williams, Vona. "Old English Handwriting." Pgs. 357-363, *Genealogy and Family History Conference*, Brigham Young University Conferences and Workshops, 1993.

Wright, Raymond S. "German Paleography." Pgs. 114-126, *Annual Family History and Genealogical Research Conference*, Brigham Young University Conferences and Workshops, 1984.

LAB ASSIGNMENT 9:   Using *GEN-BOOK®* to Retrieve Your Family Data

1.   Use *GEN-BOOK* to convert your PAF family records to a printed
      history as per your selected options in the chapter
      assignment. Be careful to make your title line brief as it
      will be printed at the top of each page. You may expand your
      actual title page once it is in *WordPerfect®*.

2.   Go into your *WordPerfect/GEN-BOOK* generated file by starting
      the *WordPerfect* program and pressing the **F5** function key to
      list files and request it to list files in drive A. After you
      find your file, press **r** to retrieve the file and see if the
      fonts fit well on the page. Make any adjustments necessary.

3.   Check your document for over-all layout. Did you capture all
      the people you desired or do you want to try another option?
      Use the Shift + F7 view option to look over the pages and see
      if you like the font and the layout. Change the font if you
      desire before you print.

4.   Print a draft copy of your book by pressing **Shift F7** and
      selecting **1** (full document). Sometimes, when you print,
      WordPerfect® will ask: "Document may need to be generated.
      Print? No (Yes)." Answer **yes**. (NOTE: If, when you press
      Shift F7, you notice that Graphics Quality and Text Quality
      are NOT at high, you should change them to "high" so that the
      best printing will take place.)

5.   Save your document as **Assnt9.**

CHAPTER TEN

Computer-Aided Genealogical Research

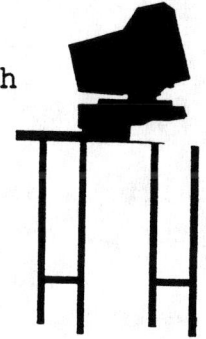

This chapter will cover:

* Computer assisted research techniques
* Organization of materials in computer data bases
* Checking for previous research using the computer
* Doing original research with computer data bases
* Finding current information on individuals
* Producing a family history report. The final product by computer technology

It doesn't take much involvement in the world of genealogy in the 1990's to recognize the impact of computer technology on family history research. From the first steps of organizing the family records to the final published history, a computer can make each task faster, easier, more accurate, and less expensive.

Genealogy & Computers for the Complete Beginner focused on using the computer as an organizational tool for entering family information and previous research. *Genealogy & Computers for the Determined Researcher* focused on using the computer as a research tool to download data from other researchers who share an interest in genealogy, and on teaching techniques for locating clues within existing documents that may not have been noted before.

This text will go beyond those initially used for the computer and focus on using CD technology for research, as well as other technology to complete a final family history for publication, video taping, or electronic storage.

Computer Assisted Research Techniques

A little program has been included with this book that will help you to analyze your data and guide you to resources for further research. Just place the computer disk in your computer and type the drive letter of that drive. Depending on your computer configuration you would type either A: or B:. Then at the A: (or B:) prompt, type GRA.

Correspondence. If you were told to write a letter to an office of vital records, a word processing program in your computer can help you to do your correspondence. You don't know how to word the letter? A computer program is there to help you.

A computer program called *Letter Links*[28] automates the process for you. It contains standardized letters which you can personalize quickly. You do not need to wonder if you are wording the information correctly or whether you are supplying all the information needed. Simply update the letter and output to your computer.

This program also contains current addresses and phone numbers for each state's division of vital statistics, plus information for

---

[28]Order from Data Tools and Services, 874 West 1400 North, Orem, UT 84057 by sending $14.95 plus shipping and handling.

U.S. territories with the current fees for copies and searches and the form of payment accepted.

The program also provides a correspondence log to track a record when copies are requested and received.

Research Calendars & Objectives. There are several methods available for preparing calendars of your research objectives. As you enter family information and research notes from the various work you have done, you are reminded of things that ought to be done. For example, as you entered a land transaction in your documentation, it reminded you that the neighbor next door had the same last name as the middle name of one of the children in the family. You want to make a note to check this other family name in the county history. In your notes you could state:

NOTE:

1. Joseph Coleman was stated as living next door in Orange County, New York in 1769. Is he listed in the Orange County, New York History. Are there any indications that his family intermarried with our Smith family?

When the time came to do research, you could simply take the family group record with the notes printed on them with you to the library or you could print the notes to a disk out of the *Personal Ancestral File*. If you are using *FamilySearch* at a local Family History Center, Library, Society or in some homes, you could print to a disk those items which you wish to search regarding the Coleman family. This might include Coleman histories, county histories, or probate records.

As you prepare your research calendars for your trip to the library, you can have all the call numbers, complete descriptions, and goals placed on one page by merging together the items off of the *Family History Library Catalog*, the *American Genealogical*

Library Computer Catalog[29], or indexes from sources mentioned below. Not only have you prepared a nice research calendar, but even better, you have prepared the report for another if you are doing this project on a client-professional basis.

Organization of Materials with Computer Assistance

The Genealogy Program. Once you have returned from your research trip (and for some people while they are on their research trip if they have portable computers), the research notes are updated reflecting negative and positive searches. This information is then moved from the word processing program back into the *Personal Ancestral File* program using *Note Tool 4.0*[30]. This program is usable with *WordPerfect, Word* or *WordStar* and uses the same keystrokes for numerous options. It is also possible to create and edit up to 800 tags and templates of commonly entered note fields. Macros (commonly used keystrokes which may be recalled by the computer as desired) may also be prepared to speed up data entry.

Inventory of Research Aids and Materials. Are you having a difficult time keeping track of your family history resources? *Resource Links*[31] is one program which makes organizing family history resources easy. The program keeps comprehensive, computerized track of individuals, artifacts, documents and certificates, books or histories, letters, magazines or newspapers, media, photographs (items/places or people), and reference materials.

---

[29] The AGLL Catalog contains the entire 3,500 pages of items available for rent or purchase from their lending library. Cost is $60 retail, but often on sale at shows. Contact AGLL, P.O. Box 329, Bountiful UT 84011-0329.

[30] Available for $19.95 plus shipping and handling from Data Tools and Services, 874 West 1400 North, Orem, UT 84057.

[31] Send $19.95 plus shipping and handling to Data Tools and Services, 874 West 1400 North, Orem, UT 84057.

An appendix includes resource categories, common resources found in the home, how to protect documents and photos, and a family history resource survey for gathering information.

Determining Previous Research

While we are on the topic of research, each time a new line is discovered, it is necessary to do a preliminary survey to determine if someone has already accomplished the research you would like to do. The computer comes to your aid again in the form of the: *FamilySearch* programs known as the *Ancestral File* (patron-submitted, lineage-linked pedigrees amounting to over 9,000,000 entries), the *International Genealogical Index* (hundreds of millions of names linked to spouses or parents and documented by sources or submitters), and the *Family History Library Catalog* surname portion which allows the researcher to locate books or microform copies of materials mentioning the line being researched.

This information may be copied to a computer disk and taken home and analyzed or moved into personal family records to aid in the research process.

Automated Archives, Inc. has produced a series of Pedigree CD's which also cover research previously accomplished by professional or individual researchers. Several computer bulletin boards (available via telephone modem), help researchers doing genealogy on similar lines, link up with each other.

Bulletin Board Systems or a BBS is another very popular method for accessing today's Information Superhighway. With the aid of a low-cost modem and the personal computer, many budding genealogists as well as experienced researchers retrieve genealogy programs, data files and information from others in a way they could never do on their own.

Bulletin boards which link together are called "nets." Messages are "local" or "echoed" from as far away as Europe. There are etiquettes and customs you should know before starting which is usually explained in their "Help" or "FAQ" (Frequently Asked

Questions) files.

The AGLL announced in 1994 a NEW national genealogical researchers computer *Bulletin Board Service (BBS)* that is totally unique to the genealogy community. Over 35 different databases and services are available to the subscriber including census indexes, marriage records, the company's microfilm catalog for browsing and ordering and a national Genealogy Message Center. You will be able to communicate electronically with the AGLL sales and customer service department. Fees $15 per month or annual $165. AGLL members can subscribe for $150. Receive one full hour per month *FREE* to use on the BBS. On-line charges are $.25 per minute after the FREE hour has been used. For more information call 801-298-5446 or 800-305-AGLL.

The German American Genealogy Quarterly put out by the Immigrant Genealogical Society of California carried an article on "Modems and Bulletin Boards." According to this article:

In most cases reading the instructions, and a one-time operating experience is about all you need...Although a modem is not a mandatory option for your system, it is advisable to look at what you gain by its use before disregarding it...the use of E-mail[32] is quicker and certainly cheaper than letter writing.

Many services are now available such as:

* CompuServe $40 startup; $8/hr. & up on line service charges. Roots Forum - Genealogy Service, 800,000 subscribers.

* GEnie sponsored by General Electric Information Services. No initial signup costs or materials. Basic services $4.95 mo non-prime-time. Genealogy Roundtable, about 300,000 subscribers.

* Prodigy, startup kit sometimes free to various prices, $14.95 mo. membership, Genealogy Bulletin Board, 1,000,000 members.

---

[32]Electronic mail messages across telephone lines.

* NGS/CIG/BBS most advanced & cooperative, sponsored by National Genealogical Society's Computer Interest Group. Receives 25,000 calls per year. Fido Bulletin Board System which is a network of volunteers with private computers called Sysops. They route messages from one to another at night. Inexpensive and volunteer motivated, very popular. And their other system National Genealogy Conference with nearly 500 bulletin boards and about 300 messages per day routing from one person to another.

* GENSOFT a companion to National Genealogical Conference including a support group of highly experienced genealogists and other experts who are messaging or monitoring and providing excellent support. Includes Genealogy Shareware Distribution System providing quick exchange of updated genealogy shareware, freeware, and some demo programs.

Even the Family History Library in Salt Lake City has set aside an area for patron BBS communications.

Okay this is now out of my "system" and into yours. I think it all comes around to marvelous ways to expand our knowledge in the field of genealogy. I believe that bulletin boards, modems, CDROM's, and computers will never take the place of a good genealogist, but they certainly make the job easier, faster, and more economical for those of us doing genealogy in a big way.

Original Research

Many computer files are available for original research including:

FamilySearch[33]

Social Security Death Index
Military Index
IGI leads

---

[33]Available at local Family History Centers, genealogical societies, or may soon be available for home use. Contact *GeneSys*, a Division of Dynix, 400 Dynix Drive, Provo, UT 84604-5650, 1-801-223-5683.

Automated Archives[34]

Census various states 1790-1870
State-wide Marriage Indexes
Native American Records
Phonedisk

Precision Indexing[35]

Census various states 1790-1910
Marriage indexes earliest to 1850
1890 Veterans Index
Lists of Passenger Ships

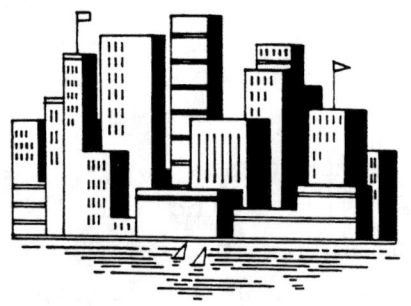

Phone directories for Canada, United States and Germany, several United States census indexes, query files, automated family pedigrees, some United States marriage records, the Biographical and Genealogy Master Index, Pennsylvania newspaper abstracts, and the National Inventory of Documentary Sources are just some of the resources currently available in the Data Center on the main floor of the Family History Library in Salt Lake City. Patrons may reserve computers in the Data Center for thirty or sixty-minute time blocks. No plans currently exist to make these sources available in family history centers.

Other projects are underway that will be incorporated in the Family History Library's computer database *FamilySearch*. One is the United States Civil Death Records project. This file will contain death records from twenty-five states, including New York, Pennsylvania, Illinois, and Ohio.

---

[34]Available from Automated Research, Inc., 327 E. 1200 S. Suite #8, Orem UT 84058, 1-800-244-1776.

[35]Contact Historic Resources, Inc., P.O. Box 329, Bountiful UT 84011-0329.

Another is the Ellis Island Passenger Arrival Lists. In 1993, the FHL began to create a *FamilySearch* resource file containing information from the Ellis Island passenger lists, 1892 to 1924. The resource file will contain the following information about each passenger: name, age, marital status, last residence, nationality, birthplace, names of relatives, name of vessel, and date and port of arrival. Other resource files which are being worked on include the 1881 Canadian census, 1880 United States census, 1881 British censuses and Civil War service records.

Some of these research systems are available on floppy disk while others are available on CD-Rom (Compact Disk-Read only memory). A compact disk can hold up to 550 million characters which equals 12-15 rolls of microfilm or 140,000 pages of text. It would take 1800 floppy disks to hold the same amount of information.[36] Searches that normally would have taken days or weeks only take minutes. Putting a $350 CD-Rom disk drive in your computer (caddy-type is better for these types of disk), turns your computer into an instant library.[37]

The *Automated Archives* CD-Rom disks contain all the federal census indexes plus some new ones such as the 1880 every name Ohio index, 1870 index for NC, MO, etc., marriage records by region;

---

[36] GENESYS, Automated Archives (AAI), November 1992.

[37] Necessary equipment: IBM compatible personal computer with at least 640K memory and a single floppy disc drive; a compact disc reader (CD-ROM); the search and retrieval software for the program you purchase; and compact disks from the company.

major genealogical works such as Virkus Genealogy; compiled pedigrees by professionals such as Ancestries; Root Cellar and Everton's Compiled Family File and soon the complete index to the *New England Historical and Genealogical Register* will be placed on CD. This includes the entire 150 volumes. By the time this goes to print several new land records series will be available listing the public domain land records in the possession of the federal government.

Samples of some of the information currently available in electronic format include those listed below. **AA** stands for Automated Archives CD's sold through Automated Research, Inc., 327 E. 1200 S. Suite #8, Orem UT 84058, 1-800-244-1776, and **PI** for Precision Indexing floppy disks sold through Historic Resources, Inc., P.O. Box 329, Bountiful UT 84011-0329.

I am giving samples of how they might be sorted by time periods, regions, or states and provinces to make them easier for the researcher to use:

SAMPLE BY TIME PERIODS

Colonial America

CD136 Census, Tax and other lists, pre 1787, AA

U.S. 1790

CD137 Census 1790 AA (all available states)
Census 1790-1850, some 1860/70, one 1880 under states below

20th Century

1960-1979 Military Index AA
1937-1991 SS Death Index AA
1994-Phone Disk AA

SAMPLE BY REGIONS[38]

U.S. & Europe
   CD017 Pre-1600's to Some 20th Century Birth Records

United States, General
   CD146 Volunteer U.S. Soldiers Military Records 1784-1811 AA
   CDJ2 Territorial Vital Records (AZ, CO, ID, MT, NV, WY, UT) AA
   CD 164 Mortality Records: 1850-1880

New England   (CT, MA, ME, NH, RI, VT)
   CD137 Census 1790 AA (all available states)
   CD138 Census 1791-1809 AA
   CD149 Census 1810
   CD141 1840 Census AA
   CD149 Vol. 1-4 Savage's FIRST SETTLERS OF NEW ENGLAND

Southern States   (AL, AK, FL, GA, KY, LA, MD, MS, NC, SC, TN,
                          TX, VA, WV)
   CD137 Census 1790 AA (all available states)

Midwestern States   (MO, WI, MI, IL, IN, OH, IA)
   CD137 Census 1790 AA (all available states)

Mid-Atlantic States (NY, NJ, PA, DE)
   CD137 Census 1790 AA (all available states)
   CDJ3 New York State Births & Deaths 1801-1992 AA
   CD139 1820-1829 No Eastern States Census Index (Federal & State)

---

[38]Some census records for one area were enumerated with another area, for example: the 1790 census for present-day Washington DC was enumerated in Montgomery and Prince George's Counties, Maryland.
   The 1820 and 1830 census records for Wisconsin were with Michigan, and the 1860 census for Wyoming was with Nebraska.
   The 1836 Iowa Territory census included Minnesota.
   The 1840 Montana census was with Clayton County, Iowa.
   The 1860 Colorado census was with Kansas, Montana was with Nebraska under "unorganized territory", Oklahoma was with Arkansas (Indian Land). Wyoming was with Nebraska. Nevada was not named, but records were with the census for Utah.

Western States (AZ, CO, ID, MT, NV, WY & UT)
    CD J1   State Marriage Records Index, Utah 1846-1992
    CD J2   Western States Vital Records

BY STATE AND CANADIAN PROVINCE

Alabama   AL
    CD136 1706, 21, 25, 64, 86, 87, 89
          Terr. Census AA
    CD151 1805-1809 Terr. Census AA
    CD150 1810,11,12,13,14,15,16,17,18,19
          Terr. Census AA
    CD154 1820-1823 Census (Terr.) AA
    CD152 1840 Census AA
    CD45 1850 Census AA
    CD26 1860 Census AA
    Early Marriages to 1825 PI
    CD3   Marriage Records AA

Alaska   AK
    CD151 1807 Territorial Census AA

Arizona   AZ
    CDJ2 Territorial Vital Records AA

Arkansas   AR
    CD150 1819 Arkansas Co, AR census
    CD154 1821-1829 Census (Terr.) AA
    CD148 1830,31,32,33,34,35,36,37,38,39
          Census AA
    CD152 1840, 41 Census AA
    CD45 1850 Census AA
    CD26 1860 Census AA
    Early Marriages to 1850 PI
    CD5 State Marriage Records AA
    CD6 State Marriages (100,000 more)
    CD227 Marriage Records Pre-1850 AA
    CD253 Land Records 1700's-1908 AA

California   CA
    CD227 Marriage Records Pre-1850 AA
          1860 Census PI
Canal Zone   CZ

Colorado   CO
    CDJ2 Territorial Vital Records AA

Connecticut   CT
    CD136 1650-1785 colonial census AA
    CD138 Census 1791-1809/Tax Lists AA

CD149 Census 1810 AA
CD140 1830 Census AA
CD141 1840 Census AA
CD40 1850 Census AA
      1860 Census PI
CD80 1860 Census AA

Delaware   DE

    CD136 1677 Upland District census AA
    CD151 1800 Census AA
    CD150 1810 Census AA
    CD140 1830, 1837 Census AA
    CD142 1840 Census AA
    CD41 1850 Census AA
    CD22 1860 Census AA
          1860 Census PI

District of Columbia   DC
    CD136 1748 colonial census AA
    CD151 1800 Census AA
    CD150 1810 Census AA
    CD154 1820-1823 Census AA
    CD148 1830 Census AA
    CD142 1840 Census AA
    CD43 1850 Census AA
    CD24 1860 Census AA
          1860 Census PI
    Early Marriages to 1825 PI

Florida   FL
    CD253 Land Records 1700's-1908 AA
    CD151 Census 1791-1809/Tax Lists AA
    CD154 1821-1829 Census AA
    CD148 1830 Census AA
    CD152 1840, 45 Census AA
    CD45 Census 1850
    CD26 Census 1860
         1860 Census PI

Georgia   GA
    Early Marriages to 1800 PI
    CD3 State Marriage Records AA
    CD226 Georgia Marriages 1700's-1850
    CD151 1792-1809 Census AA
    CD150 1810-19 Census AA

190

CD154 1820-1826 Census AA
CD148 1830-39 Census AA
CD152 1840, 45 Census AA
CD45 1850 Census AA
CD26 1860 Census AA
      1870 Census PI

Guam   GU

Hawaii   HI

Idaho   ID
    CDJ2 Territorial Vital Records AA

Illinois   IL
    CD136 1774 Hopkinton Dist colonial
          census, 1787 Terr. Census AA
    CD151 1793 Census AA
    CD150 1810, 1818 Census AA
    CD154 1820 Census AA
    CD148 1830-39 Census AA
    CD153 1840 Census AA
    CD27 1860 Census AA
          1870 Census PI: Chicago
    Early Marriages to 1825 PI
    CD2 State Marriage Records AA
    CD228 State-wide Marriage index
    CD35 1880 Cook Co Census

Indiana   IN
    Early Marriages to 1825 PI
    CD2 State Marriage Records AA
    CD228 State-wide Marriage index AA
    CD150 1810 Harrison Co Census AA
    CD154 1820 Census AA
    CD148 1830-39 Census AA
    CD153 1840 Census AA
    CD46 1850 Census AA
    CD27 1860 Census AA

Iowa   IA
    Early Marriages to 1850 PI
    CD227 Marriage Records Pre-1850 AA
    CD148 1830-39 Census AA
    CD153 1840-49 Terr. Census and Tax AA

Kansas   KS

Kentucky   KY
    CD136 1780-9 colonial census AA
    CD151 1791-1801 Census/Tax Lists AA

CD150 1810 Census AA
CD154 1820 Census AA
CD148 1830-39 Census AA
CD153 1840 Census AA
CD44 1850 Census AA
CD34 1870 Census AA
      1890 Veterans Census PI
Early Marriages to 1800 PI
CD229 Marriage Records Pre-1850 AA
CD2 State Marriage Records AA

Louisiana   LA
    CD253 Land Records 1700's-1908 AA
    CD136 1704, 21, 31, 49, 66, 85, 99
          colonial census AA
    CD151 1791, 1803, 04, 07, 07, 09
          census AA
    CD150 1810-1812 Census AA
    CD154 1820 Census AA
    CD148 1830-39 Census AA
    CD152 1840 Census AA
    CD45 1850 Census AA
    CD26 1860 Census AA
          1890 Veterans Census PI
    CD227 Marriage Records Pre-1850 AA
    CD1 State Marriage Records AA

Maine   ME
    CD136 1640-1778 colonial census AA
    CD138 Census 1791,93,94,99, 1800 AA
    CD149 Census 1810 AA
    CD140 1830 Census AA
    CD141 1840 Census AA
    CD40 1850 Census AA
    CD77 1860 Census AA
          1890 Veterans Census PI

Maryland   MD
    CD136 1640-1788 almost every other
          year colonial census AA
    CD4 State Marriage Records AA
    CD151 1796-1800 Census AA
    CD150 1810, 1819 Allegheny only AA
    CD154 1820 Census AA
    CD148 1830-39 Census AA
    CD142 1840 Census AA
    CD43 1850 Census AA
    CD24 1860 Census AA
          1890 Veterans Census PI

Massachusetts   MA
    CD136 1630-1788 almost every other
        year colonial census AA
    CD138 1791-1809 Census/Tax Lists AA
    CD149 1810 Census AA
    CD140 1830 Census AA
    CD141 1840 Census AA
    CD40 1850 Census AA
    CD51 1860 Census AA
        1890 Veterans Census PI

Michigan   MI
    CD136 1769, 78, 79, 80, 82 colonial
        census AA
    CD151 1791, 99, 1802, 05, 06, 07
        census AA
    CD150 1810 Wayne Co Terr Census AA
    CD154 1820-29 Territorial Census AA
    CD148 1830-39 Territorial Census AA
    CD153 1840 Census AA
        1890 Veterans Census PI
    CD254 Land Records (Public Domain)

Minnesota   MN
    CD227 Marriage Records Pre-1850 AA
    CD153 1840-49 Census AA
        1890 Veterans Census PI

Mississippi   MS
    CD136 1779,88,89 Natchez Dis cens AA
    CD151 1792-1809 census AA
    CD150 1810, 11, 12, 18 Census AA
    CD154 1820-28 Territorial Census AA
    CD148 1830, 37 Census AA
    CD152 1840, 41, 45 Census AA
    CD45 1850 Census AA
    CD26 1860 Census AA
        1890 Veterans Census PI
    Early Marriages to 1825 PI
    CD5 State Marriage Records AA

Missouri   MO
    CD136 1789 territorial census AA
    CD151 1807, 08 census AA
    CD150 1810, 11, 18 Census AA
    CD153 1840 Census AA
    CD148 1830-39 Census AA
        1870 Census PI: St. Louis
    Early Marriages to 1825 PI
    CD227 Marriage Records Pre-1850 AA
    CD5 State Marriage Records AA

Montana   MT
    CDJ2 Territorial Vital Records AA

Nebraska   NE

Nevada   NV
    1910 Census Index PI
    CDJ2 Territorial Vital Records AA

New Hampshire   NH
    CD136 1640, 57, 1709, 36, 40, 42, 76
        Colonial Census AA
        1790 Census PI
    CD138 1800 Census AA
    CD149 1810 Census AA
    CD140 1830 Census AA
    CD141 1840 Census AA
    CD40 1850 Census AA

New Jersey   NJ
    CD136 1643-1789 abt every year
        Colonial Census AA
    CD151 1791-1809 Census/Tax Lists AA
    CD150 1810-19 Census AA
    CD140 1830, 32, 34 Census AA
    CD142 1840 Census AA
    CD41 1850 Census AA
    CD22 1860 Census AA

New Mexico   NM
    CD152 1840 Provin. Census AA

New York   NY
    CD136 1702, 03, 14, 20 Colonial
        Census AA
        1790 Census PI
    CD138 1800 Census AA
    CD149 1810 Census AA
    CD140 1830 Census AA
    CD141 1840 Census AA
    CD42 1850 Census AA
    CD21 1860 Census AA
        1870 Census PI: Long Island
        1890 Veterans Census PI
    NY Passenger Ships by Date PI
    NY Passenger Ships alphabetically PI
    CD160 NY Valley Quarterlies Index
        1600's-1900's
    CDJ3 NY Births & Deaths 1801-1992 AA

North Carolina   NC
    Early Marriages to 1825 PI
    CD229 Marriage Records Pre-1850 AA
    CD4 State Marriage Records AA
    CD136 1684-1785 colonial census AA
        1790 Census PI
    CD151 1791-1809 Census/Tax Lists AA
    CD150 1810-19 Census AA
    CD154 1820 Census AA
    CD148 1830-39 Census AA
    CD152 1840 Census AA
    CD43 1850 Census AA
    CD24 1860 Census AA
        1870 Census PI
    CD34 1870 Census AA

North Dakota   ND

Ohio   OH
    CD2 State Marriage Records AA
    CD136 1789, Northwest Territory 1788,
        1789 Colonial Census AA
    CD151 1796-1809 Census AA
    CD150 1810, 17, 18 Census AA
    CD154 1820 Census AA
    CD148 1830 Census AA
    CD153 1840 Census AA
    CD46 1850 Census AA
    CD20 1880 Census AA

Oklahoma   OK
    CD NA 1 Native American AA

Oregon   OR
    1860 Census PI
    CD227 Marriage Records Pre-1850 AA

Pennsylvania   PA
    CD136 1692, 1727-79 Colonial Cen AA
    CD151 1791-1808 Census/Tax Lists
    CD150 1810 Census AA
    CD140 1830 Census AA
    CD142 1840 Census AA
    CD41 1850 Census AA
    CD22 1860 Census AA
        1870 Census Western PA PI
        1870 Philadelphia PI
        1870 Census Eastern PA PI

Puerto Rico   PR

Rhode Island   RI

CD136 1773-1776 Colonial Census AA
    1790 Census PI
CD138 1800 Census AA
CD149 1810 Census AA
CD140 1830, 31 Census AA
CD141 1840 Census AA
CD40 1850 Census AA
    1860 Census PI

South Carolina   SC
    CD136 1706, 20's, 30's, 40's, 1758,
        1778, 1780, 1787 Colonial
        Census AA
    CD151 1792-1809 Census/Tax Lists AA
    CD150 1810, 11, 18 Census AA
    CD154 1820 Census AA
    CD148 1830-39 Census AA
    CD152 1840, 43, 45 Census AA
    CD45 1850 Census AA
    CD26 1860 Census AA
        1870 Census PI
    CD3 State Marriage Records AA

South Dakota   SD

Tennessee   TN
    CD151 1796-1808 Census/Tax Lists AA
    CD150 1810,12,14,15,18 Census AA
    CD154 1820 Census AA
    CD148 1830, 32 Census AA
    CD152 1840 Census AA
    CD44 1850 Census AA
    Early Marriages to 1825 PI
    CD229 Marriage Records Pre-1850 AA
    CD2 State Marriage Records AA

Texas   TX
    Early Marriages to 1850 PI
    CD227 Marriage Records Pre-1850 AA
    CD5 State Marriage Records AA
    CD154 1821-29 Spanish Terr Census AA
    CD152 1840, 41, 42, 43, 44, 45, 46,
        47, 48, 49 Census AA
    CD49 1860, 70, 80, 90 Mortality
        Schedule, (plus all SSN from
        Death Masters Record 1937-Jan
        1990 AA)
        1890 Veterans Census PI

Utah   UT
        CD168 SLC Cemetery Records
        CDJ1 Marriage Records Index, 1846-1992
        CDJ2 Territorial Vital Records AA

Vermont   VT
        CD136 1763-1789 Colonial Census AA
        1790 Census PI
        CD138 1791-1809 Census/Tax Lists AA
        CD149 Census 1810 AA
        CD140 1830 Census AA
        CD141 1840 Census AA
        CD40 Census 1850
        CD78 Census 1860

Virginia   VA
        CD136 1624-1779 Colonial Census AA
        CD151 1792 Census Halifax Co, 1801
                Army Lands, 1800
                Accomack/Lancaster AA
        CD151 1810 Census AA
        CD154 1820 Census AA
        CD148 1830 Census AA
        CD142 1840 Census AA
        CD43 1850 Census AA
        CD24 1860 Census AA
                1870 Census PI
        CD34 1870 Census AA
        CD229 Marriage Records Pre-1850 AA
        Early Marriages to 1800 PI
        CD4 State Marriage Records AA
        The Virginia Genealogist Vol 1-20

Virgin Islands   VI

Washington   WA

West Virginia   WV
        CD148 1830-39 Census AA
        CD43 Census 1850
        CD24 Census 1860
        1870 Census PI
        CD34 1870 Census AA

Wisconsin   WI
        CD154 1821, 22, 29 Terr. Census AA
        CD148 1830 Census AA
        CD153 1840, 42 Census AA
        CD39 1860 Census AA

Wyoming   WY

CDJ2 Territorial Vital Records AA
1910 Census PI

            Canada

Alberta   AB
British Columbia   BC
Manitoba   MB
New Brunswick   NB
Newfoundland   NF
Nova Scotia   NS
Northwest Territories   NT
Ontario   ON
        1848/50 Census PI
Prince Edward Island   PE
Quebec   QC
Saskatchewan   SK
Yukon   YN

            Ireland

1831/1841 Census (2 counties) AA

Also available on CD:

Everton's Family File & Roots
Linked Pedigrees #1 (800,000 names)
Linked Pedigrees #2 (700,000 names)
Linked Pedigrees #3 (750,000 names)
Social Security Death Index
First Families of America, Frederick Virkus
National Zip Code & Courthouse Directories
Pro-phone
Indian Question-Native American Windows
Ani-map County Boundary Historical Atlas
Draws county boundaries during different time
periods. (Available from Automated Research, Inc., 327
E. 1200 S. Suite #8, Orem UT 84058, 1-800-244-1776.)

Handybook for Genealogists

Current Information

Sometimes it is necessary to contact living individuals such as relatives, societies, libraries and acquaintances. Again the computer comes to your aid through the services of *Phonedisc*[39] containing all the listed and some unlisted numbers throughout the United States. Phone listings for some foreign countries are also now available.

Phonedisc has a comprehensive cross reference of alternate spellings built into its director which you can flip to with a single keystroke. It can compute statistics on a single name from the database...how many "Smiths" there are in Los Angeles or even the entire country. It also has a built in cross index to various people at the same phone number as well as a built-in address cross directory to find other individuals residing at that person's same or nearby address. Zip code access can also be included.

The Final Product

It is now possible to "publish" your information in a CD-Rom format to make it much easier to access materials. Companies are watching for good genealogies to publish. Many families have produced printed volumes in the past but do not have a version available in electronic format. A printed copy with printed release forms can be submitted for evaluation and if it can be scanned and converted to machine readable format, it is accepted by producers of these products. Special projects such as the California state-wide voter registrations, etc., could also be done on such a system.

As was explained in *Genealogy & Computers for the Determined Researcher*, downloading information from a computer data base is so much easier than typing charts over and over again or mailing pounds of photocopied forms back and forth across the nation. The *GEDCOM* program allows for movement into various genealogical management programs and provides a way to share information between IBM and Macintosh users. It also allows for sharing across phone lines.

---

[39] Available from Automated Research, Inc., 327 East 1200 South, Suite 8, Orem UT 84058, 1-800-244-1776 or GeneSys, a Division of Dynix, 400 Dynix Drive, Provo UT 84604-5650, 1-801-223-5683.

The ability to produce *ASCII* texts from one word processor or program to another allows the researcher to transfer all or part of a family history from a data base of information into various word processing programs to produce reports or to publish a book. It also allows for movement into data-base management programs for manipulating and analyzing information if that is necessary. Most people have never learned all the abilities of the *Personal Ancestral File* as a data-base manager. Some which are often over-looked are PAF's Focus and Design Features, PAF's Place Indexes, PAF's Ability to download to ASCII for other searches, not to mention its low cost and support.

Reporting of findings in the form of a client report, abstracts, transcripts on one side with the original document scanned in on the other side, footnotes, indexing, family group record data and pedigree charts produced in compressed form with standard genealogical publishing layout, are all now available for the genealogist.

The following chapters will deal with the specifics regarding converting your family records to a completed family history.

Chapter Ten
Assignments: Computer-Aided Genealogical Research

Select one of the items below:

1.   If you have access to the AAI CD's search the *Master Name Index* (see
      footnote 39 for address to obtain this CD-0 index for $35) which is
      the surname index to all their other CD's. Then search the actual
      CD to see if you can find clues on your family. They are available
      in many historical or genealogical societies or family history
      centers.

2.   If you have access to a BBS, try locating a genealogy forum and see
      what information is available.

3.   Become familiar with another aspect of *FamilySearch* you have not
      used before.

LAB ASSIGNMENT 10:   Using *WordPerfect*® to Pull It All Together

1.   Retrieve the file you make in the last assignment into Document 1.
      Use Shift F3 and retrieve the introductory materials you worked on
      previously into Document 2. Go back into Doc. 1.

2.   Check your document for spelling errors by pressing **Ctrl F2,** then
      3 for document. Press **2** to skip any names that are not found in
      the dictionary.

3.   Block and move any introductory materials and acknowledgments from
      Doc. 2 into Doc. 1 at the appropriate pages.

4.   If you wish to include names, places, events, etc., in the index,
      now is the time to mark them for indexing. This is done by **Alt F5
      3.**

5.   Save your file as **Assnt10.**

CHAPTER ELEVEN

From PAF Family Records to a Printed Family History

This chapter will cover:

- *Pafability*
- *KinWrite*
- *GEN-BOOK*
- Draft copy
- Genealogy numbering systems
- Scanning materials into your family history

Several programs are now available for transferring information from the *Personal Ancestral File* to a Word Processing Program. This reduces the amount of work you have to do, makes it easy to include transcribed oral histories, historical texts, and pictures, and makes it possible to create an index to your family history.

Three programs that I have experimented with in my classes are: *Pafability*, *KinWrite* and *Gen-Book*. I finally settled upon *Gen-Book* after the producer of the program made some changes to tailor it to the projects my students were working on, but each of these programs has its advantages.

Pafability

Pafability[40] takes the documentation notes from your PAF files and prints them below the individual they apply to. This accessory program is a shareware program and is much less expensive than the others. The user has the option of creating a single line report that lists the descendants of one individual or a multiple line report listing the descendants of each ancestor of a specified individual. It also runs on all classes of MS-DOS compatible computers and supports Epson compatible dot matrix printers, Hewlett Packard LaserJet compatible printers and provides an option for creating an ASCII file for use with your own word processor.

Requirements to use this program as we do in class are *PAF 2.2/2.31*, a word processor, most any printer, and an *IBM* compatible computer, with one floppy disk drive and a hard drive or two floppy disk drives, and 512K memory.

Using this program is not easy for a beginning computer user as the menu assumes some knowledge on the part of the user. When inserting text deleting text, or adding pictures, there is no automatic adjustments to the page numbers or to the index.

---

[40]Cost as of the date of this publication was $12.00 plus applicable sales tax. Specify disk size (3 1/2" or 5 1/4"). Order from Ms. Barbara Bennett, 6426 Pound Apple Court, Columbia, MD 21045.

KinWrite

KinWrite[41] uses menus and prompts similar to *PAF's* for flexible formatting and has an automatic indexing feature. It allows a draft format with spaces for missing information, or it can "print" your report to disk to be picked up in your word processing program. You either select the prime ancestor for a descendancy genealogy, or you identify the person whose ancestors are to be reported. The program then extracts the necessary data from your *PAF* data disk, identifies family relationships, and prints the appropriate family reports by generation or by family line. Documentation notes may follow individuals if you elect to include them. The format may include RIN numbers or the ancestors of each individual.

KinWrite's text editor can customize page headers, and construct title pages, table of contents, foreword and documentation pages. Other features include a utility to help you find individuals in your *PAF* file who are not properly linked to a family, another lists the earliest ancestor of each family line, while another analyzes the longevity of the people in your file. A special side-by-side printing utility produces ancestor charts displaying any number of generations in minimal space while preserving easy traceability.

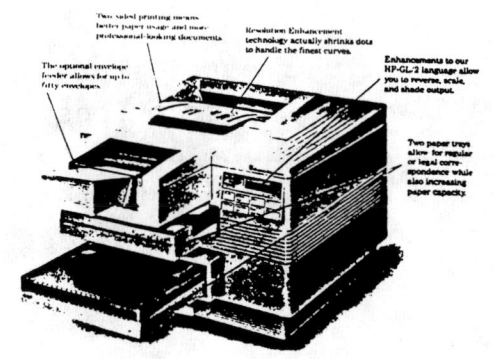

This program requires *PAF 2.0, or higher, DOS 2.0 or higher, an* IBM Graphics Printer, a Hewlett-Packard laser printer, or a printer that is compatible with one of these models; and an *IBM* compatible computer, with one floppy disk drive and a hard drive or two floppy disk drives, and 512K memory.

---

[41]Order from LDB Associates, Inc., P.O. Box 20837, Wichita, KS 67208-1837. Send $59.00 and specify disk size, (Kansas residents, add $3.48 KS State sales tax).

In the version we tested, the notes printed on separate pages, after the listing of individuals. While some may prefer this format, it often made it difficult to link a specific note to the individual to whom it referred.

GEN-BOOK

GEN-BOOK[42] provides the user with the ability to generate a family history by moving your data and notes directly from PAF into a *WordPerfect* file. It provides a variety of ID numbering systems (Modified Register, Henry, Descendancy, Ahnentafel, Multi-Surname), and reports the number of generations included. The report format may include blank lines for missing information, RIN numbers, or the ancestors of each individual. Both Tagged Notes and Source Notes may be included. Of course sensitive or private notes can be edited or deleted once the report is in *WordPerfect*.

Because of the powerful combination of *WordPerfect* features and the easy directions provided in the *GEN-BOOK* instructions, pictures, maps, certificates or personal histories can be added to the book; changes can be made to the size and style of print, the page size, and the margins; and several other books and biographies can be combined into one book.

---

[42] Order from Mr. Rex B. Clement, Clement Custom Programming, 2105 Country Lane, Auburn, CA 95603. Send $59.95 plus $4.35 sales tax for CA residents.

When finished with the report, *WordPerfect* will generate a table of contents and a two- or three-column Index of Names. *Gen-Book* requires *PAF 2.2/2.31*, *WordPerfect 5.0/5.1/5.1+ and up*, *WordPerfect For Windows*, and *Microsoft Word 2.0/6.0*.

Printing a Draft Copy

Since all of these programs use data from the *Personal Ancestral File* computer program, it is assumed that the person who is using this book has already used this program to:

a.   record family records,
b.   document records,
c.   download information from others via GEDCOM
d.   and to continue the research process.

Now is the time to print a draft copy of perhaps one or two of your family lines to see if you are missing information you would like to include for your family reunion, family holidays, client reports, magazine submissions or personal use. I suggest doing a draft print before a trip to a major library or to relatives so that you will be prepared to answer questions, such as:

a.   What pictures would look nice in this book?
b.   Could I locate copies of pictures of the time period for the same locality from non-copyrighted county histories, or from clip art books, etc?
c.   Am I missing a specific locality (date, name, etc.) for an event I could pick up at the library?
d.   Do I need some historical background as a foreword to my book?
e.   Who might I be able to interview, who would know some interesting tidbits about the family? Are there friends, acquaintances, or local historians who could be contacted?

The best way to figure out what you are missing is to use one of the accessory programs mentioned above to download your existing records from PAF into a word processor or printer. These programs take most of the tedious "writing" out of the family history project and allow you to spend your time "polishing".

All three of these programs extract the necessary information from your existing data files while they identify family relationships and print the appropriate family reports in various number systems using complete sentences in clear text with your source notes and biography included.

Both *GEN-BOOK* and *Kinwrite* allow you to add supplementary text to your book but only *GEN-BOOK* automatically adjusts the page numbering. Just wait until text, photos, maps, documents, and clip art have been entered before generating the final table of contents or index.

The first step is to ask the program to "print" your PAF family files to a disk file (rather than directly to the printer). Instructions for operating Gen-Book are given in the assignment portion of this chapter. Just follow the easy instructions on the program. It is necessary before starting the program to do the following:

1. Know what RIN you wish to start with.
2. Know if you want a descendancy book or an ancestral book.
3. Know what PATH your PAF family records are in if on your hard drive. If it is on a floppy disk, you'll need to know the letter of the drive you will be using.
4. Decide on the type of numbering system you would like to use. (The options are explained later in this chapter.)
5. Decide if you want RIN numbers to be included.
6. Decide which collateral lines you would like to include.

If you wish supplementary names (such as those included in your notes) to be included in your index, you will need to "tag" those supplementary names as your word processor requires for indexing. See your word processor manual for instructions or see the instructions at the end of this chapter. Or, if you only have a few names to add, you may wish to just type in a few corrections after the index is generated by the word processing program.

The main reasons I personally selected *GEN-BOOK* to produce the final reports in my classes were:

1. The program's ease of operation.
2. The ability to tailor the program to fit a large variety of printed reports.
3. The capability to produce an index with not only the given name of the individual but also a birth and death year.
4. The ability to have every note listed immediately after each individual citation improved readability.
5. The ease with which supplementary materials could be added, fonts changed, personalized touches added, and pages renumbered.

You may find one of the other programs works just as well for you. The producers of all three products have made the writing of family histories much easier and their appearance much more professional.

The following are sample pages produced using *GEN-Book*.

Source Notes Footnoted (This looks very nice and will pick up your tagged notes such as those marked with an ! mark, but it separates the citation from the actual note and is not recommended in our class assignments.)

Source Notes Footnoted

GENERATION NO. 4

29. Jesse Warren[4] CLEMENT [34] (14.Darius[3], 3.Thomas[2], 1.Darius, Sr.[1]) was born 30 Mar 1866 in Fairview, , Utah. He married **Sarah Matilda BRADY** [35] 16 Oct 1895 in Manti, Sanpete, Utah. She was born 23 Dec 1875 in Fairview, Sanpete, Utah, the daughter of Jordan BRADY and Mary Lavina HOWELL.

They had 6 children:

+ 44.	M	i.	Jesse Aral CLEMENT, born 8 Feb 1899.
45.	M	ii.	Warren Brady CLEMENT, born 19 Nov 1901 in Fairview, Sanpete, Utah, died 30 Mar 1909. [36]
46.	M	iii.	Gwendlyn Clay CLEMENT, he went by the name of Clay, born in Fairview, Sanpete, Utah, died 4 Jul 1917. [37]
47.	M	iv.	Salem Winton CLEMENT, he went by the name of Winton, born in Fairview, Sanpete, Utah, died 14 Mar 1909.
+ 48.	M	v.	Jordan Lowell CLEMENT, born 25 May 1910, died 1 Feb 1983.
+ 49.	M	vi.	Lyle Edison CLEMENT.

Sarah died 30 Jun 1970 in Folsom, Sacramento, California, and was buried 3 Jul 1970 in Fairview, Sanpete, Utah.
NOTES for Sarah follow:
She was an excellent story teller and her many grand children would always ask her to tell them a story.
Jesse died 1933 in Salt Lake City, , Utah, and was buried in Fairview, Sanpete, Utah.
NOTES for Jesse follow:
OCCUPATION: He was a very good carpenter and built many houses. He also made lots of fine furniture. He had a sawmill and used water power. He planted a large orchard with a variety of fruits and nuts. He was the first person in Duchesne to own an automobile.
INVENTIONS: He was also an inventor and received patents on several of his inventions. He invented an Incubator for hatching chicken eggs, and a Weeder for weeding a garden. He had a sawmill and machinery that was run with water power.
DEATH: He had always enjoyed good health, so when he got a sideache, he ignored it. After several days, when it wouldn't go away, he finaly went to a hospital in Salt Lake City, where he died from a ruptured appendix.

- - - - - - - - - -

30. Darius Albert[4] CLEMENT (14.Darius[3], 3.Thomas[2], 1.Darius, Sr.[1]) was born 30 Dec 1869 in St Joseph, Lincoln, Nevada. He married (1) **Mary Ann COX** 21 Nov 1888 in Manti, Sanpete, Utah. She was born 25 Jan 1871 in Fairview, Sanpete, Utah.

---

[34] INFORMATION: Rex B. Clement, The Ancestors and Descendants of Jesse Warren Clement and Sarah Matilda Brady; Auburn, California, 1992.

[35] Personal Knowledge of Rex Clement, 1994

[36] Death: He was killed while playing near a water powered machine.

[37] Death: He was struck by lightning while getting the horses ready to go to Duchesne.

9

If you wish to call attention to missing information to help you prepare for a research trip, try printing out a report leaving a blank line for missing information.

Blank Line for missing information

27. **Jesse⁴ Warren CLEMENT** (12.Darius³, 2.Thomas², 1.Darius, Sr.¹) was born 30 Mar 1866, in Fairview, _____, Utah. He married Sarah Matilda BRADY 16 Oct 1895, in Manti, Sanpete, Utah. She was born 23 Dec 1875, in Fairview, Sanpete, Utah, the daughter of Jordan BRADY and Mary Lavina HOWELL.

They had 6 children:

+ 42.　M　　i.　Jesse Aral CLEMENT, born 8 Feb 1899, died __ ___ ____.
　43.　M　　ii.　Warren Brady CLEMENT, born 19 Nov 1901, in Fairview, Sanpete, Utah, died 30 Mar 1909, in _____, _____, _____, and was buried __ ___ ____, in _____, _____, _____.
　44.　M　　iii.　Gwendlyn Clay CLEMENT, born __ ___ ____, in Fairview, Sanpete, Utah, died 4 Jul 1917, in _____, _____, _____, and was buried __ ___ ____, in _____, _____, _____. He went by the name of Clay. **Death:** He was struck by lightning while getting the horses ready to go to Duchesne.
　45.　M　　iv.　Salem Winton CLEMENT, born __ ___ ____, in Fairview, Sanpete, Utah, died 14 Mar 1909, in _____, _____, _____, and was buried __ ___ ____, in _____, _____, _____. He went by the name of Winton.
+ 46.　M　　v.　Jordan Lowell CLEMENT, born 25 May 1910, died 1 Feb 1983.
+ 47.　M　　vi.　Lyle Edison CLEMENT, born __ ___ ____, died __ ___ ____.

Sarah died 30 Jun 1970, in _____, _____, _____, and was buried __ ___ ____, in _____, _____, _____.
NOTES for Sarah follow:
She was an excellent story teller and her many grand children would always ask her to tell them a story.
Jesse died __ ___ 1933, in Salt Lake City, _____, Utah, and was buried __ ___ ____, in Fairview, _____, Utah.
NOTES for Jesse follow:
OCCUPATION: He was a very good carpenter and built many houses. He also made lots of fine furniture.
INVENTIONS: He was also an inventor and received patents on several of his inventions. He invented an Incubator for hatching chicken eggs, and a Weeder for weeding a garden. He had a sawmill and machinery that was run with water power.
DEATH: He died from a ruptured appendix.
SOURCE NOTES for Jesse follow:
INFORMATION: Rex B. Clement, The Ancestors and Descendants of Jesse Warren Clement and Sarah Matilda Brady; Auburn, California, 1992.

- - - - - - - - - -

28. **Darius⁴ Albert CLEMENT** (12.Darius³, 2.Thomas², 1.Darius, Sr.¹) was born 30 Dec 1869, in St Joseph, Lincoln, Nevada. He married (1) Mary Ann COX 21 Nov 1888, in Manti, Sanpete, Utah. She was born 25 Jan 1871, in Fairview, Sanpete, Utah. She was the daughter of _____ _____ and _____ _____.

14

Notes may also be endnoted which is nice for a short client report.

CHAPTER 4

Source Notes Endnoted

GENERATION NO. 4

29. Jesse Warren[4] CLEMENT [a] (14.Darius[3], 3.Thomas[2], 1.Darius, Sr.[1]) was born 30 Mar 1866 in Fairview, , Utah. He married **Sarah Matilda BRADY** [b] 16 Oct 1895 in Manti, Sanpete, Utah. She was born 23 Dec 1875 in Fairview, Sanpete, Utah, the daughter of Jordan BRADY and Mary Lavina HOWELL.

They had 6 children:

+ 44.	M	i.	Jesse Aral CLEMENT, born 8 Feb 1899.
45.	M	ii.	Warren Brady CLEMENT, born 19 Nov 1901 in Fairview, Sanpete, Utah, died 30 Mar 1909. [c]
46.	M	iii.	Gwendlyn Clay CLEMENT, he went by the name of Clay, born in Fairview, Sanpete, Utah, died 4 Jul 1917. [d]
47.	M	iv.	Salem Winton CLEMENT, he went by the name of Winton, born in Fairview, Sanpete, Utah, died 14 Mar 1909.
+ 48.	M	v.	Jordan Lowell CLEMENT, born 25 May 1910, died 1 Feb 1983.
+ 49.	M	vi.	Lyle Edison CLEMENT.

Sarah died 30 Jun 1970 in Folsom, Sacramento, California, and was buried 3 Jul 1970 in Fairview, Sanpete, Utah.
NOTES for Sarah follow:
She was an excellent story teller and her many grand children would always ask her to tell them a story.
Jesse died 1933 in Salt Lake City, , Utah, and was buried in Fairview, Sanpete, Utah.
NOTES for Jesse follow:
OCCUPATION: He was a very good carpenter and built many houses. He also made lots of fine furniture. He had a sawmill and used water power. He planted a large orchard with a variety of fruits and nuts. He was the first person in Duchesne to own an automobile.
INVENTIONS: He was also an inventor and received patents on several of his inventions. He invented an Incubator for hatching chicken eggs, and a Weeder for weeding a garden. He had a sawmill and machinery that was run with water power.
DEATH: He had always enjoyed good health, so when he got a sideache, he ignored it. After several days, when it wouldn't go away, he finaly went to a hospital in Salt Lake City, where he died from a ruptured appendix.
- - - - - - - - - -

30. Darius Albert[4] CLEMENT (14.Darius[3], 3.Thomas[2], 1.Darius, Sr.[1]) was born 30 Dec 1869 in St Joseph, Lincoln, Nevada. He married (1) **Mary Ann COX** 21 Nov 1888 in Manti, Sanpete, Utah. She was born 25 Jan 1871 in Fairview, Sanpete, Utah.

They had 1 child:

50.	F	i.	Nancy Elizabeth CLEMENT, born 18 Nov 1889 in Fairview, Sanpete, Utah.

Darius next married (2) **Betty SMITH**.

12

ENDNOTES FOR CHAPTER 4

a. INFORMATION: Rex B. Clement, The Ancestors and Descendants of Jesse Warren Clement and Sarah Matilda Brady; Auburn, California, 1992.

b. Personal Knowledge of Rex Clement, 1994

c. Death: He was killed while playing near a water powered machine.

d. Death: He was struck by lightning while getting the horses ready to go to Duchesne.

e. Info: 1860 census Lynn, Posey, Indiana Birth, marriage, and Death: A & D Amasa Carr film 1206440 p. 21 & 35 Burial: in graves 1 and 2 lot 45 in Redwood Memorial Gardens, Guerneville

f. Info: A & D Amasa Carr film _____ p. 34-35

g. Info: A & D Amasa Carr film 1206440 p. 35, 68-69 Note: Never married.

h. Info: A & D Amasa Carr film 1206440 p. 35 Note: Had no children by Charles

18

Sample *GEN-BOOK* printout of Modified Version Text set up as per instructions in Assignment at the end of this chapter.

Graphics added

GENERATION NO. 4

27. Jesse⁴ Warren CLEMENT (12.Darius³, 2.Thomas², 1.Darius, Sr.¹) was born 30 Mar 1866, in Fairview, , Utah. He married Sarah Matilda BRADY 16 Oct 1895, in Manti, Sanpete, Utah. She was born 23 Dec 1875, in Fairview, Sanpete, Utah, the daughter of Jordan BRADY and Mary Lavina HOWELL.

They had 6 children:

+ 42.	M	i.	Jesse Aral CLEMENT, born 8 Feb 1899.
43.	M	ii.	Warren Brady CLEMENT, born 19 Nov 1901, in Fairview, Sanpete, Utah, died 30 Mar 1909.
44.	M	iii.	Gwendlyn Clay CLEMENT, born in Fairview, Sanpete, Utah, died 4 Jul 1917. He went by the name of Clay. Death: He was struck by lightning while getting the horses ready to go to Duchesne.
45.	M	iv.	Salem Winton CLEMENT, born in Fairview, Sanpete, Utah, died 14 Mar 1909. He went by the name of Winton.
+ 46.	M	v.	Jordan Lowell CLEMENT, born 25 May 1910, died 1 Feb 1983.
+ 47.	M	vi.	Lyle Edison CLEMENT.

Sarah died 30 Jun 1970, in Folsom, Sacramento, California, and was buried 3 Jul 1970, in Fairview, Sanpete, Utah.

NOTES for Sarah follow:

She was an excellent story teller and her many grand children would always ask her to tell them a story.

Jesse died 1933, in Salt Lake City, , Utah, and was buried in Fairview, , Utah.

NOTES for Jesse follow:

OCCUPATION: He was a very good carpenter and built many houses. He also made lots of fine furniture.

INVENTIONS: He was also an inventor and received patents on several of his inventions. He invented an Incubator for hatching chicken eggs, and a Weeder for weeding a garden. He had a sawmill and machinery that was run with water power.

DEATH: He had a sideache that didn't go away. After several days he went to a hospital in Salt Lake City, where he died from a ruptured appendix.

SOURCE NOTES for Jesse follow:

INFORMATION: Rex B. Clement, The Ancestors and Descendants of Jesse Warren Clement and Sarah Matilda Brady; Auburn, California, 1992.

Jesse and Sarah

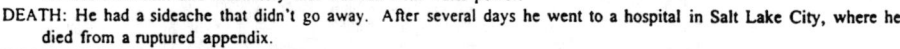

28. Darius⁴ Albert CLEMENT (12.Darius³, 2.Thomas², 1.Darius, Sr.¹) was born 30 Dec 1869, in St Joseph, Lincoln, Nevada. He married (1) Mary Ann COX 21 Nov 1888, in Manti, Sanpete, Utah. She was born 25 Jan 1871, in Fairview, Sanpete, Utah.

12

Sample *GEN-BOOK* printout of Table of Contents

TABLE OF CONTENTS

Sample *GEN-BOOK* printout of Index (3 column with birth and death years)
(Notice the females with their maiden name given in parenthesis, for example, Mary Lavina (Howell) who married a BRADY is listed under both HOWELL and BRADY.)

INDEX OF NAMES

Various Numbering Systems

Reference was made earlier in this chapter to various numbering systems which these programs produce. Brief descriptions of these systems and samples will follow.

Register: The Register system of publishing a family history was invented by the New England Historic Genealogical Society over 100 years ago, and is used as the standard method of displaying a genealogy in their periodicals. The oldest ancestor is always number 1 and children are numbered in sequence. Each descendant is listed with his or her own children directly below them, and there are only two columns created: one for adults and one for children. Only those descendants who are also listed as adults will be assigned a number. Each family group uses lower case Roman Numerals to number children in order of birth. The names of descendants are written with all letters capitalized. Only the given names are listed for the children.

A major flaw of the Register system has been that adding a child to a family group will cause the numbers to change *for every descendant thereafter*. Therefore, genealogists normally do not assign register numbers until they are completely ready to go to print.

Sample Register System:

Sample taken from *Genealogies of Barbados Families* published by Genealogical Publishing Company. Notice the numbers 3, 4, 5, and 6 beside those children who will actually be covered in the book. Abel, #3, is listed at the top of the page and further down with his own wife.

Children of Reynold[2] and Mary (Skeet) Alleyne, born in Barbados :—

3. i. ABEL 3.
   ii. REYNOLD, of St. Philip, Barbados. Will dated 25 Oct 1675 proved 1688 at Barbados. Abstract; Eliza and Edward Skeat, children of Col. Edward Skeat. My sister Mrs. Mary Rous. My sister Elizabeth Alleyne. Brother Abel Alleyne Mrs. Mary Skeat. Mr. Alleyne Culpepper and Francis Culpepper. Nephew Reynold Alleyne.
   iii. DIX. The name Dix appears in the copied record of his father's will but in the entry of his marriage to Priscilla Benson he is named Lt. Bix Allen. He was probably named after his fathers' friend David Bixe*
   iv. MARY, Married Major Thomas Rouse of the *Cliff*, St. John, Barbados. Living in 1662.
   v. ELIZABETH, born soon after 16 June 1650 and referred to in father's will, then unborn.

Mary (Skeet) Alleyne, widow of Reynold Alleyne,[2] married secondly John Turner of St. Philip, Barbados. and predeceased him, leaving issue named in her husband's Will dated 26 Nov. 1673 Pr. 14th June 1675.

Children of Mary (Skeet) Alleyne and John Turner:

(1) ANNE TURNER, Md. Tobias Frere, their son John Frere, Lieut General and President of the Council of Barbados. Married Elizabeth his cousin.
(2) MARY TURNER Md. 1st. Col. Thomas Farmer, Md. 2nd. Col. Thomas Spiar whose will dated 28 Nov. 1682 mentions Abel Alleyne brother-in-law. Mary Spiar daughter, and to her heirs the plantation etc., called Mount standfast, Barbados. Thomas and Mary Spiar had issue :—

   (i) Mary Spiar, married Robert Stewart, whose child, Mary Stewart, married Sir Mark Pleydell Bart.
   (ii) Elizabeth Spiar Md. John Frere aforesaid son of Tobias Frere & Anne Turner his cousin.
   (iii) Rebecca Spiar Md. William Terrill of Cabbage Tree Hall, St. Lucy Barbados and had issue a Daughter. Mary Terrill, Md. John Alleyne her cousin. Their son Sir John Gay Alleyne.

(3) ABIGAIL or ELEANORA TURNER Md — Lighthouse of Bridgetown, Barbados.

3. ABEL ALLEYNE[3] *(Reynold[2] Richard.[1])* Married 12 Jan. 1665/6 Elizabeth Denzy, daughter of Thomas Denzy, at St. John, Barbados.

Elizabeth Denzy, Bapt 27 July 1652, daughter of Thomas Denzy, whose will is dated 1674. Barbados. She died 25 Sept 1705 at St. James, Barbados.

Children :

4. i. THOMAS 4, bapt. April 1668 at St. Philip, Barbados. Died 10 Feb. 1717 at Barbados, Married Judith Thornhill.
5. ii. REYNOLD Born 1672 at Barbados. Died 2 Oct. 1722 at St. James, Barbados Married Elizabeth Isabella Gay.
6. iii. BENJAMIN Buried 22 April 1721 at St. James, Barbados. Married (1) Arabella Pilgrim, (2) Anne Kirton.

*Priscilla Benson was the only daughter of Robert Benson of St. John, Gent and Katharine his wife.

8

Modified Register: This method is used by the National Genealogical Society. Every descendant receives a number and those who will be continued as adults are indicated with a plus sign. All names of adults and spouses are printed with bold, upper/lower case type.   Since NGS editors do not use abbreviations, but spell out words such as born, married, died, the modified register follows this convention.

Modified Register System

GENERATION NO. 4

27. Jesse[4] Warren CLEMENT (12.Darius[3], 2.Thomas[2], 1.Darius, Sr.[1]) was born 30 Mar 1866, in Fairview, , Utah. He married Sarah Matilda BRADY 16 Oct 1895, in Manti, Sanpete, Utah. She was born 23 Dec 1875, in Fairview, Sanpete, Utah, the daughter of Jordan BRADY and Mary Lavina HOWELL.

They had 6 children:

+ 42.	M	i.	Jesse Aral CLEMENT, born 8 Feb 1899.
43.	M	ii.	Warren Brady CLEMENT, born 19 Nov 1901, in Fairview, Sanpete, Utah, died 30 Mar 1909.
44.	M	iii.	Gwendlyn Clay CLEMENT, born in Fairview, Sanpete, Utah, died 4 Jul 1917. He went by the name of Clay. Death: He was struck by lightning while getting the horses ready to go to Duchesne.
45.	M	iv.	Salem Winton CLEMENT, born in Fairview, Sanpete, Utah, died 14 Mar 1909. He went by the name of Winton.
+ 46.	M	v.	Jordan Lowell CLEMENT, born 25 May 1910, died 1 Feb 1983.
+ 47.	M	vi.	Lyle Edison CLEMENT.

Sarah died 30 Jun 1970, in Folsom, Sacramento, California, and was buried 3 Jul 1970, in Fairview, Sanpete, Utah.
NOTES for Sarah follow:
She was an excellent story teller and her many grand children would always ask her to tell them a story.
Jesse died 1933, in Salt Lake City, , Utah, and was buried in Fairview, , Utah.
NOTES for Jesse follow:
OCCUPATION: He was a very good carpenter and built many houses. He also made lots of fine furniture.
INVENTIONS: He was also an inventor and received patents on several of his inventions. He invented an Incubator for hatching chicken eggs, and a Weeder for weeding a garden. He had a sawmill and machinery that was run with water power.
DEATH: He had a sideache that didn't go away. After several days he went to a hospital in Salt Lake City, where he died from a ruptured appendix.
SOURCE NOTES for Jesse follow:
INFORMATION: Rex B. Clement, The Ancestors and Descendants of Jesse Warren Clement and Sarah Matilda Brady; Auburn, California, 1992.

- - - - - - - - - -

28. Darius[4] Albert CLEMENT (12.Darius[3], 2.Thomas[2], 1.Darius, Sr.[1]) was born 30 Dec 1869, in St Joseph, Lincoln, Nevada. He married (1) Mary Ann COX 21 Nov 1888, in Manti, Sanpete, Utah. She was born 25 Jan 1871, in Fairview, Sanpete, Utah.

They had 1 child:

48.	F	i.	Nancy Elizabeth CLEMENT, born 18 Nov 1889, in Fairview, Sanpete, Utah.

Darius next married (2) Betty SMITH 10 Oct 1905, in Fairview, Sanpete, Utah. She was the

12

Henry: In this method the first person is number 1. His or her children would be number 11, 12, 13, 14, etc. Children of number 11 would be 111, 112, 113 and so on. In order words, the number indicates a generation as well as a birth order. You can read a Henry number such as 13113 from right to left as the 3rd child of the 1st child, of the 1st child, of the third child of number 1. If a family has over 9 children, the 10th child would be an "A", and 11th a "B", etc. In all other ways, the Henry system appears like the Modified Register system which indicates continued adult lines using a plus sign, etc.

Henry System

GENERATION NO. 4

.14A161 Jesse[4] Warren Clement (.14A16.Darius[3], .14A1.Thomas[2], .14A.Darius[1]) was born 30 Mar 1866, in Fairview, Sanpete, Utah. He married Sarah Matilda Brady 16 Oct 1895, in Manti, Sanpete, Utah. She was born 23 Dec 1875, in Fairview, Sanpete, Utah, the daughter of Jordan Brady and Mary Lavina Howell.

They had 6 children:

.14A1611	Jesse Aral Clement	b. 8 Feb 1899	d.
.14A1612	Warren Brady Clement	b. 19 Nov 1901	d. 30 Mar 1909
.14A1613	Gwendlyn Clay Clement	b. 16 Apr 1905	d. 4 Jul 1917
.14A1614	Salem Winton Clement	b. 18 Nov 1908	d. 14 Mar 1909
.14A1615	Jordan Lowell Clement	b. 25 May 1910	d. 1 Feb 1983
.14A1616	Lyle Edison Clement	b. 1 Dec 1915	d.

Sarah died 30 Jun 1970, in Folsom, Sacramento, California, and was buried 3 Jul 1970, in Fairview, Sanpete, Utah. Jesse was a Carpenter. Jesse died 13 Mar 1933, in Salt Lake City, Salt Lake, Utah.
NOTES for Jesse follow:
OCCUPATION: He was a very good carpenter and built many houses. He also made lots of fine furniture.
INVENTIONS: He was also an inventor and receivied patents on several of his inventions. He invented an Incubator for hatching chicken eggs, and a Weeder for weeding a garden. He had a sawmill and machinery that was run with water power.
DEATH: He died from a ruptured appendix.
Update: this is an update.
SOURCE NOTES for Jesse follow:
INFORMATION: Rex B. Clement, The Ancestors and Descendants of Jesse Warren Clement and Sarah Matilda Brady; Auburn, California, 1992.

- - - - - - - - - -

.14A162 Darius[4] Albert Clement (.14A16.Darius[3], .14A1.Thomas[2], .14A.Darius[1]) was born 30 Dec 1869, in St Joseph, Lincoln, Nevada. He married Mary Ann Cox 21 Nov 1888, in Manti, Sanpete, Utah. She was born 25 Jan 1871, in Fairview, Sanpete, Utah.

They had 1 child:

.14A1621	Nancy Elizabeth Clement	b. 18 Nov 1889	d.

Mary Ann died 12 Oct 1928, in Fairview, Sanpete, Utah, and was buried 16 Oct 1928, in Fairview, Sanpete, Utah. Darius died 19 Jul 1959, in Kennewick, Benton, Washington, and was buried 22 Jul 1959, in Kennewick, Benton, Washington.

12

Ahnentafel: *Ahnentafel* is a German word which means *ancestor table*. The first person is always number 1 and each ancestor is then assigned a unique ID number that is related mathematically to that individual. This is a most efficient method of displaying a pedigree but is not as easy to read. To find the father of any person, double that person's number. To find a mother of any person, double the person's number and add one.

Ancestors by Ahnentafel

GENERATION NO. 1

1. **Jesse Warren Clement** was born 30 Mar 1866, in Fairview, Sanpete, Utah. He was the son of **2.Darius Salem Clement** and **3.Louisa Kelsey**. He married Sarah Matilda Brady 16 Oct 1895, in Manti, Sanpete, Utah. She was born 23 Dec 1875, in Fairview, Sanpete, Utah, the daughter of Jordan Brady and Mary Lavina Howell.

They had 5 children:

M	i.	Jesse Aral Clement	b. 8 Feb 1899	d.
M	ii.	Warren Brady Clement	b. 19 Nov 1901	d. 30 Mar 1909
M	iii.	Gwendlyn Clay Clement	b. 16 Apr 1905	d. 4 Jul 1917
M	iv.	Salem Winton Clement	b. 18 Nov 1908	d. 14 Mar 1909
M	v.	Lyle Edison Clement	b. 1 Dec 1915	d.

Sarah died 30 Jun 1970, in Folsom, Sacramento, California, and was buried 3 Jul 1970, in Fairview, Sanpete, Utah. Jesse died 13 Mar 1933, in Salt Lake City, Salt Lake, Utah.

GENERATION NO. 2

2. **Darius Salem Clement** was born 24 Nov 1834, in Dryden, Tompkins, New York. He was the son of **4.Thomas Clement** and **5.Elizabeth Betsey Foote**. He married **3.Louisa Kelsey** 27 Nov 1859, in Union Fort, Salt Lake, Utah.

3. **Louisa Kelsey** was born 9 Aug 1844, in Nauvoo, Hancock, Illinois, the daughter of **6.Easton Kelsey** and **7.Abigail Finch**.

They had 3 children:

1. M	i.	Jesse Warren Clement	b. 30 Mar 1866	d. 13 Mar 1933
M	ii.	Darius Albert Clement	b. 30 Dec 1869	d. 19 Jul 1959
M	iii.	Thomas Alma Clement	b. 13 Mar 1879	d. 30 Jun 1957

Louisa died 17 Nov 1919, in Fairview, Sanpete, Utah, and was buried 20 Nov 1919, in Fairview, Sanpete, Utah. Darius died 22 May 1917, in Mesa, Maricopa, Arizona, and was buried 25 May 1917, in Mesa, Maricopa, Arizona.

GENERATION NO. 3

4. **Thomas Clement** was born 1 Apr 1792, in Washington, New York. He was the son of **8.Darius Clement** and **9.Mehitable Griswold**. He married **5.Elizabeth Betsey Foote** 15 Mar 1812, in Dryden, Tompkins, New York.

5. **Elizabeth Betsey Foote** was born 8 Feb 1794, in East Windsor, Broome, New York, the daughter of **10.David Foote** and **11.Irene Lane**.

They had 6 children:

F	i.	Nancy Clement	b. 31 Oct 1815 d. 26 Mar 1847

2

Perhaps you will simply want to take information you have already typed into your *PAF* notes and bring it into the word processing program for inclusion into your history. This is very easy to do using the PRINT TO FILE option in *PAF*. Just note the RIN of the individual whose notes you want to transfer, select **P** to **Print** at the PEDIGREE SEARCH screen, tap #1 **Select Printing Option** at the PRINT FORMS AND REPORTS menu, tap #2 **Print to Disk File**, and type in the disk drive you wish to copy notes to, and give the file a name. Now return to the **PRINT FORMS AND REPORTS** menu, select #3 Range Print, select #4 Notes for Individuals, and at PRINT NOTES FOR MULTIPLE INDIVIDUALS menu type in the RIN number or numbers you wish to print.

Scanning Materials Into Your Family History

Pictures convey information and impressions in a way that can not be accomplished with words alone. Given a choice between a printed page with a picture and a page full of text, we will instinctively look at the picture first. It isn't any wonder that we all desire pictures to be a part of our text.

All scanners measure light reflected off the subject image using built-in lamps that shine light on the image you are scanning. A row of light sensors, measures the light that bounces off the image. Dark areas of the subject image reflect less light than bright areas. A scanner's

resolution is determined by the size and number of its sensors. Most scanners have between 100 and 400 sensors "dots-per-inch" or "dpi". Some scanners have controls to let the user set the scanning resolution. The high-resolution limit is limited by the number of sensors in the scanner, but the scanner can scan at lower resolutions by combining outputs from *several* of the sensors into a single value. Combining pairs of sensors gives half the resolution; every third sensor gives one-third resolution, and so on.

With a hand scanner, a rubber roller turns as the scanner is pulled across the paper. A mechanical detector inside the roller determines when it has advanced enough to collect a new line of image data. Because they are moved by hand, some users have problems moving them straight and with uniform speed.

At 400 dots-per-inch, a 4-inch wide hand scanner will produce 400 x 4 or 1,600 values per row. At 400 rows per inch this results in 640,000 values per inch of a four-inch wide picture. Slow computers, such as 286 or 386SX machines may have difficulty reading this data as fast as the scanner is producing it. This only applies to hand-held scanners, since other types of scanners are controlled by the computer and will slow down or even stop if the computer can't keep up.

Some hand-held scanners have buffers to hold the data if the computer starts lagging behind. If the scanner does not have a buffer and computer lags behind, some data may be lost, resulting in a dark line or shrunken image. Most hand held scanners have an indicator that flashes if the computer can't keep up. If the light flashes, move the scanner more slowly. Because the hand-held scanners are quite compact, and travel over the surface of the scanned image, they can generally be used quite successfully to scan books and other material which present problems for other types of scanners.

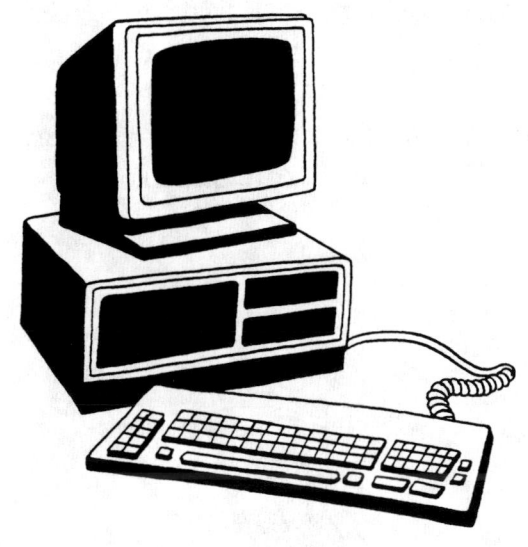

A flat-bed scanner, uses a stepper motor that moves in precisely controlled increments to position the scanner head at the next line to be scanned. The image to be scanned is placed face down on a glass bed (usually 8.5 x 11 inches). A cover is laid over the image and the scanner sensor is moved under motor control from one end of the page to the other. These scanners are the largest, and cannot effectively scan books or large documents.

Like most other areas of computer technology, scanners are rapidly changing. Prices continue to drop while resolution and capabilities continue to expand. It won't be long before skanners will be a popular tool to the family historian, but most genealogists are waiting for the technology to improve a bit more before purchasing their own machine.

Just as pictures contain more information than words, it takes much more space to store pictures than to store words. To use a scanner you will need a computer with substantial amounts of space on a fast hard disk. A medium to high quality monitor and fast video card are also needed to ensure accurate display of the images. A 386 computer running at 33 Mhz should provide a minimum acceptable performance level for modest-size image files. The minimum RAM size required is 4 MB.

Going to 6 or 8 MB of RAM can make a large difference in performance, because multiple copies of the image data must be created during the image manipulation. If the RAM space is not available, these images must be constantly saved to and read from the hard disk which makes the process much slower. You should have at least a 256-color VGA display.

Black and white newspaper pictures are printed using "half-tone" techniques that spread out solid black dots to make them appear gray. Regular black and white photos use true scales of gray varying from white to black. Printing grayscale pictures presents problems for black/white printers. The effective resolution of a 300-dpi black ink laser printer drops to around 53 dpi when printing a grayscale or color  picture. For a large printed image this can provide a good appearance, but for small images, 53 dpi is inadequate.

Color printers capable of printing shades of gray retain their full resolution when printing grayscale images. Dot-matrix printers produce poor quality grayscale images. Printed dots aren't as dark or as uniform as a laser, and each dot is much larger than a laser-printed dot. A 300-dpi laser or bubble printer is capable of producing barely acceptable quality images, but there is a significant difference in the quality of output produced by different programs printing the same image file.

To get excellent reproduction, you will need to use a 133 or 150 line screen, but anything over 100 **dpi** must be presented as a screened negative. *ADOBE PhotoShop* or *Digital Dark-Room* can create electronic (EPS) files which can be used to make *screened negatives*. Since these files are huge, they will need to be held in place by a smaller TIF[43] file and then presented separately. The preferred screen for negatives is 133 line.

What Do Publishers Think of Scanned Photographs? They report that by scanning photographs into your document you may be compromising quality and not saving money in the process. While they admit, scanning is terrific for black and white items which do not have gray shading such as maps, documents, and line drawings, photographs or anything containing shades of gray, will need to be scanned **and then put through another program,** such as *ADOBE PhotoShop* or *Digital Dark-Room*, to obtain the halftone attributes (a line screen), so the image will be printable.

They further indicated that *screening*, standardly done at 85, 100, 120, 133, and 150 dpi [dots per inch], is a separate process from "scanning in your image" at a certain dpi. Once photos are screened, they cannot be reduced without distorting the image. Therefore, before you screen your photo, you'll need to know how big the photo will be in your book and choose a text area that will allow the publisher to work with your screen photo at 100%.

If you want to save the entire approximately $14.00 per photo or $15.50 for larger book sizes, screening/stripping cost of photographs, select an 85 or 100 line screen when you use your *ADOBE PhotoShop* or *Digital Dark-Room* program. Give the publisher a positive printout of your text with screened photographs in place. You need to watch for consistent darkness of the pages

---

[43]A file format developed by Microsoft and Aldus to support desktop publishing. It is considered a rather complex standard with many optional configurations which may result in some incompatibility and trouble transferring TIF files between computer systems.

throughout or else the publisher will have trouble getting good reproduction quality. Light photos will remain light and dark photos will remain dark. If they adjust the exposure to compensate for the lightness or darkness of the photos, the text will come out too light or too dark. The obligation for photo results will rest primarily with you.

Some techniques they suggested were: do not place light and dark photos on the same page. As a rule, even darkness throughout will give you adequate reproduction quality.

Cost. The publisher I spoke with indicated that creating screened negatives from your EPS files can cost you in time. It can take up to 6 hours of computer time to run out a single photo file. Also, the output film is quite a bit more expensive than regular film. You will pay between $3-7/photo, depending on the size and complexity of the photo. **In addition,** there will be a $4.50/each stripping charge for merging halftone negatives with text negatives, unless they are taking the text from your disks and the photo file is embedded with a TIF file (an image storage file which appear to be supported by the publisher's typesetting applications.)

Larry Ledden[44] indicated that the EPS image storage system developed by Adobe® for typesetting applications is extremely inefficient for the desktop publisher which may account for the previous paragraph in which the publisher suggested usage of that program. As Larry indicated, "Many software packages cannot display EPS images on screen, but can only print them."

I listened to a presentation by Larry at the GEN-TECH Conference in Texas in 1994 and was impressed with his knowledge on the subject of photographic scanning. As he mentioned during that class, disk storage is a significant issue when you are working with scanned images. Image files are quite large and there are many file formats to select from for saving your scanned images.

---

[44] *Complete Guide to Scanning* by Larry Ledden from Family Technologies, pg. 65.

Larry referred to image files as *digitized imagery*. Those that he recommended for existing PC formats included BMP developed by Microsoft® specifically for the Windows® environment. Nearly all compatible software supports this format. OS/2 uses a variant of the BMP format. BMP supports images of all color depths as well. Another was TIF developed by Microsoft and Aldus®.

A third was PCD developed by Kodak® for the Photo CD products. Perhaps you have seen advertisements of how Kodak will develop photographic film and store the digitized images on a CD in PCD format. CD players have been released which can play audio CDs and play PCD images for display on a standard TV. It is accepted by professionals in the photo processing industry.

Electronic photo files require high level computer hardware: A minimum of 100 MB hard drive, minimum 4MB ram, 33 mhz for computer speed, a color monitor with a 24 bit graphics card, a mouse, and perhaps a removable hard disk cartridge system--(Syquest is the industry standard if you have a lot of photographs). You will also need a flatbed scanner, since hand held scanners cannot give a consistent enough image for quality photo work. Let us do your photos if you want the best possible reproduction quality. If cost is more of an issue than quality, use screened positives to be shot with the text and use EPS files for 133-line screen, but expect to pay $3-11.50/each for them. And, remember the printed quality will depend on the quality of the files we receive.

To get good quality photos, you must scan at the proper dpi. Calculate a dpi based on the line screen to be used and the percentage of reduction or enlargement to be used. Here's the formula: 2 x the line screen x the output size. In other words, if you're planning to use a 133 line screen and enlarge a photo to twice its original size, you would multiply 2 x 133 = 266 x 200% = 532 dpi. If you're reducing the photo to half its size and are using a 100 line screen, you would figure 2 x 100 = 200 x .50 - 100 dpi.

This means you'll need to know before you scan the photo, how big it will appear in the book and whether you're going to use screened positives or screened negatives. You'll need to make cropping decisions before you scan, as well. Incorrect decisions about scanning will result in poor quality printed photographs.

Can disks just be sent to publishers? Disk-to-film, and, in another few years, disk-to-plate technology is the wave of the future for commercial publishers. It allows passing the conventional camera and stripping work (a potential time saver) and gives high resolution typography (better than your computer printer can produce). There is a down side, too. Making changes after your book is at press becomes more complicated and  costly, and you will probably end up paying more.

Publishers suggest saving your document in a *PostScript* file format. (*PostScript* is a language that describes entire page layout). You must be using *Adobe Type 1* or *III PostScript* fonts. To avoid an extra "strip up charge", your software must be able to interface with the publisher's equipment.

When you submit your files, make sure they will work, and if they don't there's a charge for fixing them. About 98% of files received need some correction; therefore, generally, you will be paying something extra at this stage. Workable files are run

228

through equipment which outputs high resolution (2540) dpi negatives.

If the software used to make the files is compatible, they can run it through their large format imposetter (a machine which composes type and also lays out the negatives for printing in one large sheet.) For incompatible software programs, they may use a standard imagesetter to produce single negatives. The imagesetter gives the same high resolution type as the imposetter, but you'll have to pay extra $4.50 per page to have your single page negatives laid out.

While most commercial publishers are switching to electronic prepress technology which requires high resolution type because they have the resources to invest in specialized software programs and the training to use them, individuals producing only one or a few books may wish to wait until this technology produces real cost saving before embracing the entire field.

Thus far we have discussed only the finest quality of family histories comparing the accounts of various experts in the field. However, for many of us who are engaged in our family histories and who do not intend to publish more than 20 to 25 copies of our book, typesetting of our book is really not even considered. Photocopying, laser printing and scanning may prove quite adequate for what we have in mind at this particular time. Particularly when our goal is to locate others working on this same line at this time so we might tie up loose ends while we preserve what we have gathered along the way.

Taking advantage of local college courses on the subject of scanning, joining a neighborhood or community computer users group, or working side by side with a knowledgeable friend will provide you with many hours of free advice and experience.

Sample GEN-BOOK Default Pages

```
              GEN-BOOK   Ancestors   Defaults List No. 1
A.  Name of the Registered GEN-BOOK user = KAREN CLIFFORD
B.  Sub-Directory path to PAF data files = C:\PAF\CHAT
C.  Sub-Directory path to put WP files = C:\WPP\DOC\
D.  Version of WordPerfect 5.0/5.1 & above = 1
E.  File Name of the Book = chatbk2   Default File Name = SYSDATA.002
F.  Title:The Ancestors of              Author:Compiled By
        Anne Bassett Stanley Chatham        Genealogy Research Associates
                                            Karen Clifford, A. G.
G.  Rin of the Individual. = 3 = Anne Bassett STANLEY
H.  Number of generations to be included. = 25
I.  Number of Columns in the Name Index. = 2
J.  Ancestors By Generation , Descend(Multi-Surname) = d   Multi-Surname
K.  Print Source Notes? = y Letter size = s Line for Line = w  Inline
L.  Print Tagged Notes? = y Letter size = s Line for Line = w
M.  Print "His parents are unknown."? = n
N.  Print a dashed line between individuals? = y
O.  Print RIN No. in curly brackets after name? = y
P.  Print descendants in parentheses? = n   Include ID Number? = y
Q.  Starting ID number. = 1
R.  Exclude RINs = 0 0 0 0 0 0 0 0 0 0
S.  Multi-lines of descent? = 7688 2521 45 85 2671 1534 7527 7107 0 0
T.
X.  Exit program, Quit.  Y Go to Defaults List No. 2.  Z Generate Book.
        Enter the letter of the Default that you want to change.

              GEN-BOOK   Ancestors   Defaults List No. 2
AA.  Blank Line missing date & place. = n  Add Burial Info = y  Age Limit = 50
BB.  List Children in Tabular form? = N  Print Spouses? = y
CC.  Print PAF ID No. in square brackets after name = n
DD.  Print Name Title Field? = y  Add to Name? = y
EE.  Print "NOTES for XXXX follow:" = y
FF.  Add [Birth-Death] to Index entry? = y
GG.  Print AT place or IN place. = i
HH.  Exclude MRINs = 0 0 0 0 0 0 0 0 0 0
II.  New Chapter each Generation? = y   Starting Chapter Number = 8
JJ.  Surname in All Capital Letters? = y
KK.  Add ID Number to Index entry? = n
LL.  Tab Individual's Name left? = y
MM.  Add "County" when missing City? = y
NN.  Print M/F for children? = y
OO.  Separate Source Notes? = n
PP.  Indent Notes? = n    Strip excess spaces from notes? = y
QQ.  Change State Codes to Names? = y
RR.  Print Death and Burial BEFORE children? = y
SS.  Table of Contents add Principal each Generation = y
TT.  Print Explanation = n   Acknowledgments = n    Introduction = n
UU.  Add Wife's married names to index? = y
XX.  Exit program - Quit.   YY Go to List No. 3  ZZ Generate Book.
        Enter the letters of the Default that you want to change.


              GEN-BOOK   Ancestors   Defaults List No. 3
AAA.  Print Christening information? = n
BBB.  Print LDS Baptism Info.? = n   Endowment Info. = n    Sealing Info. = n
CCC.  Print Spouse in Bold? = y
DDD.  Set Margins for 6 X 9 page? = n
EEE.  Print Individual's notes first? = n
FFF.  Amount of Space before Children. = 2
```

          GEN-BOOK Descendancy Defaults List No. 1
A. Name of the Registered GEN-BOOK user = Karen Clifford
B. Sub-Directory path to PAF data files = c:\paf\mort
C. Sub-Directory path to put WP files = c:\wpp\doc\
D. Version of WordPerfect 5.0/5.1 & above = 1
E. File Name of the Book = adambk2   Default File Name = SYSDATD.002
F. Title:Adams Family   Author:Compiled By
          Connections   Genealogy Research Associates
          of Patrick County, VA   Karen Clifford, A.G., Owner
G. Rin of the Individual. = 1094 = John ADAMS
H. Number of generations to be included. = 5
I. Number of Columns in the Name Index. = 2
J. Descend By Generation, Descendants, or Henry? = g
K. Print Source Notes? = y Letter size = n Line for Line = w   Inline
L. Print Tagged Notes? = y Letter size = s Line for Line = w
M. Print "No children have yet been identified"? = n
N. Print a dashed line between individuals? = y
O. Print RIN No. in curly brackets after name? = y
P. Print Ancestors in parentheses? = y Include ID Number? = n
Q. Starting ID number. = 1
R. Exclude RINs = 0 0 0 0 0 0 0 0 0 0
S. Multiple starting points? = 0 0 0 0 0 0 0 0 0 0
T.
X. Exit program, Quit. Y Go to Defaults List No. 2. Z Generate Book.
      Enter the letter of the Default that you want to change.

          GEN-BOOK Descendancy Defaults List No. 2
AA. Blank Line missing date & place. = n Add Burial Info = y Age Limit = 50
BB. List Children in Tabular form? = N Print Spouses? = y
CC. Print PAF ID No. in square brackets after name = n
DD. Print Name Title Field? = y Add to Name? = y
EE. Print "NOTES for XXXX follow:" = y
FF. Add [Birth-Death] to Index entry? = y
GG. Print AT place or IN place. = i
HH. Exclude MRINs = 0 0 0 0 0 0 0 0 0 0
II. New Chapter each Generation? = y   Starting Chapter Number = 1
JJ. Surname in All Capital Letters? = y
KK. Add ID Number to Index entry? = n
LL. Tab Individual's Name left? = y
MM. Add "County" when missing City? = y
NN. Print M/F for children? = y
OO. Separate Source Notes? = n
PP. Indent Notes? = y   Strip excess spaces from notes? = y
QQ. Change State Codes to Names? = y
RR. Print Death and Burial BEFORE children? = y
SS. Table of Contents add Principal each Generation = y
TT. Print Explanation = y   Acknowledgments = y   Introduction = y
UU. Add Wife's married names to index? = y
XX. Exit program - Quit.   YY Go to List No. 3 ZZ Generate Book.
      Enter the letters of the Default that you want to change.

          GEN-BOOK Descendancy Defaults List No. 3
AAA. Print Christening information? = n
BBB. Print LDS Baptism Info.? = n   Endowment Info. = n   Sealing Info. = n
CCC. Print Spouse in Bold? = y
DDD. Set Margins for 6 X 9 page? = n
EEE. Print Individual's notes first? = y
FFF. Amount of Space before Children. = 2

GEN-BOOK Descendancy Defaults List No. 1

December 12, 1994

A. Name of the Registered GEN-BOOK user = Karen Clifford

B. Sub-Directory path to PAF data files = a:

C. Sub-Directory path to put WP files = b:

D. Version of WordPerfect 5.0/5.1 & above = 1

E. File Name of the Book = berrybk2   Default File Name = SYSDATD

F. Title:Descendants of   Author:Compiled By

    John & Elizabeth (Harris) Berry   Carolyn Berry

    1775-1899

G. Rin of the Individual. = 17 = John BERRY

H. Number of generations to be included. = 3

I. Number of Columns in the Name Index. = 2

J. Descend By Generation, Descendants, or Henry? = g

K. Print Source Notes? = y Letter size = s Line for Line = w   Inline

L. Print Tagged Notes? = y Letter size = s Line for Line = w

M. Print "No children have yet been identified"? = n

N. Print a dashed line between individuals? = y

O. Print RIN No. in curly brackets after name? = y

P. Print Ancestors in parentheses? = y   Include ID Number? = n

Q. Starting ID number. = 1

R. Exclude RINs = 0 0 0 0 0 0 0 0 0 0

S. Multiple starting points? = 0 0 0 0 0 0 0 0 0 0

T.

GEN-BOOK Descendancy Defaults List No. 2

AA. Blank Line missing date & place. = n Add Burial Info = y Age Limit = 50

BB. List Children in Tabular form? = N Print Spouses? = y

CC. Print PAF ID No. in square brackets after name = n

DD. Print Name Title Field? = y Add to Name? = y

EE. Print "NOTES for XXXX follow:" = y

FF. Add [Birth-Death] to Index entry? = y

GG. Print AT place or IN place. = i

HH. Exclude MRINs = 0 0 0 0 0 0 0 0 0 0

II. New Chapter each Generation? = y   Starting Chapter Number = 1

JJ. Surname in All Capital Letters? = y

KK. Add ID Number to Index entry? = y

LL. Tab Individual's Name left? = y

MM. Add "County" when missing City? = y

NN. Print M/F for children? = y

OO. Separate Source Notes? = y

PP. Indent Notes? = y   Strip excess spaces from notes? = y

QQ. Change State Codes to Names? = n

RR. Print Death and Burial BEFORE children? = y

SS. Table of Contents add Principal each Generation = y

TT. Print Explanation = y   Acknowledgments = y   Introduction – y

UU. Add Wife's married names to index? = y

GEN-BOOK Descendancy Defaults List No. 3

AAA. Print Christening information? = n

BBB. Print LDS Baptism Info.? = n   Endowments = n   Sealings = n

CCC. Print Spouse in Bold? = y

DDD. Set Margins for 6 X 9 page? = n

EEE. Print Individual's notes first? = n

FFF. Amount of Space before Children. = 2

GGG. Move Page Number up into the Header? = n

HHH.   =

III.   =

JJJ.   =

KKK.   =

Chapter Eleven
Assignments: Converting Your PAF Data to a Formal Family History

Select the following default options which will allow you to print to a disk using the Modified Register Version. Tailor-make changes to those items which are underlined.

GEN-BOOK Ancestors Defaults List No. 1
DEFAULT LIST NO. 1

A.   Name of the Registered GEN-BOOK user = **Karen Clifford**
B.   Sub-Directory path to PAF data files = **b:**
C.   Sub-Directory path to put WP files = **a:**
D.   Version of *WordPerfect* 5.0, 5.1, 6.0 = **1**
E.   File name of the book = **(no more than 6 characters with last two bk, i.e. smithbk)**
F.   Title: **The Ancestors**   Author: **(Your Name)**
                    of
          (Your full name)   (or whatever you select. You have three lines for title and author.)
G.   RIN of Individual. = <u>**1 = Karen Clifford**</u>
H.   Number of generations to be included = <u>**22**</u>
I.   Number of Columns in the Name Index. = **3**
J.   Ancestors by Generation, Descend (Multi-Surname) = **g**[45]   ID numbers sequential = **y**
K.   Print Source Notes? = **y** Letter size = **n**[46] Line for line = **w**
L.   Print Tagged Notes? = **y**   Letter size = **n** Line for line = **w**
M.   Print "His parents are unknown."? = **y**
N.   Print a dashed line between individuals? = **y**
O.   Print RIN No. in curly brackets after name? = **y**
P.   Print descendants in parentheses? = **y** Include ID Number? = **y**
Q.   Starting ID number. = **0**
R.   Exclude RINs = **(you may exclude up to 10 RINs, give RIN #)**
S.   Multi-lines of descent? = **(give the RIN numbers included)**

The GEN-BOOK *Descendancy* Defaults List has only three differences: J (select g), P (y to print ancestors in parentheses, and S (multiple starting points if you have them).

───────────────────

[45]GEN-BOOK uses four of the descending numbering systems: 1) Modified Register System which is designated with the letter "g" 2) the Henry System which is designated by the letter "h" 3) Descendancy order with same ID numbers as Modified Register System with default of "d" and "n" and 4) Descendancy Order using sequential numbering system with default of "d" and "y".

[46]N=normal, S=small, w=word wrapping feature is set up to remove paragraph markers set up in the PAF program.

DEFAULT LIST NO. 2

AA.   Blank line for missing date & place = **n** Add burial info = **n**
      Age limit = **(you determine age limit or leave as is)**

BB.   List children in tabular form? = **y** Print Spouses? = **y**

CC.   Print PAF ID no. in square brackets after name = **n**

DD.   Print Name Title Field? = **y** Add to Name? = **y**

EE.   Print "NOTES for XXXX follow:" = **y**

FF.   Add [Birth-Death] to Index entry? = **y**

GG.   Print AT place or IN place = **i**

HH.   Exclude MRINS =

II.   New chapter each generation? = **n** Starting chapter number = **1**

JJ.   Surname in all capital letters? = **y**

KK.   Add ID number of Index entry? = **n**

LL.   Tab individual's name left? = **y**

MM.   Add "County" when missing city? = **y**

NN.   Print M/F for children? = **y**

OO.   Separate source notes? = **n**

PP.   Indent notes? = **y** Strip excess space from notes? = **y**[47]

QQ.   Change state codes to names = **y** (CA=California)

RR.   Print death and burial BEFORE children? = **y**

SS.   Table of contents add principal each generation = **y**

TT.   Print explanation? (on how to use the system selected) = **y**
      Print acknowledgments (page heading only)? = **y**
      Print introduction (page heading only)? = **y**

UU.   Add Wife's married names to index = **y**

XX.   Exit program - Quit   YY. Go to List No. 3   ZZ. Generate book

GEN-BOOK Ancestors Defaults List No. 3

AAA. Print Christening information = **y**

BBB. Print LDS Baptism Info?=**n** Endowment Info.=**n** Sealing Info.=**n**

CCC. Print Spouse in Bold? = **y**

DDD. Set Margins for 6 x 9 pages = **n**

EEE. Print Individual's notes first? = **n**

FFF. Amount of Space before Children = **2**

GGG. Move Page Number up into the Header? = **n** ZZZ Generate Book

---

[47] When selecting "w" (Wrap-Around) on defaults K & L, this setting allows you to indent the note. It automatically tabs the beginning of the note to the right and the rest of the note will wrap around to the left margin, in paragraph form. Then you can tell GEN-BOOK to strip the excess spaces (more than one) from your notes but your PAF files will not be changed, i.e.:
NOTES for Jesse follow:

   1870 CENSUS: CA, Monterey, Salinas, pg. 254, household 211: Jesse Jones, 45, white, male, born CA.

   OCCUPATION: He was a very good carpenter and built many houses. He also made fine furniture.

LAB ASSIGNMENT 11:   Using *WordPerfect*® to Index

1.   Retrieve the file you saved in Assignment 10.

2.   Insert spaces for pictures or clip art. Try striking **Shift F8** then **1** then **7** then **4** and **1** to make the left margin indent to 4" or reverse that to make the right margin indent to 4". Repeat to return the margins to the correct size.

3.   If you decide to add entries to the Table of Contents such as biographies, charts or other information, first turn on reveal codes **Alt F3**.

   Then tag the first letter of the word or phrase to be included in the table of contents by positioning the cursor on the first letter of the word or phrase, turn the block on **(Alt F4)** move the cursor right just past the end of the word of phrase but do not include any bold or underline marks unless you want them to appear that way in the Table of Contents.

   Mark the text **Alt-F5** select **1** (Table of Contents), then enter the level number (1 = a chapter level; 2 would be a chapter subheading; and 3 is the last setup possible.) See sample Table of Contents pages in previous chapters.

4.   Generate an index (these instructions are for 3-column name index only), by pressing **Home, Home,** and **Down-arrow,** which will take you to the end of the file. Press **Alt F3** to turn the reveal codes on. Watching the lower screen, position the cursor immediately AFTER the words "INDEX OF NAMES". The press **Ctrl F8** (font), **4** (base font) and select a font that is 12 or 15 cpi (compressed size) or 5-7 point size. Select **F10** to save and return to document.

   Now press the following **Alt F5** (mark text) **6** (generate) **5** (generate indexes) **y** (existing indexes will be replaced). Press **Alt F3** to turn off reveal codes.

5.   Print the file. Save as **Assnt11**.

CHAPTER TWELVE

Preparing a Video History

This Chapter will cover:

- Preparation
- Visuals
- Music
- Length
- Narrative
- Type of equipment
- Environment

Preliminary Preparations

Using the same techniques that you used in writing a family history, determine who your audience will be and what message you wish to communicate. Is your goal to put together a life story of an individual; to tell of his/her immigration to the United States; to show the growth of a person as a child up through marriage, work, and death; or to share the solution to a major mystery in your family's history?

Write down your main goal and any sub-goals that you would

237

Write down your main goal and any sub-goals that you would like to have go along with that central theme. Secondly go into your word processing program and set up a table to organize the work as indicated in table 12.1.

Use the column on the left to identify each major segment of your production. The second column is where you will type the actual dialogue and place in the musical cues which you will use.

VIDEO PRODUCTION PLANNER

Table 12.1

SCRIPT		Describe Picture	Approx. Time
Title			
Introduction			
Transition			
Detail			
Transition			
Detail			
Transition			
Detail			
Conclusion			
Credits			

The next column is where you will put down which pictures or other visuals you will be filming as you read the script. In the right column estimate how long each segment will be.

You won't want to forget, however, to make a title page or an introduction to your video. Be creative and think of ideas which would visually describe your theme. For example, if this family was living by the seashore you might consider writing the title of your video in the sand and letting the tide wash over it. I did  one where I used a lovely deep blue fabric with a nice sheen to it which I laid on an easel. The names and titles were then printed on white paper and cut out in the shape of clouds. Below the clouds on blue was a beautiful picture depicting the family whose story was to be told.

At the end of your project, give credits for those who provided help or pictures. In order to have the correct information for the credits, it is a good idea to collect everyone's names, addresses and phone numbers who helped you or contributed to the project as you go along. Include the date and place of production. Although full-motion video may be more interesting, most of us have more photographs than old films. Production and editing are also easier using a series of photographs, so that is how you ought to begin.

Also allow several minutes for music and background at the end, and the words THE END in some humorous or serious way so that people will know it is the end of your video.

Visuals

In the several family histories that I have put together I have discovered that you can use one picture every five seconds. This would amount to 12 pictures per minute of video taping. However, some pictures have much more detail than others (a group shot, for example) or if there is much about the picture you are trying to point out, then it might be better to spend 10 seconds on a particular picture.

As you are describing migration movements, consider using drawings or maps. You could use a picture of a map but usually there is too much detail for the observer to see the points you want to highlight. As you are considering town scenes, think of post cards or pictures from out-of-print county histories. There are many things that can be used to depict the scene that you are describing by voice.

Music

A nice touch to your video is background music appropriate to the setting or the time period that is taking place. Once you have your manuscript written, write into your script music tapes. I incorporated accordion and violin music into my Finnish family history because that music was a part of my background. Civil War scenes could use military or specifically Civil War music, etc.

Length

A good video shouldn't last more than about 15 minutes, but putting together a 15-minute video takes at least two to three hours of work **after** all the materials are gathered together.

Compare the content and length of your manuscript with the pictures, maps, background history, music, etc. you've selected. If you do not have enough materials to accomplish the task, write the items necessary on a research calendar so that you can obtain them either from relatives, or as you visit libraries or repositories.

Narrative

You could try reading the narrative as you film each video segment, but that puts a lot of pressure on the narrator. Normally, the narration and music will be "dubbed in" after the filming is completed. That is why you need to know how long you will film each picture and how long the narrative for that segment lasts.

Type of Equipment

First you need to know what your equipment can do before you decide what you are going to do with that equipment. Study the instruction manual and practice each feature a few times so you can see how it is going to work. With some basic equipment and some production assistance you can put together a very nice video.

videographer

The basics include:

1. A video camera.
2. A tripod to hold the camera still while filming pictures and slides.
3. A camera with a "dub" feature (or you can buy a VCR that has a dub feature in it).
4. A TV or video monitor.
5. A stop watch.
6. Bright lights.
7. A tape recorder with either an internal or external microphone. The external one is better because the sounds are much clearer,
8. An easel that you can use to support the pictures.
9. Some black fabric, velvet or felt, to cover the easel and provide a backdrop for the pictures.

If you wish to add scenes from an old super 8 home movie, you will need a film projector and a screen. A better quality copy is possible if you purchase a special transfer box. You project the film into the box and a video camera attaches to the side of the box to make the video copy. If you have some 35 mm slides that you would like to add, these can be done the same way.

Before I found out about this simple little box I used to show them right on a flat wall instead of a screen and then take videos. This worked very well if the lights were low, so the pictures did not look "washed out". This method was adequate, but the transfer box makes the process even easier.

Audio Mixing Console. There is also a nifty little gadget that allows you to combine audio sounds from two different sources. For example, you might want to have some music background along with your narration. Most camera and VCR equipment only allows you to record from a single source. However, you can combine two signals and then dub them into your production. The professional way to do this is to use a stereo mixing console, which can sometimes be found for under $150. You might also be able to rent one. You could also begin with the low cost approach. Just place the instrumental background music on one tape recorder in the background, while the narrator speaks into the microphone. This is sometimes tricky, because if you don't have someone else helping you to turn the music on and off at the right time, it may require several tries to get it right. Also, the quality may be unacceptable as you can get a "wow and flutter" in the music.

The best quality recording will be achieved using the dub feature on your camcorder or your VCR. These audio signals may be shaped by amplifiers, mixers, and graphic equalizers. Both machines should have instructions for helping you. The higher quality is achieved with the use of patch cords. The patch cords are plugged into the equipment jacks that send the signal directly from one piece of equipment to another without being broadcast into the air and then re-recorded.

Lighting. Now is the time to take your camera and practice in different lighting situations. Try with regular house light, then with a brighter fluorescent light or halogen lighting, and finally with outside light coming in through a window to find out the best affect. Remember that light during different times of day produces different colors.

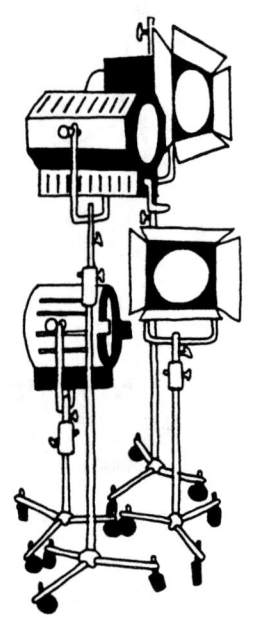

I found when I was doing the video, that the lights can become very, very hot. You don't want to bump into them and burn yourself. I try to use as bright a light as possible and am very careful to check each picture to make sure that it is not reflecting a light off of its surface.

Zoom Lens.   Practice using the zoom lens. I found it really nifty to use this feature with a detailed postcard or family picture. For instance, with a picture of a barn or house, I might begin by focusing on a bucket and talking about the chores being done on the farm, and then expanding the field of view to first take in the barn and later the people until the picture is completely visible.

Fader.   Some camera's VCRs come with fader buttons that let you fade out one picture and on with the next. This is an inexpensive way to transition from one picture or segment to the next.   The most expensive equipment will provide several transition options.   Some come with a fader feature for the sound tract. The more features you have, the more time you'll have to spend before you become proficient with your equipment.

Background Environment

Lets speak for a minute about the room where our video will be put together. It is very important that it is quiet.   I put notes on the front door when I'm doing an oral history or making a video taping asking people to please not ring the

door bell, but to just quietly walk in or come back.

There are other noises in the background that you want to watch for like washing machines running, the ticking of a clock, the furnace starting up. These distracting sounds should be caught before you get long into your dubbing of the sound levels. Once you get ready to set up, make sure you label all your material so that it matches the script that you have prepared.

People Considerations

It is very helpful if you can have one or two people helping you. One person can run the camera while another does the narration following the script, and perhaps a third person can set up all the pictures and other items that you wish to photograph or even line up living people if necessary.

Also, if you have some people that you are going to videotape live, try to do some of the still materials first. Then visit with them to put them at ease.

I don't believe it is a good idea to take their materials and actually show it to them ahead of time because the spontaneity of the moment is lost. Rather just have them pick up a picture and ask them questions about the picture. Do you recognize who these people are? When was this taken? Any events that happened during the day that this picture was taken that you can remember? Try to pick pictures the person is familiar by just having them glance at them and say, "Are you acquainted with any of these people?" If they answer "yes" then respond, "We will talk about them later."

If you are going to make copies of your video, make sure you make all copies from the original "master" copy. Each copy made from one VCR to another will be less clear and a little more grainy than the tape it was copied from. Using a video stabilizer will improve the quality of your copies. Video stabilizers cost between $30 and $100.

Chapter Twelve
Assignment: Preparing a Video History

Select one of these two ideas:

1.   Now that you have analyzed your research, organized your
     documents, summarized your findings, determined who your
     audience will be and studied some successful techniques for
     producing a video, make a brief outline of what would go into
     a video production planner.

     A.   INTRODUCTION (some of these may apply)

          1.   Event
          2.   Time period
          3.   Person(s) involved
          4.   Title
          5.   What graphics could enhance this idea?

     B.   TRANSITION (from one family, generation, idea to another)

          1.   Place
          2.   Time period
          3.   Person(s) involved
          4.   Event
          5.   What graphics could enhance this idea?

     C.   DETAIL

          1.   Place
          2.   Time period
          3.   Person(s) involved
          4.   Event
          5.   What graphics could enhance this idea?

(Repeat B and C as needed to end of history)

D.   CONCLUSION (for example)
    1.   What do you now feel about the individual?
    2.   What characteristics do you admire in the family?
    3.   Have your family traditions carried on?
    4.   What research would you like to see done next?
    5.   Humor or quotation.

E.   CREDITS

2.   Select and read some books on producing video histories such as *Video Family History* by Dwayne and Pat Sturm done by Ancestry Inc. Report on some ideas you would like to do when you get around to doing a family video.

LAB ASSIGNMENT 12:   Using *WordPerfect*® to Incorporate Interest

1.   Place mock-up sizes of pictures or clip art in place and
     determine if ready for finalizing.

2.   If pictures are too large, adjust your margins at this time.

3.   Decide on the pictures or fonts for the front cover.

4.   If you have made any corrections to your file, or you wish to
     include pictures in your index, you will need to regenerate
     your index at this time.

5.   Save your file as **Assnt11**.

CHAPTER THIRTEEN

Other Forms of Family Histories

This Chapter will cover:

- Family Health Histories
- Calendar ideas
- Photo histories
- Art histories

We should take time periodically, to "finish" a family history project. This may take a great deal of self-control to finally say, "Stop! I've done enough on this line. It's time to let others add their two cents worth." Nearly every student who does just this, comments with great enthusiasm on the benefits of being forced to reach closure on one aspect of their research. Not only does it allow them to share their

findings, but the process focuses them on their central research goals.

How can we go about sharing our results besides through an extensive written, oral, or video history? I'd like to devote this chapter to some techniques others have used to share their histories in a different or unusual format.

Family Health Histories

The July 1994 issue of *Good Housekeeping* magazine carried an article entitled "Finding My Parents Saved My Life" by Lisa Collier Cool. This story was about a young lady whose father discovered he had an inherited disease and insisted his adopted daughter try to find her own parents in case she too had inherited health problems. What actually prompted her to action, however, was the illnesses of her children and some learning disabilities.

As is the case in many adoptive records, both truth and error were listed on her adoption papers. Through the help of ALMA (Adoptee's Liberty Movement Association) she located her mother through extensive study of California's vital records. When she met with her mother, she found out that her mother had some learning impairments as well.

Finding her father turned out to be more frustration, and the search took "an odd and gloomy twist". It was 8 years after the death of her birth father that she noticed his surname appearing over and over in the obituaries of people dying before age 40. She was then 38, but thought only men had heart trouble so put it out of her mind.

Coming home from a meeting one evening, in 107 degree weather, she started sweating heavily and later found herself so weak she couldn't undress. She felt a sharp pain across her shoulder blades and a strange sensation along her left arm.

An alarm went off in her head of her father's family's early deaths. She put her embarrassment aside and had her husband rush her to the hospital. She was in great pain, but no one paid much attention to her until she told them of her family history. Then they reacted. Fortunately their assistance came in time, for she had suffered a severe heart attack. She still maintains that the knowledge of her family's medical history saved her life.

Medical family histories are becoming more prevalent today. They can be found in popular magazines, and an entire issue of the National Genealogical Society Journal was devoted to the topic in July, 1994.

A few pointers to keep in mind while doing research for a family health history include:

1.   Research the whole family including collateral lines, because they may show the affects of the same genes, only generations earlier.

2.   Learn to conduct thorough oral histories at the same time. Great tact may be necessary to try to determine the primary cause of death - not what might appear on the death certificate. For example, a suicide might have been linked to a brain tumor or other serious illness.

Besides standard pedigree information, medical histories need to include the age at which any individuals were diagnosed with a disease, their ethnic origin, religion and all marriages[48].

_____

[48]I would suggest the article "How to Be a Family Health Historian" by Anita A. Lustenberger in the *National Genealogical Society Quarterly Special Issue* Vol. 82 No. 2 June 1994.

Oral histories of living relatives are a good place to begin, then follow up with research in records containing medical information such as obituaries, insurance records, vital records, coroner's records, etc.

All the information is then analyzed, patterns of illness highlighted and put in an easy to read format. Present your report to a medical practitioner for review, and then share the results with family members so appropriate precautions may be taken as needed.

One should exercise care to avoid overgeneralizing or complicating a healthy relative's appreciation for insurance by creating the impression that there is a pre-existing condition.

NGS's special journal edition also covered medical holdings in the National Archives. Some major collections are Patient Records Prior to WWII; a report on 520 rolls of film of over 40,000 collected genealogies prior to 1940 on genetics, recently microfilmed by the Genealogical Society of Utah, and a Genetics Resource Guide for the Family Health Historian.

Calendar Ideas

Each year our local genealogy society has a Genealogy Christmas Ideas evening. I made up calendars using photos of deceased relatives. Next to the photo was either a little history about the person, a favorite recipe of theirs, or some other bit of poetry, insight gleaned, etc.

If you are only doing a few of these, a different photo can be used with each month of the year. If you are making several you can reduce costs by placing two monthly calendars on each opposite page, or place the entire year calendar on a single page. Including everyone's birthday as a calendar entry generated a lot of interest and these were VERY POPULAR!

I used a computer calendar program like *Calendar Creator* and placed my relatives birth dates in it. Now it updates every year automatically and I just need to add new births, marriages and deaths. The latest

version of this program allows you to scan in and print accompanying photos with your family calendar.

To create a special calendar for a newly married couple, I placed their wedding picture in the calendar itself by cutting a frame from heavy weight paper and slipping in the picture. The newly married bride really appreciated everyone's birthdates in her husband's family.

Photo Histories

Once you have spent a sizeable fortune on film and development, it is a real shame not to put these visual treasures into a displayable format. I attended a home demonstration on how to do just this at a friend's house recently. The company is called *Creative Memories* and their products are of archival quality, yet they go beyond the rather stiff and staid photo preservation materials usually associated with document preservation.

All materials were acid-free including the colorful background papers cut into various shapes, the stickers, the scrapbooks and filler pages in a multitude of shapes. Instruction was provided on how to crop pictures, angle pictures to create groups, use wavy scissors to cut off corners, and use colored strips for accents.

It was the application of background history for the pictures put into the books that caught my attention. The novice photo historians attending were told to look at the pictures and answer these questions:

Who is this person?
        What are they doing?
                When did this happen?
                        Where did this take place?

Did anything memorable happen about the time this picture was taken?

        What was going on in the world?
                What are my memories about this day:
                        What did I smell or taste?
                        What did I see or hear?
                        What did I feel?

The final results were very impressive. As the pictures were first edited to eliminate the poor quality or repetitive snapshots, individuals focused in on the high points of the events depicted. They then laid the photos out on the page to please themselves.

Pictures were then cropped using templates to make interesting shapes, by rounding the corners, or by cutting curvy borders on those that needed it.

We then selected colored acid-free paper to include as a "mat" or a template frame for our pictures, but plenty of space was left to write our headlines and stories about the pictures.

256

Many people mounted their pictures with double-stick photo "splits" rather than messing with paper cement or adhesive corners. We then proceeded to write on the pages with pigma ink pens of various colors because these pens will not fade over time.

The final touch came with the application of stickers that gave a decorative fun accent to the pictures, especially where the acid-free stickers matched the theme of the page. The pages were then protected from sticky fingers and spills with page protectors. At least 48 hours "curing" time is suggested before adding page protectors to pages with paper cement on them.

Page protectors are also recommended whenever cards, certificates, invitations, etc. were placed in books. Otherwise, the acid from these items will migrate across to the facing page and damage an item there.

I enjoyed looking at everyone's books and recounting their family histories in photo format. But it was the words along with the pictures that brought this all together for me. I particularly enjoyed making my own family history books in 8 x 10 size which fit very nicely beside my other history books on my book case.

 You may be wondering why I seem so excited about acid-free paper. The main causes of deterioration of paper and photographic materials are light, relative humidity, pests, heat, air pollution and improper storage and handling. Once we have realized the value of our family history materials, we should try to create and maintain a reasonable environment for them.

In most localities an interior closet of the house is the best place to store family treasures. The environment fluctuates least there and it is dark. Properly maintained air conditioners or air cleaners can reduce pollution and good housekeeping practices should prevent insect and mildew damage.

Most paper has a high acid content, and will destroy itself over time. Therefore, paper storage materials for your family records should have an alkaline pH, an alkaline buffer and no groundwood content that may become acidic. Cover sheets should not give off an odor (as that is one indication that chemicals are present that could hurt your pictures). Several national paper supply companies now sell acid-free, archival materials.

Art Histories

In my two decades of active involvement in family history studies, no single publication has affected me quite as much as the artistic family histories produced by Rien Poortvliet entitled *In My Grandfather's House* and *Daily Life in Holland in the Year 1566 and the Story of My Ancestor's Treasure Chest.*[49]

In My Grandfather's House is done in original paints by the author (over 240 pages of them with well over 500 paintings and drawings) along with a handwritten description of each. The first page opens with:

Here is Uncle Dirk's farmhouse and the two bridges over the Boezem River, which was teeming with sticklebacks. The wide bridge was for the little steam tram that chugged by every two hours. Sometimes if the engineer saw you fishing, he would toss a piece of coal into the water right in front of you.

Rien Poortvliet then portrays his Uncle Dirk, the farmhouse, the two bridges, the river and even a little boy fishing.

---

[49]Published by Harry N. Abrams, Inc, 100 Fifth Avenue, New York, NY 10011.

Slowly he takes you back in time through his paintings of the dress, the customs, his pedigree and even, as on page 48, "...*the house built in 1659 where Keesje Bok - standing with his sister - was born...*" together with a sketched map of the tidal flats Keesje's father fished.

On page 108 he sketches his great grandfather and explains the customs of "tenths" at the same time. By page 118 he has drawn a complete sketch of the home and barn and the food storage customs of this island people.

Nestled in the middle of the book on pages 132-133 he presents a type of descendancy chart starting about 1560 and coming forward to 1986. This was followed up with a possible cause for the high infant death rate *"the cradles were too close to the ground and drafty...and wet diapers were not washed, just dried and reused"*.

The book concludes with a tenth great grandfather who, fortunately, did enough mischief in his lifetime to be included in enough records to be remembered today. The author's love for his family is evident by the manner in which he tied his family together.

Daily Life In Holland In The Year 1566 and the Story of My Ancestor's Treasure Chest is a wonderful sequel. Here another 208 pages of paintings tell the story of his personal struggle to find documents to continue his family history. (You see by now he is hopelessly hooked on his genealogy pursuits). He weaves an entire tale around the contents of a probate settlement.

This is a fascinating reconstruction of events with many more pages of Dutch customs, buildings and people. It ends with:

"He was very happy: the armoire was his, and he had the document to prove it. And, believe it or not, today, more than four centuries later, that same piece of paper lies right in front of me on the table".

These books prepared by Mr. Poortvliet truly put love into the Poortvliet Family History. We may not have the artistic skills of Rien Poortvliet, but we can put stories on paper, voices on tape, and scenes on video. There is something about the *visual* that touches others. I see evidences of it around me everywhere: the framed crest, the pedigree chart; the cross-stitched pedigree sampler; oil paintings of ancient ancestral homes or individuals; the vivacious grandmother with the painted sweatshirt or research bag bearing her ancestors' names.

All these visual evidences give a feeling of belonging, and giving a form of gratitude or reverence for past sacrifices. As we put together our final family history project on one of our lines, may we too find ways through words to express our appreciation for those who came before.

Chapter Thirteen
Assignment: Other Forms of Family Histories

A.   Go back and add graphics or pictures to beautify your Family
      History Project.   These might include:

      1.   Maps of places mentioned.
      2.   Charts such as census rosters, military lists, analysis
           of families in an area, etc.
      3.   Pictures of places or people from family sources, county
           histories or postcards.
      4.   Clip Art of similar situations or people from purchased
           books
      5.   Sketches of places visited or hand drawn maps.
      6.   Copies of old documents.

B.   Layout the placement of your photographs and illustrations.

LAB ASSIGNMENT 13: Using *WordPerfect*® to Print the Final Product

1.   Retrieve Assnt 11, make sure all corrections have been made, new index generated, page numbers start on the correct page, headers and/or footers are in place, proper font has been selected, your name, address and date have been included, etc.

2.   Print the file.

3.   Turn it into the teacher as your first draft of your family history.

CHAPTER FOURTEEN

Publishing the Final Product

This Chapter will cover:

- Locating a publisher
- Submitting your manuscript
- Recovering your expenses
- Self-publishing
- Copyright

Locating a Publisher

Locating a publisher is often as easy as looking on your own bookshelf. You are probably purchasing the type of books you are writing. Who published those books? They are the people you will want to contact. Particularly watch for publishers of the type of book you are interested in producing. Examples for genealogy and family history books include:

Genealogical Publishing Company, Baltimore MD.
Heritage Press
American Genealogical Lending Library
Ancestry

Submitting Your Manuscript

Write for permission to send a copy of your manuscript or it may be returned unopened. Don't feel bad if you are rejected. That particular publisher may not cover the area of the United States you are dealing with. Try another publisher.

It is assumed your materials are neatly typed in double space for comments and suggestions if you wish them. Leave at least a one inch margin on all four sides and be sure each page is numbered. It is good to place a header or a footer on each page with the title of the book in case the pages get out of order and mixed with other manuscripts.

It is usually preferable to submit the manuscript unbound in a small box. Have a title page with a proposed title and your name, address and phone number. Send a good xerox copy and keep your original.

Be patient as you wait for a response. The fact that you have not received your manuscript back is usually a good sign since someone is probably looking at it. Busy publishers may take several months to respond. After that it is very much in order to write and ask if they have had time to review your manuscript and that any progress report would be appreciated.

Recovering Your Expenses

Royalties run between 5 and 15% with the most common at 10%. They are usually paid once or twice a year on actual copies sold. Free books, bad copies, returns, and bad debts are not included.

Although you may feel your family history would be valuable to everyone else with your surname, these particular books may have a very small general market unless you know about a specific market in advance. Do you know of a reunion of 1,000 individuals of which 250 have already paid in advance for a copy of your book? This information may help you determine if you should go to a publisher or to a company to help you do self-publishing.

If you are planning and publishing and printing your own book, try mailing out a flier to relatives ahead of time telling them of your plans and asking for commitments to purchase the book at a lower pre-publication price.

On your order form ask for names and addresses of other relatives who may wish to be notified and include a printout of the information on the family your are mailing the information to asking if they would like to update any information or perhaps include a picture. This way they know yours is not a come-on product for a listing of telephone numbers, and they know they are included.

Run a small advertisement in the local newspaper of the area in which your ancestors resided also telling of your intentions and offering a pre-publication price. Also place a small ad in the *Genealogy Helper* magazine offering the same. All of these methods will provide you with other contacts and a way to recover your publishing expenses. Don't forget to include at least $3.50 for postage and handling as well as tax in some states.

Professional Assistance. Gateway Press is an example of a company who helps you to publish your own materials. It is an affiliate of the Genealogical Publishing Company established in 1970 to meet the demands of patrons looking for a place to publish their family history books.

They provide a video entitled *Prepare to Publish* to alert you to the potential problems and solutions to preparing a genealogical or historical manuscript.[50]

How much time should I expect to wait for my book to be on the market. "Longer than anticipated." If you want a book in 3 months, plan on nine and you'll get six. All kinds of things can go wrong such as a break down in equipment, a loss of photos, delays in receipt of materials for the cover page, etc.

Individually Produced. Perhaps you wish only 10 to 50 copies of your book to be bound. Companies specialize in original limited editions with handbinding. All is done with archival quality and natural materials. One such company I have worked with is: Edwin Michael Wing and Mina Yamashita, PO Box 6145, Santa Fe, New Mexico 87502.

Computer generated books from PAF may often contain long quotes from copyrighted materials. It is up to the author to write and obtain written permission to quote from other authors if you have used extensive quotes. Quoting a sentence or two does not need permission. Paraphrasing in your own language would avoid extensive quotes. One would commonly write to

---

[50]Available by writing Gateway Press, Inc., 1001 N. Calvert St., Baltimore MD 21202 301-837-8271.

the publisher for permission to quote from copyrighted materials.

Copyright

Copyright means the copyright holder has the right legally to print, reprint, copy and sell or distribute copies of the work.

Book manuscripts are not copyrighted until after they are published. However, they are protected by "common law" until they have been published. You may type a warning on the first page that the material is not to be copied without permission of the author.

If a publisher is financing your publication, he usually retains the copyright. A copyright is obtained by printing the proper notice in the book on the title page or the reverse side of the title page. Then the application form from the Library of Congress is filled out and notarized. Two copies of your book are sent along with the fee of $20.00 to the Copyright Office.

All published copies should bear a notice of the copyright or the rights in a work can be permanently lost. Usually a statutory copyright runs for 28 years and then it may be renewed for another 28 years if an acceptable renewal application and fee are received in the Copyright Office during the last year of the original term of copyright.

While you are writing your history you can protect it by writing "Copyright 1993 John A. Smith" at the bottom of each page.

(The date should be the year when you began writing, and your name would replace "John A. Smith".) This is called "common law copyright" and will protect your work until it is printed. When it is printed, the copyright notation needs to appear on the title page only.

After you have finished writing your book and want to print it and distribute it to family and friends, you should protect it further by filing official copyright papers with the Copyright Office, Library of Congress, Washington, D.C..

If you intend to offer your book for sale, you should also register the work with the Copyright Office in the Library of Congress. The number of the Copyright Form Hotline is (202) 287-9100. Use this number for ordering forms and for individual help in filling out the forms. They can answer most of your questions. Since copyright laws and fees change from time to time, it would be wise to consult the Copyright Office for the latest information. If you wish to write the Copyright Office, the address is: Copyright Office, Library of Congress, Washington, D.C. 20559, (202) 479-8700. More on the Library of Congress follows.

Sharing Your Research

There are several ways to share the knowledge you have gained from your research on your family history. Some even protect your rights as an author. Who knows? Perhaps your history will become a best seller or even be made into a movie!

Library of Congress

One of the largest and most valuable research libraries in the world is the Library of Congress. It is especially important for its United States history collection

268

which also contains the papers of almost all the United States presidents from George Washington to Calvin Coolidge.

The Library of Congress also gives publishers cataloging data to be printed directly in books, usually on the back of the title page. As indicated earlier, the library also loans other libraries books that are unobtainable elsewhere as well as supplying photocopies of other materials.

The library administers the copyright laws from one of its departments, the Copyright Office. Two copies of every publication for which an author requests copyright protection must be deposited in the library. From the accumulation, the library selects items for its own collection. The Copyright Office does not grant copyrights. It just registers claims. Forms and instructions can be obtained from the United States Copyright Office, Library of Congress, Washington D.C. 20559.

The complete Library of Congress complex presently covers about 71 acres of land. To a genealogist who learns its cataloging system, it is one of the grandest places to research. Is it no wonder that it is a place you would like your own book placed. Someday a hundred years from now, your descendants might read a book you wrote and in their eyes, you will come alive. So share a book by depositing two copies in the Library of Congress.

Local Historical and Genealogical Societies

Consider your own research. If you did as most of us, you wrote to local societies requesting information on a particular family. There are times when many of you have discovered a wealth of information gathered by others. You were led to that particular locality because your family lived there.

Often, the families we research spend several generations in one town or county of the United States. If that local county or region has an established historical or genealogical society, consider giving them a copy of your book. In this way other family members over the years who also try to find their families may be lead to you and your resources.

Books such as *Meyer's Directory of Genealogical Societies in the U.S.A. and Canada, Eighth Edition*[51] by Mary Keysor Meyer can help you find such societies. Don't forget to furnish them with purchasing information in case some of their members would like to order a copy of your book. You might also write a BRIEF summary of your book, and suggest they include it in their local newsletter or periodical.

Family Organizations

As we all know, during our research phase we often come across many families with the same surname as our own that do not necessarily belong to our family. Sharing this information can be of mutually benefit to all concerned. I once wrote to a Locke Family Organization for information on a family I was researching for a client. They were able to supply an obituary on the family I was researching which opened up a whole new line.

---

[51]Published by Mary Keysor Meyer, 5179 Perry Road, Mt. Airy, Maryland 21771.

To help you find information on family organizations, use the book *Directory of Family Associations, 1993-1994 Edition*[52] by Elizabeth Petty Bentley.

Another way to find family organizations is using the *Ancestral File* itself. Individuals are encouraged to register an interest in a particular surname so that others may contact them. So even if you do not have extensive research on a particular line, submit the surname and what you do know about the family so others might contact you.

Family History Library

Ancestral File Submissions. The Ancestral File is a computerized file created from family group records and pedigree charts that have been submitted to the Family History Library since 1979. The purpose of the Ancestral File is to help families coordinate their research and reduce the cost of duplicated efforts.

I submit all the miscellaneous materials I have researched on the *Ancestral File* in order to help others as well as to keep a place for reference myself. Presently, I receive at least one letter a day in regard to names submitted! They come from all over the country and even foreign countries. Whether you publish a book or not, you should share your research electronically. Just follow the steps outlined below.

Ancestral file submissions may be produced from any versions of the *Personal Ancestral File* computer program as well as other computer programs. At the **Access Menu** of PAF, select **2 - Genealogical Information Exchange** or GIE.

At the **Genealogical Information Exchange Menu** select **1 - Ancestral File Submission.** Ancestral File Submission is used to prepare your family records data for submission. It checks whether

---

[52] Published by the Genealogical Publishing Co., Inc., 1001 N. Calvert St., Baltimore, MD 21202.

the names in your Family Records meet the minimum standards for merging with the Ancestral File. It also checks for inconsistencies in dates and lets you know what problems might exist. Problems should be corrected before submitting your data to the Ancestral File.

Have available the following materials to produce a submission diskette:

1. Your Family Records data disk.

2. A copy of your Family Records data disk.

3. Two blank, formatted disks.

Place the Family Records data disk into "drive A", and place one blank formatted disk in "drive B". At the **Ancestral File Submission Menu,** it will give you the date automatically set by your computer. If the date is incorrect on the screen, correct it.

Indicate which drive contains your Family Records data disk. The program may already give this information, particularly if you are storing your family records data on your hard drive. In our sample above, the submission disk would be "b" and the data disk would be in "a". The file name for submission is automatically created using the first few characters of your last name as placed in your name and address fields. You can change this name to whatever you would like, however.

Notes which have been tagged (usually with an exclamation point as the first character, and the events all in CAPS followed by a ":") will be used as source documentation. If you do not have a "!" as the first item in the notes, these notes will not be copied by the GIE program.

The present version of the Ancestral File program does not process your documentation, but hopefully it will at a later time. If you feel at this point that the source documentation of your data is not sufficient you may press "F2" twice to exit the program and work on it. When you have revised the documentation you may return and redo the steps indicated above. If you feel your source documentation is sufficient, press the "F1" function key to continue.

The Ancestral File submission menu will then ask "What type of submission do you wish to create?".

1. Ancestor submission
2. Descendant submission
3. Family submission
4. All records
0. Return to the Main Menu

Each time you select 1, 2 or 3 from this menu, you create a separate submission that is starting a file and the program will bring you back to the main menu. Try to avoid duplicating individuals as you select submissions.

If you select that you would like to do an **Ancestor submission** then you would start with one ancestor and go back as far as you want. This would leave out second and third cousins, however. Those 2nd and 3rd cousins could be picked up, however, by selecting a **Descendants submission**. This would submit records of the descendants of an ancestor. Finally, you may only wish to submit the records of one family including a father, mother and children to the Ancestral File by selecting **Family submission**.

Ancestor Submission. If you select **1. Ancestor submission**, you would press **1** and you would need to indicate the individual you want as the beginning ancestor. You would, therefore, need the RIN number to begin or ask the computer to find the individual by name.

Next you would need to select the number of generations you want to include in the submission; the limit is 50 generations. The program will then copy the data onto your submission diskette. In addition to adding the direct line families to the temporary file, the program will add the brothers and sisters of the direct line ancestors and their families, spouses and children.

Descendant Submission. If, however, you wish to locate all the 1st cousins and 2nd cousins, etc., you would select **2. Descendant submission.** Again you would indicate the RIN number of the individual you wanted as the beginning individual for the descendants listing which would usually be the furthest person the pedigree surname you are tracing.

You would then verify that this person is truly the RIN you desired. Again you would select the number of generations you want to include (the limit is 50), and the program will copy the data onto your submission diskette. Since the descendants of an ancestor include all of the brothers, sisters, children and their spouses, the list of names copied to the temporary file could be quite large depending on how many individuals you entered.

Family Submission. Perhaps, you wish to submit the records of one family. You would select **3**, find the one MRIN that you wish to select, verify that it is who you want and the program will copy the data onto your submission diskette. Of course, if you wish to stop without making any submission, you would strike the "0" key.

Next, the information will be printed on the screen to see if the data can be merged with the Ancestral File. **OK** (okay) will indicate that the data if sufficient. If there is missing or conflicting information, a **See comments** will be placed in the right hand column.

You will then look at the detailed report which is shown when the checking is complete. The report begins with the first person on the list highlighted and lists the results or problems at the bottom of the screen. You can use your arrow key to look at the details for this individual. If the details for a particular individual is more than will fit on one screen, you can use the side arrows to move the message onto the screen.

You are then given the option to do several things:

1. Finalize the submission.
2. Print the complete list of problems.
3. Stop and fix the problems before submitting the names.

You would **F1** to finalize, **F2** to quit or **F3** to print the comments. If you decide to finalize, it will ask for your complete name, address and phone number. The program will not continue until a name and address have been included. Your telephone number, if included, will be made available through the Ancestral File for others to contact you about their genealogical data. The stake name and stake unit number are for members of The Church of Jesus Christ of Latter-day Saints to indicate their local church unit.

When you select the **F1** function key, the program begins creating the submission. Up to this point the program has only stored the RINS of the individual in the submission. It now must extract the data for each individual and put it on the submission diskette. There will be a screen which indicates that the submission is being created.

When the submission is finished you will see a note indicating it is done and asking you to press **enter**. A message will then be presented that will tell you how many individuals are being sent in, how many marriages, and the total bytes free on the diskette and whether or not you want to create another submission. Once you notice the available space on your diskette, you may choose to either submit another line or you may want to go to another diskette.

You may make a printed copy of all the people you have submitted, or if you do not want a printed report you press **n** for **no** at the bottom of the screen.

Finally, the Ancestral File diskette will not be completed without instructions. The PAF program will even help you type these instructions out. It will tell you what to include and what to say. It will also ask if you want the computer to print these instructions for you. Just type **y** for **yes** when it asks.

The program will indicate the type of computer you have, the type of operating system and how many diskettes are being submitted as well as your name and phone number. Usually the *Personal Ancestral File* program will read the instructions right off the computer and complete the form for you. If you have any special handling concerns, you should mention them on the notes field allowed.

It actually takes much longer to write out the instructions for submitting the information to the Ancestral File than to actually do it. It is a wonderful way to share your information with others and costs are kept to a minimum. You may also submit corrections to information you submitted earlier, or to other's research that you find in the Ancestral File.

Creating a Permanent Electronic Record

There are companies today who are seeking to publish family histories in compact disk (CD) format. The advantages over costly bound books are obvious, but there are other advantages. Storing your work in electronic format provides the capability of an "every word" index and a permanent storage format. However, mixing pictures and text may be a problem. If you are interested in pursuing this option, contact any company that produces CD's.

Selected Bibliography

Ames, Stanley Richard. *How to Write and Publish Your Family History Using Word Perfect*. Interlaken, NY: Heart of the Lakes Publishing, 1988.

Andereck, Paul and Richard Pence. *Computer Genealogy: A guide to Research Through High Technology*. 2nd ed. Salt Lake City: Ancestry, 1991.

Hartley, William G. "Family History Writing and Publishing." Pgs. 153-158, *Annual Family History and Genealogical Research Conference*, Brigham Young University Conferences and Workshops, 1984.

Lackey, Richard S. *Cite Your Sources.*. New Orleans: Polyanthos, 1980. (Style book written specifically for genealogical projects.)

McColgin, Michael. "Genies and the Magic Preservation Lamp." Session F-62, *New Horizons a Conference in the Southwest Syllabus* The Federation of Genealogical Societies, 1992.

Schreiner-Yantis, Netti. "Marketing Your Publication." Session W28, *Syllabus*, Part I, National Genealogical Society Capital Conference, 1990.

Szucs, Loretto Dennis. "How to Publish a Family History and Safe Expectations about Marketing It" Session S-105, *New Horizons a Conference in the Southwest Syllabus* The Federation of Genealogical Societies, 1992.

Zinsser, William. *On Writing Well: An Informal Guide to Writing Nonfiction*. 3rd ed. New York: Harper & Row Publishers, 1985. (Correct writing principals with a chapter on word processing.)

Chapter Fourteen
Assignments: Publishing and Sharing the Final Product

1.   Read the qualifications for submission of a manuscript in the front of any genealogical publishing catalog.

2.   Assume that a publisher has agreed to publish your materials. Submit your manuscript to a fellow student as though you were submitting it to a publisher.   Include a copyright notice. This manuscript will be judged on accuracy, interest, clarity, eye appeal and consideration of your reading audience.

3.   Describe your plans for advertising and collecting book orders for your new book.

4.   Submit the new information you have learned about your family through the Ancestral File portion of the PAF program.   It is not necessary to single out the changes only.   Resubmit all the names in order to update the information in the files.

LAB ASSIGNMENT 14: Using *WordPerfect*® to Correspond with Printers

1. Draft a letter to a publishing company describing your project
    and asking permission to send a copy of your manuscript for
    review.

2. Type up a review of a fellow student's manuscript. Be kind
    but honest.

APPENDIX 1:   Research Calendar

RESEARCH CALENDAR

Goal _____

_____

SURNAME/SUBJECT _____   CLIENT_____

RESEARCHER   _____   AREA   _____

Repository Call #	Date	Description of Source	Ind Con	Object of Search	Time Period, Search	Note	Ext #

RESEARCH CALENDAR

Surname / Subject ______________________

Locality ______________________

Goal: ______________________

____

____

Date	Repository / Call #	Description of Source	Indexed / Condition	Object of Search	Time Period of Search	Note	Extract

KAREN CLIFFORD
23040 Guidotti Drive
Salinas, California 93908
(408) 484-9426

RESEARCHERS

10/92

APPENDIX 2:   Sample Pages from Student Histories

The following samples came from my students last semester. They include:

1.   Sample Title Pages[53].

    a.   The Descendants of James Cotter by Mary Foletta page 286.
    b.   The Descendants of James Cotter by Mary Foletta page 287.
    c.   Descendants of John & Elizabeth (Harris) Berry by Carolyn Berry page 288.
    d.   Family Ties (Genealogy Research Associates) page 289.
    e.   Ancestors of Richard P. Spencer was done modifying the Title Page program mentioned below (see footnote 53), Special Edition Collection page 290.
    f.   My Loving Challenge same as "e." above, Special Edition Collection page 291.
    g.   Job Rainwater same as "e." above, from Collection #1 page 292.
    h.   James Berry Chandler same as "e." above, from Collection #1 page 293.
    i.   John Stewart Family same as "e." above, from Collection #2 page 294.
    j.   James Agee Smith same as "e." above, from Collection #2 page 295.
    k.   Jesse & Jeffrey Jordan same as "e." above, from Collection #2 page 296.

2.   Sample "How-to-Read This Book" pages produced in part by *GEN-BOOK* but added upon by student Karen L. Robert on page 297.

---

[53] An easy yet lovely way to make your own title page is to use templates for *WordPerfect* 5.1 & 6 which are available in four collections (each collection includes 10 finished title pages each). You may order these from Keepsake Publishing, 9712 Mirage Circle, Garden Grove, CA 92644 (714) 636-3536 for $10 per Collection plus $1 shipping & handling (CA residents add sales tax 78 cents each disk). See samples of these pages under e-k Sample Title Pages.

3. Sample Acknowledgments and Dedication Pages.

   a. By Karen L. Robert page 299.
   b. By Mary Foletta page 300.
   b. By Ardell Lynds page 301.
   c. By Carolyn Berry (both) pages 302 and 303.

4. Sample Table of Contents Pages.

   a. By Ardell Lynds on dot matrix page 305.
   b. By Mary Folleta on an ink jet printer page 306.

5. Sample Introduction Pages.

   a. Introduction used as a research report by Beverly Tucker-Miguel pages 307-309.
   b. Introduction used to elicit responses from others by Robert G. Chapman, M.D. page 310.
   c. Introduction used to thank others for sharing information and for organizing that information to return to them in the hopes of helping the family extend a line backwards. This book was 125+ pages long by Karen Robert page 311.
   d. An oral history incorporated into an introduction by Carolyn Berry page 312.
   e. An introduction using dot-matrix printer, giving background on the family and story to follow by Ardell Lynds on page 313.
   f. An introduction expressing impression on the family and stating a goal by Mary Folleta page 314.

6. Sample insert boxes using *WordPerfect* **alt** + **F7,** 2 (tables) 1 (create) then tell how many rows and how many columns you want. A box is 1 row, 1 column. A box used to point out research goals by Mary Foletta may be seen on page 315.

7. Sample picture and historical interest inserts into the *GEN-BOOK* text.

a. Edward Northrop Chapman by Robert G. Chapman, M.D. pages 317-318.

b. James Abercrombie by Karen Robert page 319 (notice the scissors and the inventory connection).

8. Sample reference pages.

   a. Bolding date and event to emphasize information by Robert G. Chapman, M.D. pages 321-323.

   b. Sample maps by Robert G. Chapman, M.D. pages 324-325.

   c. Sample clip art maps and text by Carolyn Berry pages 326-327.

   d. Sample bolding of date and event as well as complete citations listed in notes by Karen Robert page 328.

9. Sample appendix where a pedigree chart was placed to guide the reader, by Robert G. Chapman, M.D., page 329.

10. Sample Index of Names pages.

    a. Two column by Mary Foletta page 331.

    b. Three column page 332-333.

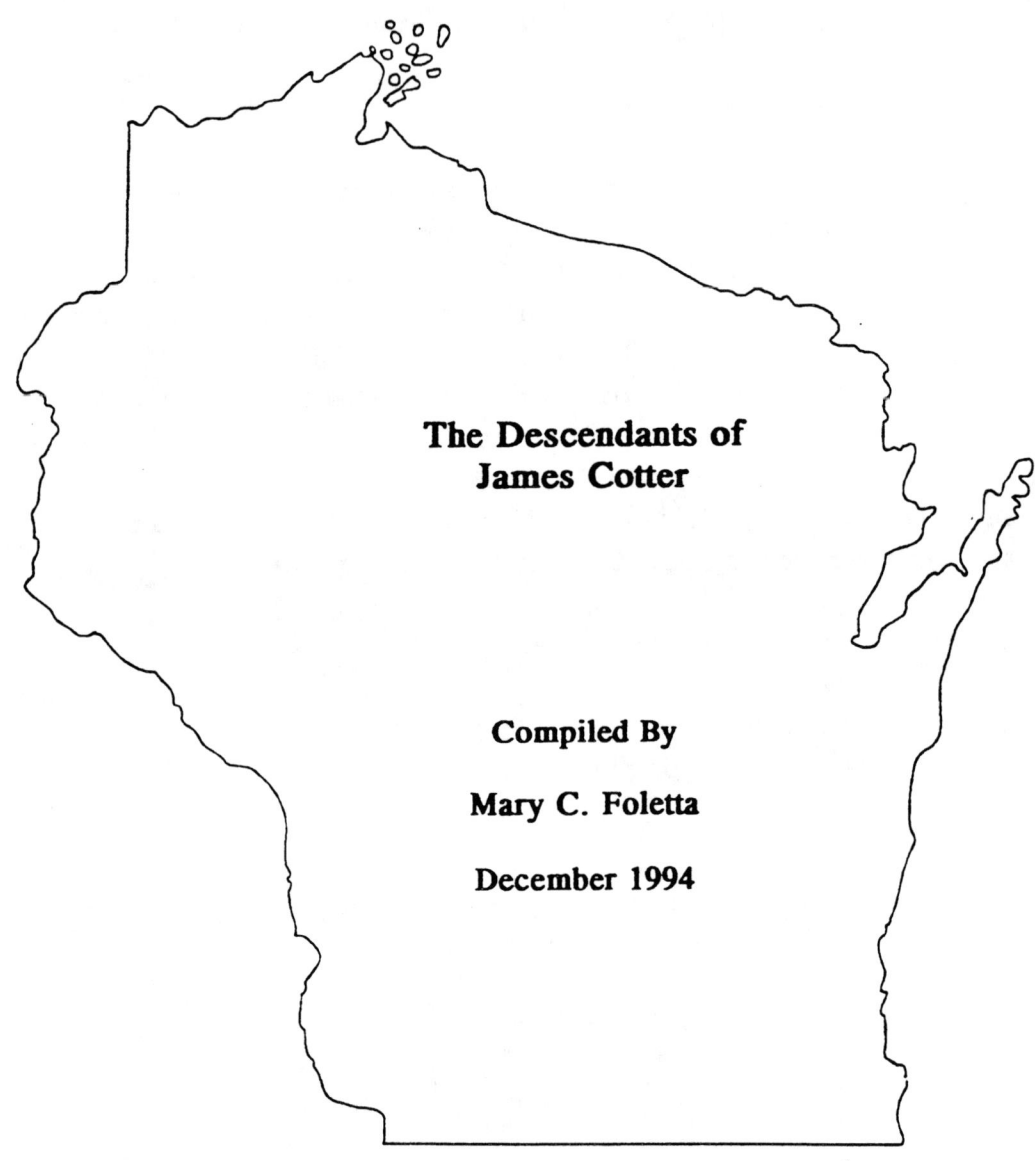

The Descendants of
James Cotter

Compiled By

Mary C. Foletta

December 1994

The Descendants of James Cotter

1895 to 1994

Compiled by
Mary C. Foletta
December 1994

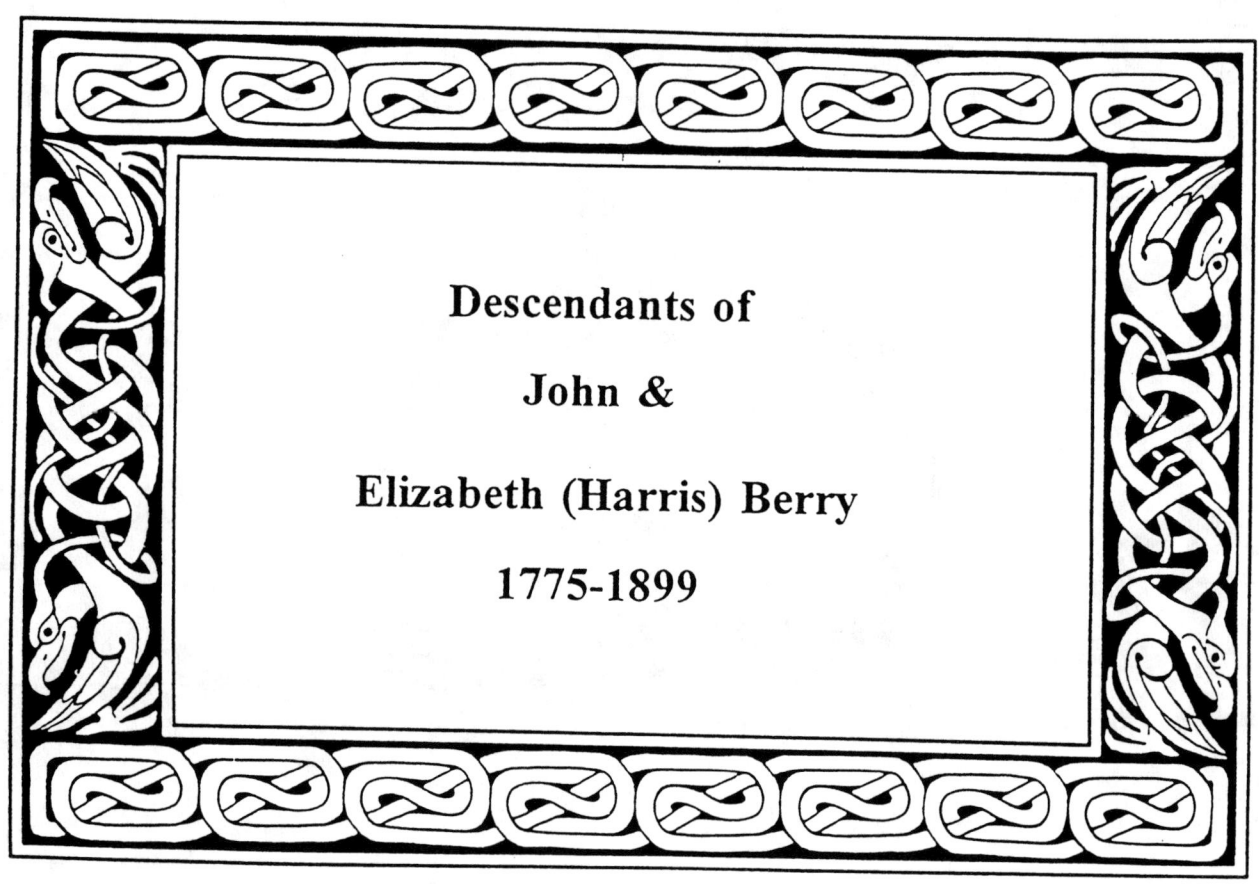

Descendants of

John &

Elizabeth (Harris) Berry

1775-1899

Compiled By

Carolyn Berry

1994

288

FAMILY TIES

The Descendants of

Roland Ernest

&

Kathryn Lucile Kasper Carlson

with their

link to

General Ulysses S. Grant

ULYSSES S. GRANT

289

THE SURRENDER OF LEE TO GRANT AT APPOMATTOX COURT HOUSE

Ancestors
of
Richard P. Spencer

Son of Walter Lee Spencer
& Gertrude Eliza Midyette

Compiled by

Richard Payne Spencer
1994

My *LOVING* *CHALLENGE*

Finding Descendants
of
Charles Albert Cannon
&
Ruth Louise Coltrane
North Carolina Natives

By
Mary Ruth Cannon Spencer

Ancestors and Descendants of
Job Rainwater
(1785-1863)
of Georgia

Compiled By

Ilene (Chandler) Miller

Prepared by:
Ilene (Chandler) Miller
9712 Mirage Circle
Garden Grove, California 92644

James Berry Chandler
A Story of His Life
1861-1939
b. Louisiana, d. Thatcher, Arizona

Prepared for:
The James B. Chandler Family Reunion
August 5, 1994

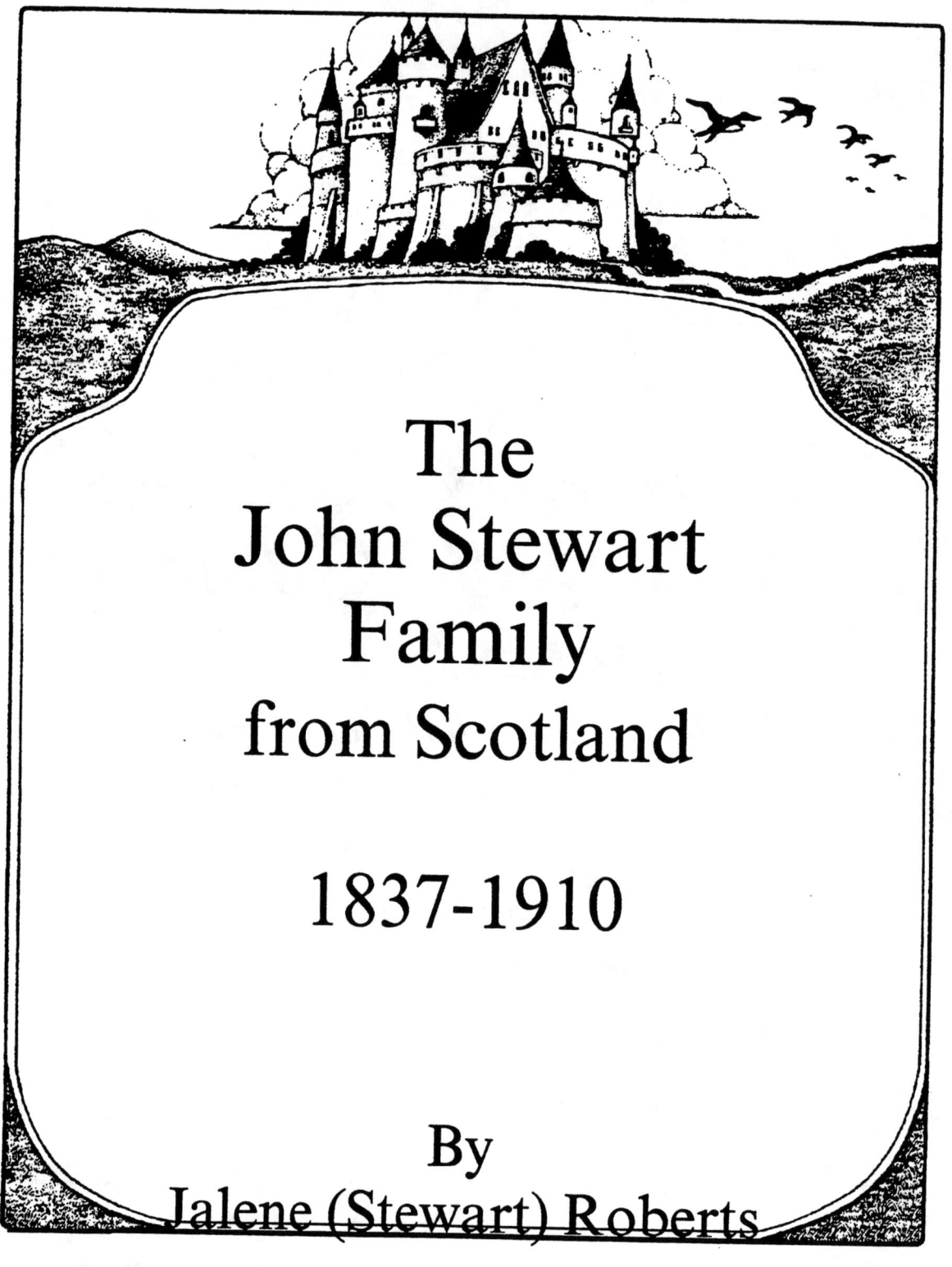

The
John Stewart
Family
from Scotland

1837-1910

By
Jalene (Stewart) Roberts

English Heritage
of
James Agee Smith

1787—1875
b. Sullivan County, Tennessee
d. Washington County, Utah

By
Ilene (Chandler) Miller

Ancestors of Jesse & Jeffrey Jordan

Compiled by

Judy (Chandler) Jordan
1995

Reading This Book

The format or style used in this book is known as the **Modified Register System,** which has been refined by the National Genealogical Society.

Three types of numbers are used: one to uniquely identify the individual, one to indicate the generation into which that person falls, and one to denote his or her birth-order within the nuclear family. The identification numbering system used in this book is called **By Generation.** The starting person is 1, his first child is 2. All the children are listed as generation number two, the grand-children are listed as generation number three and so on. Each person is assigned an ID number in sequential order by generation.

When an individual is introduced in his/her separate sketch, the name appears in boldface letters with the surnames in all capital letters.

Young David ABERCROMBIE

The name is preceded by the identification number.

9. Young David ABERCROMBIE

The last given name is followed immediately by a superscript number indicating the number of generations from the starting individual in this book.

9. Young David² ABERCROMBIE

In parentheses following the name is a list of direct ancestors back to the starting individual. Only the given name is listed, preceded by his/her ID number, and followed by the generation number in superscript.

9. Young David² ABERCROMBIE (1.James¹)

When the list of children is presented, the plus (+) sign indicates that more about this child will be presented in his/her separate sketch. The ID number is printed, followed by M/F indicating the sex. Next a small roman numeral in front of the name designates birth-order. Next the name is followed by the birth and death dates.

+ 9.   M   viii.   Young David ABERCROMBIE, born 7 May 1804, died 11 Feb 1888.

The index is arranged alphabetically by surname. Under each surname, the given names are alphabetically arranged. The name is followed by the year of birth and death in square brackets. The number to the right indicates the page where this name appears. The wife appears under her maiden name and under her married names with her maiden name in parentheses.

Sample Acknowledgments and Dedication Pages.

Acknowledgments

First, I wish to thank my genealogy teacher, Karen Clifford, without whose knowledge, patience, and friendship I would never have come this far in such a short time. I also wish to thank Ann Sanford for helping me find out how to accomplish my goal of becoming a genealogist and letting me pick her brain from time to time. Two close friends of mine, Loreta Blank and Donna Catterick, who are also studying to become genealogists, will be glad when this book is finally complete so they will not hear the surname Abercrombie.

I wish to thank all of the Abercrombies who have sent me information, C. L Abercrombie, Ella May Hunter, Beverly Martin, Ardith L Ott, and Linda Roholt. Without their help this book would not be possible. I would also like to thank the Chestatee Regional Library of Gainesville, Georgia for the volumes of information they have sent to me.

Acknowledgment

This book is an out growth of my interest in genealogy. It is a small but important record of those members of the Cotter family who have, just by their existence made a contribution to this book. To them I am extremely grateful.

First, I wish to thank my genealogy teacher, Karen Clifford, for she has been such an inspiration and good example to me. Second, I want to thank my three wonderful daughters, Cherie, Cynthia, and Catherine for all their encouragement and help. Last, I would like to thank my dear friend Patrick Iman for his immeasurable support.

Mary C. Foletta

Acknowledgments

I wish to thank all of those people who have helped me collect the information for this book. To my parents, Henry and Phyllis (Pease) Parkman, for all the help trying to answer all of my "do you remember" questions. To Marjorie (Hart) Hayden who started collecting informtion on the descendants of Sampson Hart many years ago. .To Marguerite Hart who took over the task from Marjorie and has helped bring the data up to date. Also for her enthusiasm and desire to see the book in print. To the late Thelma (Peasley) Richards who gave me access to many letters and a family bible that helped to locate members of the family that left Maine. To my aunt, the late Meredith (Parkman) Wood, who provided me with many family pictures. Also to Helen (Ham) Littlefield who provided me with a darling picture of my grandmother as a young child and to Elizabeth (Hart) Fisher who helped identify old pictures. And last, but not least, Stephen J. Chapman, who provided me with the marriage date of John Hart & Betsey Gullifer, and over the past ten years has provided me with information on all the families that I am researching. There are many others, too many to mention, who also provided me with informtion and inspiration. To all of you, I say a heartfelt, THANK YOU and GOD BLESS.

Acknowledgments

Robert E Becker, Iona Faulk, Arlene Johnson, Verda Berry Thomas, William Moultrie Berry, Jo Ann Turner, Mary Jo Berry, Karen Clifford, Ray Clifford, Virginia De Marce, William B Claycomb, Mary Ray, June Welch, Claude Norcross, H L Jones, Karen W Myers, Helen Darrah, Jo McCurdy, Carolyn Bartels, Martha Reavis DeWitt, Jimmy Thomas, Smith Higgins, Lynne Bernard, Lorene Berry, R L Byler, Rhoda Fone, Annette Eliason, Ruth Lewis, Dorothy Koenig, Mildred Bailey, William G Scroggins, Don Cofer, Kenneth Berry, Russell Berry, Pat Roy, Forrest F Anderson, Karen Berry, Cleo Whitworth, Doc Harris, Edith Cunningham, Dorothy Franks, Mary W Dalton, Thelma Yeates, Edith Wentz, Wilma Di Betta, Lily Freeman Walker, Faye Lightburn, Margaret Scoggins, P H Gillaspy, Norma Middendorf, Glenda Housh, Betty Williams, Kathy & Bill Vockery, Laura Wells, Phyllis Johnson, Carol Hulen, Phyllis Sears, Doris New, James Powell, Georgia Munro, Bobbie Thompson, Mrs. Fred Meinershagen, Charles O'Dell, Dorothy Boone Patterson, Dolores Blaze, Rene McGuire E KY U, Christine S Agee, Barbara Augspurger, Hugh Denny, Ms B J Gooch U of KY Libraries, Mona Hays, MO State Archives, John Hurm, Jackie Little, Rosemary Kutch, Paula Whitmer, Mildred Adams, Minnie Parsons, Shirley Haynes, Cora Huntress, Ray Copher, Martha Billings, Arlene Stone, Jack Mayer, W Jane Stroehmer, Marie Edgar, Elaine Rowland, Gypsy Lee Cosby Jones, Zora Evans, Mary Givan, Rosemary Delmore, Phil & Alice Goodwin

Dedication

Dedicated to my father, Charles Thomas Berry, who couldn't have cared less, but he would have been proud.

TABLE OF CONTENTS

TABLE OF CONTENTS

I N T R O D U C T I O N

I decided to write my first family history on Joseph Ephraim Hartsell as my final project for Family Research Studies at Monterey Peninsula College. I selected Joseph for several reasons. The first reason is that he fit the criteria of an ancestor born before 1850. The second reason was because I wanted to know more about the man my father was named after. My grandmother, Grayce Thomas Koehler, told me in an oral interview I conducted in 1986 that she always planned to name a son after her granddaddy.

The objective I had when I selected J. E. Hartsell was to find his parents. This turned out to be relatively easy. The 1850 census of Stanly County, NC, shows Joseph E, age 8, listed in household of James L. Hartsdale, age 22 (he was actually 32), with Elizabeth, age 36. The 1860 census of Stanly County, NC, shows Joseph, age 18, listed in household of James L. Hartsell, age 42, with Elizabeth, age 46. The 1862 enlistment of Joseph shows he enlisted from Rowan County at the age of 21. The 1878 marriage record lists Joseph E. Hartsell (age 33) as son of James L. and Elizabeth Hartsell. The 1880 census of Stanly County, NC, shows James L. Hartsell, age 63, listed with Elizabeth, age 66. The 1924 obituary of Joe E. Hartsell states "he was the son of the late Mr. and Mrs. James Hartsell." The article also stated that "he was a well known Confederate veteran, having served in a volunteer company of which his brother, the late Jack Hartsell, was captain." The 1924 death certificate of Joe E. Hartsell stated that the maiden name of his mother, Elizabeth, was Taylor.

Once I found Joseph as a child in the 1850 census I was able to pick up his siblings in that census and following censuses. I came up with 10 different children. Looking at some of the dates a few more could have died in infancy. I know that Joseph joined the Methodist Church as a youth, so his parents were probably Methodist as well. His parents, as well as two sisters and two brothers, are buried in the same Methodist cemetery where he and his wife are buried.

At this time I would like to give you some background information about Stanly County, the rural area of North Carolina where my story takes place.

AREA AND TIME SETTLED:
Stanly County is in the central southern area of North Carolina. Originally, the county was Craven, which was formed out of Prec. Bath County in 1712. New Hanover County was formed out of Craven County in 1729 followed by Bladen County in 1734. In 1750, Anson County was formed out of Bladen County. In 1779, Montgomery County was formed out of Anson County, then in 1841, Stanly County was formed out of Montgomery County and remains to this day.

NEIGHBORHOOD SETTLEMENT:

English settlers came from VA, and upriver along the Cape Fear, Yadkin, and Pee Dee Rivers to the southern portion of the county.

Scotch-Irish, German, and Dutch settlers traveled the Great Wagon Road from PA, NJ, and other spots along the way settling in the western townships.

French settlers settled in the eastern region near the Yadkin River.

RULING GOVERNMENT:

The ruling government during the settlement of this area was the Crown. Between 1729 and 1776, NC was a crown colony. Seven of the eight original proprietary shares were sold to King George II. However, Earl Granville refused to sell. Those lands were confiscated when the American Revolution began. In 1800, a lawsuit was filed by his heirs in federal court, but they lost. By 1817, the suit was abandoned.

In 1777, land offices were set up in every county to grant land formerly owned by the Crown and Lord Granville. A man could get 640 acres for himself, 100 acres for his wife, and 100 acres for each minor child.

NC law is based on English common-law and the state constitution was formed in December, 1776. The legislature is called the General Assembly with a Senate and a House of Commons.

RELIGIOUS BACKGROUND OR AFFILIATIONS OF SETTLERS:

Methodist was the first to organize. Fifteen Methodist churches had been organized by the antebellum period.

POPULATION AND SLAVE OWNER INFORMATION:

In the 1860 census, Stanly County had only 7,801 inhabitants. Stanly County had the lowest number of slaves in the state. In fact, during 1830-1860, the slave population actually declined going from 18% of the population in the Stanly County region of then Montgomery County to 15% of the population in 1860. In 1850, the 228 slaveholders had only one to five slaves. By the end of the war the population had been reduced down to a little over 6,000 people. The Hartsell family did not own slaves.

PROMINENT LEADERS:

The prominent leaders of the Crown were King George II and King Goerge III. The prominent leaders in NC were the governors. The governors under the rule of the Crown were: 1753-Matthew Rowan, 1754-Arthur Dobbs, 1766-William Tryon, 1773-Joseph Martin.

The governors under the Republic Government were: 1777-Richard Carswell, 1780-Abner Nash.

A BRIEF CHRONOLOGY OF STANLY COUNTY

10,000 BC   Native American Hardaway Culture

c 1746   Settlers begin to move into the Fork section (in the "V" formed by the confluence of the Rocky and Pee Dee Rivers below Norwood in what was then Bladen County and is now Stanly County

1750   Anson County established out of Bladen County

c1750-1770   Western Stanly settled by people of German origin

1779   Montgomery County formed out of northern Anson County

1780   Military action between Patriots under William Davidson and Tories at Colson's

1826   Post Office established at Smith's Store

1841   Stanly County formed on 11 January 1841 out of Montgomery County West of the Yadkin/Pee Dee River

1850   Population 6,922 including approximately 1,488 slaves (21.5% of the population)

1860   Population 7,801 including approximately 1,217 slaves (15.6% of the population)

1861-1865   War Between The States - Stanly County supplies six companies for the Confederate Army - in all more than 700 men

1870   Population 8,315

1915   Furr City incorporated as Oakboro (Croson Furr was son-in-law of Joseph E. Hartsell. Land originally belonged to Joseph Hartsell. Descendants of Joseph Hartsell, Croson Furr, and Duncan Kennedy (another son-in-law) still live in and around Oakboro

1926   Joe Thomas Tucker born to Arlie Rufus Tucker and Mary Grayce Thomas Tucker, granddaughter of Joseph Hartsell

INTRODUCTION

As I grew up in the Chapman family I heard much about the Chapman ancestors in Connecticut. My grandfather, Edward M. Chapman, wrote a small book entitled *The Chapmans of Old Saybrook, A Family Chronicle*; and there was a sizeable tome *The Chapman Family, Descendants of Robert Chapman, one of the First Settlers of Say-Brook, Conn.* by Rev. Frederick W. Chapman published in 1854.

No such works existed for my mother's side of the family, the Johnsons of northern New York. I heard rather little about her Johnson ancestors. We lived in Colorado, far from other relatives on either side of the family. My limited knowledge of the Johnson family came from watching old family movies and from a few visits to Saranac Lake when I was in school in the east.

My aunt "Patsy", Agnes Johnson, provided me with her family record files before her death in 1990. These provided a lot more information than I had expected and have been an invaluable help in leading me to her direct line of ancestors as far back as Isaac Johnson, who was one of the first settlers of Stratford, New Hampshire, in 1772. My own efforts have been largely to find documentation in support of Patsy's notes and to make a few, usually minor corrections in them. I have been able to identify Isaac's father, Joseph, in Stratford, Connecticut, correcting information given in the very useful 1925 Stratford, New Hampshire town history.

Using these sources plus written histories of the places of residence and migrations of the Johnson family over the past 250 years, I have endeavored to provide an interesting narrative about my mother's ancestors for my own family and relatives. Each chapter covers one generation and includes additional information on collateral ancestral lines which I believe to be of interest. Documentation on which I rely is listed at the end of each chapter. I have made no effort to present all available details on these collaterals, but have concentrated on presenting the direct Johnson line and their children. In a number of cases the list of children is incomplete.

If my readers have additional information or corrections to make for the material in this book, I shall greatly appreciate hearing from them.

Robert G. Chapman, M.D.

47 La Rancheria
Carmel Valley, CA 93924
December, 1994

310

INTRODUCTION

I am the granddaughter of Meekie Anna Abercrombie, number 390 in this book, and the daughter of her son John Leonard Lewis. I was born 6 Jul 1941 in Madera, Madera, CA. I have had two marriages and three daughters. At this time in my life I have an opportunity to follow a dream I have had since I was 10 years old, to work on my family history. I am presently enrolled in an advanced genealogy class in Monterey, CA. I plan to take a specialty class next semester in Southern research. My goal is to be an Accredited Genealogist.

This book is an accumulation of information I have received from Abercrombies all over the United States and information I have found through my research. I am writing this book at this time as a project in my current class and decided to take this opportunity to send what I have accumulated to the people who have helped me.

I still have a lot of research to do before I can write my final book. I will be researching South Carolina and other southern states for information about the Abercrombies during the 1700's. Any information that any of you might have would be greatly appreciated.

You will find information in boxes. This information is theory, conjecture and assumption on my part. I would welcome comments about these items.

I apologize for any errors in this book. Please feel free to send any corrections to me, as I would like this book to be as accurate as possible. Corrections and additions can be sent to:

Karen L Robert
4850 Freedom Blvd
Aptos, CA 95003

Phone (408) 724-6751

311

INTRODUCTION

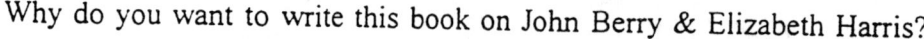

Jeremiah XII Chapter 9 "Mine heritage is unto me as a speckled bird..."

Why do you want to write this book on John Berry & Elizabeth Harris?

I want to preserve the information that I've been researching the last twenty plus years. I'm hoping that the book will be inexpensive enough to produce that I will be able to send it to societies & libraries & to the people who contributed their information over the years & this will create an interest & maybe other family members will connect & fill in some of the gaps.
I also want to have a history available for my children & grandchildren so that if they become interested, they won't have to start from scratch

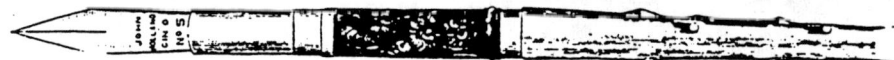

Will this be new information or more of a compilation of information you have gathered through the years?

The information as such is not new. It's compiled from old histories of counties in Missouri published in the 1800's & census records, cemetery records, & a few Bible records. Most of the family Bibles were destroyed in the Civil War. What is new is the combination of the data from various sources which allowed me to eliminate the incorrect information that I found.

Had you never found any information on this couple before?

I've been able to find a considerable amount of information about this couple but it has involved a lot of research trying to eliminate the records of other John Berrys. There were many John Berrys in early Kentucky, Virginia, & Missouri. We still have not determined who John's parents were in spite of generations of work on this family. Elizabeth Harris' family is well-documented. Unfortunately, the primary book on the Harris family left Elizabeth out of the list of children of Robert Harris & Nancy Grubbs. Fortunately, "The Boone Family" by Spraker included Elizabeth on the list of children even though they didn't know if she married John or James Berry.

How many children did John & Elizabeth have ?

They had nine children that we have verified. The Spraker book only lists 8. There were probably more. I've been able to determine enough of the birthdates to tell that there were no children who survived during the period around 1806 when they moved to Missouri from Kentucky. Then there was another gap in 1814 when the War of 1812 was being fought in Missouri. The
family was "forting up." None of the histories that I have found mention this, but I think that there must have been a number of miscarriages during these hard times.

312

INTRODUCTION

The research into the ancestry of my paternal grandmother's Hart family started nearly twenty years ago. It was my goal at that time to research all of my paternal and maternal ancestry, and carry that search from the present generation back to the first know immigrant ancestor into this country. Im many instances I have been fortunate enough to have accomplished that goal, but in searching for the ancestry of my third great grandfather, John Hart, I have have not succeeded in reaching that goal.

We know from the census records that John was born in Maine sometime around the years 1767 to 1770. We also know that he lived in Waterville in Kennebec Co, at one time a part of Winslow, in Lincoln County, and that he spent his final years in Pittsfield, in Somerset County.

The death records of two of his sons, Eben amd Allen, indicate that their father was born on Swan Island. Swan Island is now called Perkins Island and is part of Dresden, situated in the Kennebec River, near the town of Bowdoinham.

This area of Maine is now in Sagadahoc County, but was in Lincoln county from 1760 to 1854. Very few town records were kept in those early years and some of those that were recorded have since been destroyed or disappeared. The French and Indian Wars were still going on until after the American Revolution in 1776, families moved into Maine while things were quiet and then when the skirmishes with the indians flared up, they would move back to Massachusetts, until it was quiet again, some families never returned. Surviving was the order of the day, not going into town to record a birth, marriage or death.

No records has been found that show any family living on Perkin's Island by the name of Hart. Two of the families that did live there were the Pushors, a French Huguenot family, and the Nobles. Both of these families moved up the Kennebec River and lived in and around Fairfield, near where the Gullifers lived, John's wife's family. Both the Pushor and Noble families had connection with the John Hart family. Other families, the Pattees, Toziers, Cobbs, Roses, that migrated north along the Kennebec River, also lived in the same area in Kennebec County that John Hart lived.

There was a Morris and Mary Hart family living in Georgetown, south of Perkin's Island, that had sons John & Thomas born in 1743 & 1745. Probably this son, Thomas, was the man who married in 1771, Jean Ren in Georgetown. Also in Georgetown a Nathaniel Hart & Martha Cobb married in 1762. In Winslow in 1785, a Benjamin Hart and Hannah Ren were married. Perhaps this Benjamin was the Mr. Hart mentioned in MARTHA BALLARD'S DIARY as visiting the Ballards on the evening of 4 Dec 1786. Was it his wife, the Mrs. Hart, who died in March 1790 also mentioned in Martha's diary? Who were the descendants of these couples. Are any of the these Harts related in anyway to the John

INTRODUCTION

My goal has been to find out about the COTTERS. This is my mother's paternal line. Searching for my grandfather, grandmother, brothers, sisters, aunts, and uncles helps bring a closeness that is hard to put into words.

More information abounds in all the materials that I have thus far aquired. As I search I seem to have more and more doors open to me. But I am quickly realizing that I need to slow down and take one item at a time being carefull to read it, search it, transcribe it and most of all remembering that this is MY family and MY history that I will be writing about.

From the "HISTORY OF OUTAGAMIE COUNTY," Published in 1911 by the Goodspeed Historical Association of Chicago:

> In the old town of Lansing were settlements of people
> from various localities and countries, who while coming simultaneously were
> often referred to as distinctive
> settlements. In that portion of the town of Lansing, now known as center, Irish
> people came from Columbiana County, Ohio, they acquired the name, Ohio
> settlement, and for several years dominated the affairs of the town, not alone
> because they were the first and most numerous
> But because of their deep interest in the welfare
> and progress of the towm along education, religious,
> and the material lines of improvements ....the Cotters
> and Hephner's were neighbors in Ohio and formed the
> nucleus of the Ohio settlement in Center.

In a newspaper clippings I found in my grandmother Sarah Bley Cotter's scrap box, dated 10 may 1963. It said " The early settlers were people of one mind, all anxious to promote each others welfare and lending a helping hand to all in distress. Although sickness was rare, death would come and break the circle of friendship; and the sorrows of one family were felt and shared by all. The soil was rich, the climate healthful, the settlers poor. All worked with a hearty good fruit from the labors and sacrifices of the pioneers of center."

I don't think I need to add any more to this description of my ancestors, this describes my family still today

314

Sample Boxes

JAMES (JIM) COTTER OWNED A FARM IN WI. WHEN HE DIED IT WAS LEFT TO HIS CHILDREN. HIS SON JOHN E. COTTER BOUGHT OUT HIS BROTHERS AND SISTERS. THIS WAS TOLD TO SARAH HAMBEY BORCHARD BY HER MOTHER, MILDRED M. COTTER HAMBEY ON 1993.

NEW RESEARCH GOALS: SEARCH OH FOR THE COTTERS LIVING COLUMBIANA CO. BEFORE 1845.
SEARCH PENNSYLVANIA FOR THE COTTERS LIVING THERE BEFORE 1840. SEARCH POSSIBLY NEW YORK FOR THEM COMING TO THE UNITED STATES.

NEW RESEARCH GOALS: LOOK FOR LAND RECORDS AND PROBATE RECORDS IN OUTAGAMIE CO., WISCONSIN ON 12 MARCH 1902. IN THE PROBATE RECORD IT MIGHT LIST JAMES COTTER'S SIBLINGS. ON THE 30 MAY 1994, I FOUND TWO JAMES COTTER'S ON A 1889 PLAT MAP OF OUTAGAMIE CO., CENTER TOWNSHIP, WISCONSIN, FILM # 1597750 AT FHL, HOLLISTER, CA.,
USE THIS MAP TO SEARCH LAND RECORDS. *(SEE MAP PAGE 4)*

NOTES for Julia follow:

1859 BIRTH: Julia Mullen born Mar 1859, Vermont, on 1870 Wisconsin census, Town of Osborn, # 0553229

NEW RESEARCH GOALS: SEARCH VERMONT FOR HER BIRTH RECORD. I SEARCHED ALL OF VERMONT AND NEW HAMPSHIRE TO FIND HER PARENTS ON A CENSUS, THEY ARE NOT FOUND.
CHECK TO SEE IF ANY CONNECTION BETWEEN JULIA AND THOMAS J. MULLEN LISTED IN HISTORY OF OUTAGAMIE CO, WISCONSIN, 1912, # 0928279; COULD POSSIBLY BE HER BROTHER. *(SEE HISTORY PAGE 15)*
I SEARCHED ALL THREE FILMS # 0549882, # 0549883, # 054884, FOR RENSSELAER CO, NEW YORK, 1850 CENSUS, WAS UNABLE TO FIND PATRICK MULLEN WITH SON THOMAS J., THE INDEX TO RENSSELAER CO. NEW YORK WAS OF NO HELP, THE FILMS WERE POOR COPIES AND MOST PARTS UNREADABLE AND WITHOUT PAGE NUMBERS.
1860 STATE CENSUS: ORDER FROM WI STATE HISTORICAL LIBRARY, 816 STATE ST., MADISON , WI, # 933,651 IS INDEX.
1865 STATE CENSUS: ORDER FOR WALWORTH CO, WI.
SEARCH THE 1870 WI CENSUS FOR JULIA WITH HER PARENTS, SHE WOULD BE ABOUT 11 YEARS OLD. *(SEE MAP PAGE 5)*
RAH! I FOUND HER...LISTED WITH HER PARENTS IN 1870 IN OUTAGAMIE CO. MY SUSPICION ABOUT THOMAS POSSIBLY BEING HER BROTHER WAS CORRECT. SOME OF THE INFORMATION IN THE HISTORY WAS INCORRECT SO I WAS SENT ON A FEW DEAD ENDS. SOMEHOW I OVERLOOKED ORDERING THAT FILM, I HAVE ALL OTHERS ONE.

THE ANCESTORS OF JANET GALBRAITH JOHNSON 1897-1979

Edward Northrop CHAPMAN

Edward was born in Worcester, MA, and spent much of his childhood in Lyme, CT, were his father was minister of the First Congregational Church of Old Lyme. He had his schooling at Black Hall in Lyme and after initial failure on exams for Yale he spent an extra year at Holbrook School in Ossining, NY, thereafter gaining admission to Yale on conditions. While at Yale he was arrested for a "bottle night" disturbance, a story he later loved to tell his children. He served in the Connecticut National Guard, 10th Field Artillery in 1916, and graduated from Yale in the class of 1917. He attended Harvard Medical School, receiving his M.D. degree in 1921.

During the summer after graduation he worked with Dr. (Sir Wilfred) Grenfell in Newfoundland and Laborador (Pilley's Island Hospital), then served an internship at Hartford Hospital in Connecticut, planning to become a pediatrician. These plans ended when he developed tuberculosis in 1924. He was treated at Trudeau Sanatorium in Saranac Lake in the home town of Janet JOHNSON whom he married in 1925. They travelled to Colorado Springs, CO, on their honeymoon and remained until 1927 when they returned to Mt Magregor Sanatorium in New York where he served as staff physician. His tuberculosis flared up and they returned to Colordo Springs in the fall of 1928 to stay.

Nort, as Edward was known, put his interest in investments to work at first on his own and then with the Cowles Commission for Research in Economics until it moved to the University of Chicago in 1939. He had survived the market crash in 1929 largely because of his rule personally never to borrow money to invest. This allowed him to ride out the market swings. He was able to support his family through the 1930's in comfort, buying and remodeling a house, and providing Jan with live-in help through that whole time. In 1940 he returned to investment work on a personal level, publishing articles in *Barron's* and the *Commercial and Financial Chronicle* and later serving as

317

investment advisor to one of the banks in Colorado Springs. In the medical field his health did not permit engaging in private practice but he developed considerable interest in public health matters, publishing articles leading to improved sewage treatment in Colorado, and later served the state in the field of maternal and child health and in tuberculosis care.

Nort always longed to live in California. In 1934 he spent a year there with his family, first in Claremont and then in La Jolla. Away from Colorado's altitude and climate his tuberculosis flared up, so he returned to Colorado for the next 30 years. After the children were away at school, he and Jan began to take vacations in the winter to Carmel, CA, and after Nort's retirement in the early 1960's they moved permanently to this California town. By this time his tuberculosis appeared to be cured, but he had been left with pulmonary emphysema causing shortness of breath. He made only a few more trips to visit his favorite Colorado mountain byways because breathing at that altitude became too difficult. He and Jan lived at first in Carmel a few blocks from the ocean, but after a few years, preferring a less foggy climate, they moved the short distance into Carmel Valley where they built a house above the Village. Health problems led them to change their residence to Carmel Valley Manor in the Valley where they spent their final years. In the last year Nort began to have fainting episodes from which he was slow to recover, seeming to lose his drive to breath. This bothered those around him much more than it did him. It was in one of these brief spells, without a struggle, that he died on his way to the bathroom at their Carmel Valley Manor apartment in 1978. He was 83 at his death.

Hawaii cruise, 1961

+ 8.   F   vii.   Mahala ABERCROMBIE, born 1798.

+ '9. M   viii. Young David ABERCROMBIE, born 7 May 1804, died 11 Feb 1888.

NOTES for James follow:

In 1769 Isaac Abercrombie bought a tract of 100 acres on Rabun Creek in what was later Laurens Co, SC. John and James Abercrombie witnessed the deed. Isaac Abercrombie moved from here to Anson Co, NC before 1790 as he is in the 1790 census in NC. About 1795 Isaac Abercrombie sold that tract of land to the 2nd James in the 1790 census, this deed witnessed by John Abercrombie and Hastings Dial, before James Abercrombie, Justice of the Peace. Isaac was then living in Anson Co, NC. This James later made numerous land deals and finally dropped out of the records. He sold the land on Rabun Creek in 1798 and appears no more in Laurens Co records. His wife was Ann.[1]

1785 PLAT MAP: SC, 96 Dist, North side of the Saluda River, Plat Book B 1785-1787. FHL, SLC, UT: James Abercrombie, date of warrant 19 Apr 1785; 640 acres; surveyed on 12 July 1785; surveyed 202 acres by Robert Hanna; Number 1650, page 115. From the plat map the neighbors are: Patrick Cunningham, Donald Williams, William Boyd, Benjamin Evans.

1785 PLAT MAP: James Abercrombie, date of warrant 19 Apr 1785; 640 acres; surveyed on 19 July 1785; surveyed 230 acres by Jonathan Downs; Number 1650, page 176. From the plat maps the neighbors are: James Abercrombie, David Allen, Richard Pugh, George Hastings, John Williams. Rayburns Creek runs through the property.

1790 CENSUS: SC, Laurens County: From the living children that I have found the Census should be as follows: James Abercrombie; males 16+, 1; males <16, 1; females, 4. The closest on in SC that I could find was: James Abercrombie; males 16+, 1; males <16, 2; females, 5.

1800 CENSUS: SC, Laurens Co: I have not been able to find him in the census. I think he may have gone to GA by this time since Young David Abercrombie was born in GA by 1804.

1800 CENSUS: GA, Jackson and Hall Co: The Federal Census for GA had been lost for 1790, 1800 and 1810.

1801 PURCHASE: GA, Jackson Co, FHL Film # 0325675: Estate of Joseph Neal, 31 Jan 1801, Inventories of Estates, Jackson Co, GA 1800-1832. James A Crombie bot 1 pair sissors, 12 1/2 cents.

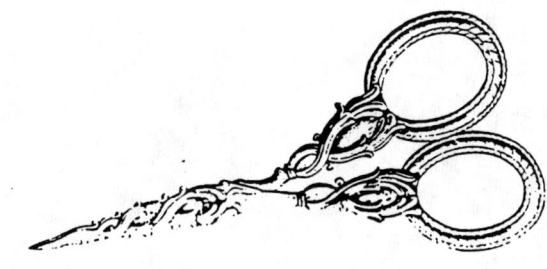

1803 TAXES: GA, Jackson Co, <u>Georgia Pioneers Genealogical Magazine</u>, Vol VIII, February 1971, No 1, copy at FHC, Monterey: Jackson County, digest of Taxable Property for 1803. Names listed to overcome in some degree the loss of census records. Capt Joseph Mc Connell's District. Abercrombie, James. James Abercrombie also paid taxes for someone else but name not listed.

---

[1]Letter from Annie Laurie Ewald in Washington, DC, 23 Jun 1967 "Georgia"s Landmarks, Memorials and Legends," by Lucien Tamar Knight 1914, Volumn 2.

Sample reference pages.

Walter and his family were living in Saranac Lake on Academy Street at the time of the 1900 Federal Census. This residence at 16 Academy Street, near the center of the Village, was undoubtedly the one he referred to in his letter of 15 Apr 1900 in which he asks Cory [probably his brother Corydon] to provide part of a loan for purchase of a house for $ 1500. He served several terms as Town Clerk for Harrietstown, the township in which Saranac Lake Village is located, and at the time of his death he was serving as Assessor. In 1912 he was appointed to the first of two terms as Postmaster for Saranac Lake. He belonged to the Franklin County Republican Party, the Masons, Knight Templar, the Shrine, and was a charter member of the Saranac Lake Elks.

He died in 1928 at the age of 54 after an acute intestinal illness and general peritonitis of only a few days. A medical specialist called in from Plattsburgh said there was nothing he could offer for treatment. He was buried in the Burke Center Cemetery in Burke, NY.

Grace GALBRAITH

Grace was born the sixth daughter of Thomas GALBRAITH and Elizabeth REYNOLDS in 1875 in Rowe, a town in the northwest corner of Massachusetts. Her father had moved to that area from Canada in 1869 to work on the Hoosac railroad tunnel, built for probably the same rail line that Walter JOHNSON worked for as a telegraph operator. Grace lived to be nearly 91 years of age. She was living in Florida, Massachusetts, near Rowe and North Adams, when she married Walter in 1895. Her first child, Marion, was born in Massachusetts. Janet, her second child was born in Saranac Lake, New York, in 1897, where she and her family moved and remained.

Grace and her family lived their whole Saranac Lake life at 16 Academy Street, the home Walter arranged to purchase for $ 1500 in 1900. Two more children, Millar born in 1901, and Agnes born in 1908, were born while there, making a family of six. Marion, the eldest, married Charles NEUBAUER, a salesman, about 1918, and they had two children Sylvia, born in 1919,

and Charles, born in 1922. Marion later moved to Tucson,

12

Arizona, with her second husband Anthony SABATELLO and it was there that she died. Three wives are listed for Millar: Margaret, Lucille and Ann WALTHAM. He lived near Saranac, but had no children. He died at age 66 in 1968 in Long Beach, Harrison Co., Mississippi. Agnes, the youngest, never married, living at home with her mother. Patsy, as our family knew her, had great interest in the out-of-doors, loving her beautiful Adirondack mountains and lakes. She showed me how to use snow shoes and I still remember climbing Mt. Marcy with her on a 10 degree below zero day. My camera shutter almost refused to work it was so cold. She and grandmother JOHNSON, whom we knew as Bamy (Bah-me), kept a warm, friendly house, later taking in boarders to help with expenses. After Bamy's death at the advanced age of 90, the house was sold and Patsy lived her last years in a nearby apartment building. She was the custodian of many of the family papers, providing them to me on my last visit to her. Grandmother Grace JOHNSON died of coronary heart disease in 1966 leaving one child (Agnes), five grandchildren and eight great grandchildren. She was buried at the family plot in the Burke Center Cemetery in Burke, NY.

references

Walter:

1873 BIRTH: JOHNSON Family Bible, pages in my possession:
Births: Walter Eugene JOHNSON - Burke NY June 30, 1873.

1880 CENSUS: NY, Franklin Co., Burke, 9&10 June, ED77 S11 L46:
JOHNSON, Walter E W M 7 b NY son of Nelson and Agnes C JOHNSON, S, at school, F&M b NY.

1892 HISTORY: Seaver, F J, Historical Sketches of Franklin Co and its Towns, 1918 Sutro fiche G3 LH3447:
Saranac Lake Village incoporated 1892, Harrietstown township

13

1895 MARRIAGE: MA, Berkshire Co., Florida; Record of Marriage No. 61796, for Walter E JOHNSON and Grace C GALBRAITH; 1895, vol 451, pg 53, no 3; copy in my possession:
Walter E. JOHNSON and Grace C. GALBRAITH, Florida, Mass., June 10th, 1895 groom 22 yrs, white, res Florida MA, 1st marr, Tel. operator, bpl Burk NY, F A.A. JOHNSON; bride 19 yrs, white, res Florida MA, 1st marr, occup At Home, bpl Rowe MA, F Tom GALBRAITH; Jerome Ward, Clergyman.

MARRIAGE: JOHNSON Family <u>Bible</u>, pages in my possession:
Walter Eugene JOHNSON of Plattsburgh NY and Grace GALBRAITH of Hoosac Tunnel, Mass.

1900 LETTER: Saranac Lake, 15 Apr 1900, to Cory from Walter on Branch & Callanan stationery:
Request from Walter to "Co" [Cory, probably Walter's older brother Corydon] asking for $500 loan on paper endorsed by Branch & Callanan to enable Walter to buy house "a short way from the Berkeley House" for $1500. He will borrow remaining $1000 from the loan assoc for $10 per mo (6%). The house rents for $15/mo. "I am pretty sure we will move this spring any way..." "...and if I staid here no longer than say three years, I would have the loan down to $1000..." Cory's handwritten response at bottom: "Allright that would be a great idea I think. Be sure the loan assoc don't get more than 6%."

1900 CENSUS: NY, Franklin Co., Saranac Lake Village, Academy St, 12 June, ED78 S16 L67:
JOHNSON, Walter E, W M 26 M b NY Jun 1873, F&M b NY; married 5 yr, 2 children (Marion G b MA Dec 1895, Janet G b NY 1897); wife Grace G b MA Jul 1875; her F Scotland, her M b Canada; Walter a bookkeeper; employer not legible (J___let Door Factory?).

1912 NEWSPAPER: <u>The Adirondack Enterprise</u>, Thurs, 1 Feb 1912, photocopy in my file, includes a good portrait picture:
WILL AIM TO PLEASE Public is Well Satisfied with W. E. JOHNSON Postmaster of Saranac Lake [new appointment]. Appt conf by U.S.Senate on Thurs. He has been resid of Saranac Lake 14 yrs, working for Branch & Callanan, builders. When the firm was recently incorp he became stkhldr and elected director. Has been memb Village Board of Health and town clerk of Harrietstown for several terms. "a self-made man". Born in Burke 1873, attended public schools and Franklin Academy of Malone. Became telegraph operator for several yrs with various stations on Fitchberg RR. Later returned to Plattsburgh where he became bookkeeper in the First National Bank there, From Plattsburgh he removed to Saranac Lake. He has a wife and 4 children.

1920 CENSUS: NY, Franklin Co., Saranac Lake, 4&5 January, ED92 S3 L43:
JOHNSON, Walter M W 46 M husb of Grace JOHNSON b NY,F b NH,M b NY,owns home free; occup on census: contr & bldgs "Branch & Oil Co", self empl; NOTE: discrepancy on F's bplace - other records show NY.

1928 DEATH: NY, Franklin Co., Saranac Lake, NY State Dept of Health, #4520, for Walter E. JOHNSON, copy in my possession:
Walter E JOHNSON death Jan 2nd, 1928, general peritonitis caused probably by Ptomaine poison; 16 Academy St, Saranac Lake; res in city 30 yrs; wife Grace GALBRAITH; b June 30, 1873, age 54 yr 6 mo 8 dy; contractor & building, Branch & Callanan; bpl Burke NY; f Nelson W JOHNSON, bpl Brasher NY; mo Agnes C HARE, bpl Schuyler Falls NY; info from Victor L JOHNSON, Saranac Lake; burial Jan 4, 1928, Saranac Lake NY, C J Stickney, undertaker lic 4418, Saranac Lake.

14

also son-in law Solomon W BARBER 27 b Apr 1873 VT, 2yrM,telegraph operator, and their dau Elizabeth E 4/12 b Jan 1900; also grndch Mary L KING 12 b MA July 1887 & Philip M KING 9 b MA July 1890 whose F b NY & M b Canada(Eng)

1920 CENSUS: MA, Franklin Co., Charlemont Town, High St, ED95 S3 L81 6 Jan: GALBRAITH, Elizabeth W F Wd 71 noncit,b Canada,F&M b England, rents home; only other in house Harold Rice, boarder, W M S 29 b MA, F b MA, M b Canada; wood turner

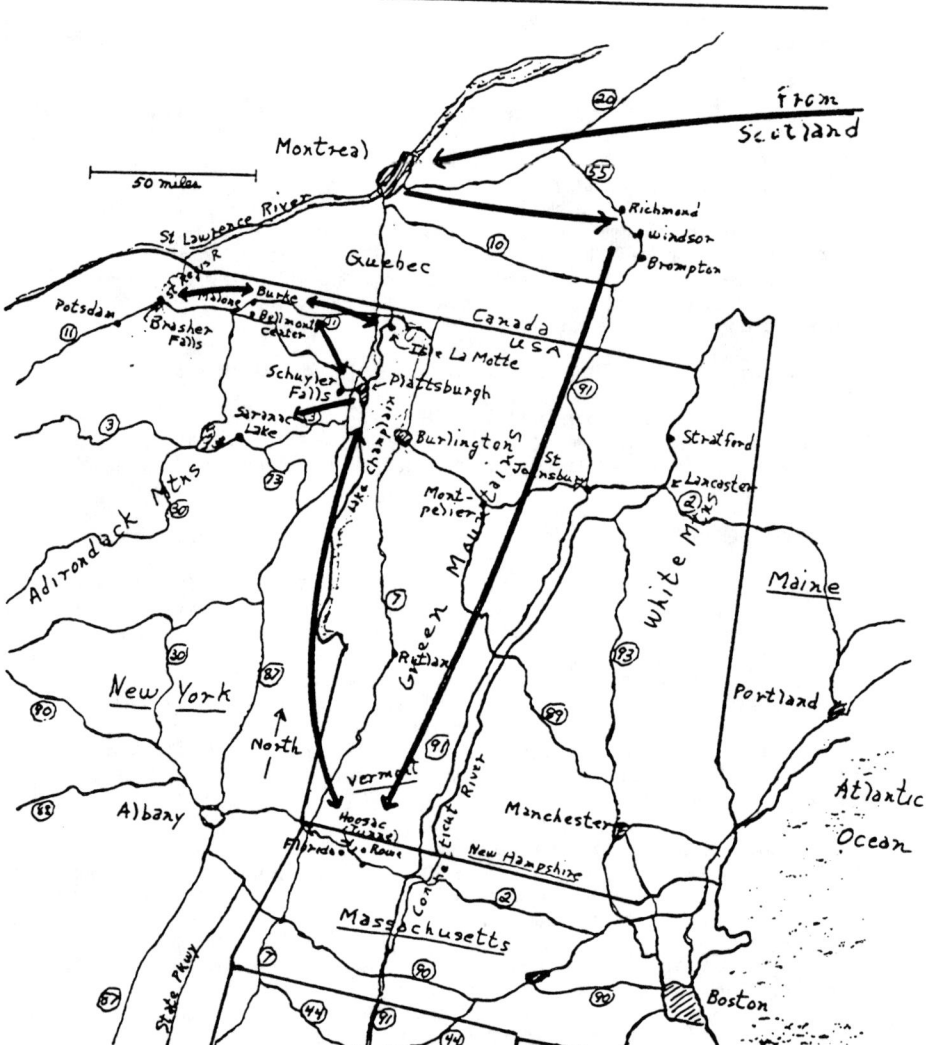

JOHNSON, HARE and GALBRAITH migrations 1830-1920

29

324

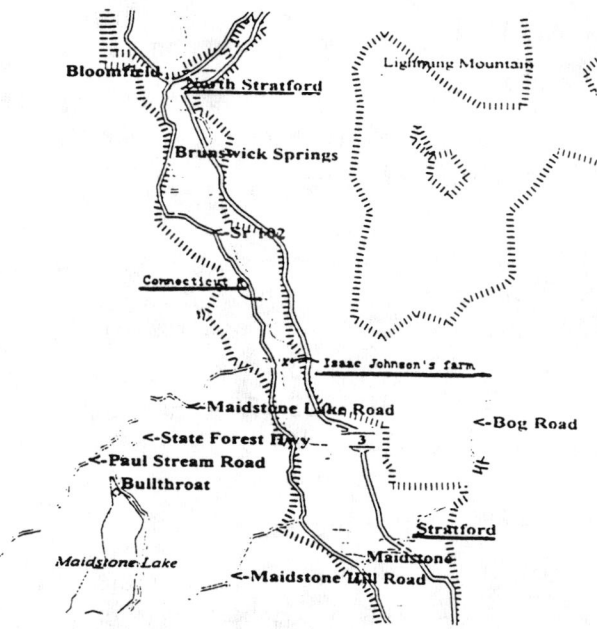

Farm location at Stratford, NH

Phebe GRANT

Phebe GRANT was born 27 April 1745, the daughter of a Congregational minister. She married Isaac JOHNSON in New Haven, CT, on 15 September 1762 in the North Congregational Church also known as the Church of Christ in White Haven Society. She and Isaac lived in the Stratford, CT, area where they had 6 sons and 1 daughter, their last child.

Their first child, Grant, was baptized 26 January 1764 in the church in Easton, CT, close to Monroe and Moose Hill. Phebe and her family went with Isaac to Stratford, NH, in 1788 or 1789, where she lived until her death 27 April 1808.

Descendants of Isaac JOHNSON

Jeannette Thompson in her History of the Town of Stratford NH 1773-1925 provides portraits of three of Isaac JOHNSON's descendants.

Marcus D JOHNSON (1805-1864), Isaac's grandson, a surveyor by profession with probably more practical knowledge of the topography of the Stratford area than anyone else at the time, served the town in many civil capacities. His wife, Evelina Ann Maria MARSHALL

70

325

CHAPTER 1

Descendants of John & Elizabeth (Harris) Berry 1775-1899

Listing 70 descendants for 3 generations.

GENERATION NO. 1

1. John¹ BERRY {17} was born 11 Nov 1775 in Albemarle Co, VA. John died Sep-Oct 1840 in Brownsville, Salt Pond Twnshp, Saline Co, MO, and was buried 1840 in the 1st cemetery, later reinterred in Fairview, Sweet Springs, Saline, MO. He married **Elizabeth Betsy HARRIS** {18} 12 Apr 1797 in Madison County, KY. She was born 1780-82 in Madison Co, KY, the daughter of Robert HARRIS {28} and Nancy GRUBBS {29}. Elizabeth died 1838 in Brownsville, Saline, MO, and was buried 1838 in the 1st cemetery, later reinterred in Fairview, Sweet Springs (old Brownsville), Saline, MO.

They had 9 children:

+ 2.	M	i.	Thomas G. BERRY {19}, born 1798/1810, died after 1844.
+ 3.	M	ii.	Tyre Harris BERRY, Rev. {15}, born 25 Oct 1800, died 13 Sep 1871.
+ 4.	M	iii.	Higgason H BERRY {21}, born 1802, died after 1845.
+ 5.	M	iv.	Milton David BERRY {20}, born 11 Jul 1803, died 6 May 1889.
+ 6.	F	v.	Eliza BERRY {131}, born 10 Jan 1805, died 13 Jul 1878.
+ 7.	F	vi.	Lucy J BERRY {128}, born 1810, died Oct 1842.
+ 8.	M	vii.	Robert H BERRY {22}, born 30 May 1811, died 20 Jul 1867.
+ 9.	F	viii.	Nancy Stone BERRY {25}, born 20 Feb 1814, died 5 Oct 1864.
+ 10.	F	ix.	Elizabeth Taylor BERRY {26}, born 11 Jan 1820, died Apr 1900.

NOTES for Elizabeth follow:

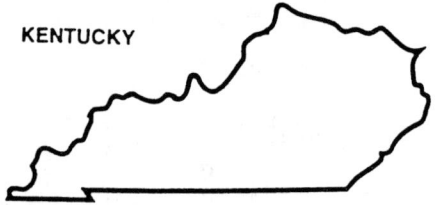

KENTUCKY

1780 BIRTH: letter 29 Oct 1994 from Rosemary
- Kutch; info to her from Arlene Johnson, Lee's Summit MO
Elizabeth Harris was born 1780-82 Madison Co KY

1780-90 HISTORY: W H Miller, History & Genealogies, Richmond, KY 1907 p 261
"In the period 1780-90 there was a great migratory movement from VA & other states to the new & fertile regions of KY, 'The Dark & Bloody Ground'. Among the emigrants from Albemarle & adjacent counties of VA, were Christopher Harris, Sr, his 2nd wife Agnes McCord, besides a greater number of his sons & daughters, in two sets, numbering in all 17 & a host of grand children, who composed an amazing throng for 1 family to swell the population of the new country...many at later dates moved to the Territory of MO. Christopher Harris, Sr travelled a great deal over the KY wilds & entered lands on the waters of the Licking river, but settled & established his home in Madison Co KY, where he owned lands on Silver, Muddy & Downing Creeks, in addition to a large body of land in Albemarle...Schedule of his family who came besides collateral branches of the Harris family...Robert Harris (wife Nancy Grubbs)." These were Elizabeth's parents. Christopher was her

326

F	xi.	Rebecca BERRY {1370}.	
F	xii.	Elizabeth BERRY {1371}.	
.	F	xiii.	Florence Leone BERRY {1372}.

NOTES for Anna follow:
   his 2nd marriage according to Bill Berry KC MO 1991 m after the Civil War also spelled Haire

NOTES for William follow:
   Virgil Andrew Berry wrote William M Berry served during the Civial War in Co G & B MO Cav under Col John F Plillips Later US District Judge Western Dist for MO now deceased written about 1939 or 40 He spelled his father's name Moultry think his son uses Moultrie (William M Berry Kansas City) Cemetery Record Dresden Cemetery difficult to read researcher's notes War Record Co G 7 MO S.M. Cav Married by Rev Tyre H Berry Minister of the Gospel

- - - - - - - - - -

41. **Tyree Milton³ BERRY** {231} (Milton², John¹) was born 15 Mar 1848 in Pettis County, MO. Tyree died 5 May 1946 in Eureka, Greenwood, KS, and was buried in Eureka County, Greenwood, KS. He married **Lucinda B LOYD** {704} 25 Jul 1878 in Lamonte, Pettis, MO. She was born 26 Jan 1855. Lucinda died 13 Sep 1927 in Eureka, Greenwood, KS.

They had 11 children:

F	i.	Willia Maud BERRY {380}, born 21 Apr 1879, died 9 Oct 1879.
F	ii.	Martha Alberta BERRY {1024}, born 3 Sep 1880, died 12 May 1961.
F	iii.	Mary Elizabeth BERRY {1025}, born 10 Nov 1882, died 5 Sep 1961.
M	iv.	Charles Milton BERRY {1022}, born 8 Dec 1884.
F	v.	Lula May BERRY {1026}, born 8 Dec 1884, died 1884.
F	vi.	Lucille BERRY {1027}, born 18 Sep 1886, died 20 Sep 1951.
F	vii.	Lenora Belle BERRY {1028}, born 18 Jul 1889.
F	viii.	Laura Evelyn BERRY {1029}, born 13 Jul 1891, died 5 May 1966.
M	ix.	Lloyd Andrew BERRY {1030}, born 22 Sep 1893, died 28 Dec 1951.
F	x.	Living BERRY {1031}.
F	xi.	Leona Grace BERRY {1032}, born 20 Nov 1899, died 16 Oct 1906.

NOTES for Tyree follow:
   1860 census Tyre M was attending school

- - - - - - - - - -

42. **Elizabeth³ REAVIS** {209} (Eliza², John¹) was born 27 Nov 1823 in Boone County, MO. Elizabeth died 13 Feb 1894 in MO. She married **Thomas Chilton WARREN** {220}. He was born 1805 in KY, the son of Martin W WARREN {1305} and Sarah DUNBAR {2292}. Thomas died 5 May 1890 in MO.

They had 1 child:

F	i.	Martha J WARREN {201}, born 1847, died 1930.

227-229: Letters from Indian agent Hugh Montgomery, received 3 Jul 1817 by Governor William Rabun: Sir, I have just returned from the Frontiers, and have sat down to give you the names of the white persons (heads of families) who I find living on the Indean Lands adjesant to this County -- Jackson... on and near the Chestetee (river) are Freeman Overbee, Danl Short, Noah Langly, John Martin, and Jese Martin and at and above the shallow ford are William Stoker, William Baity, a man by the name Mason, an other by the name of Hains, another by the name of Hawkins, and John Wagoner, James Abercrombie Senr, James Abercrombie Junr, Benjn Morris, Henry Morris, John Diffy...I did not see all of them, but a greater part of them that I did, promised to come in, some few will, say about one in ten, the ballance will not.

1817 LETTER: GA, <u>Whites among the Cherokees, Georgia 1828-1838</u>, written by the participants, collected and edited by Mary B Warren and Eve B Weeks, Sutro Library, San Francisco, CA, pages 227-229:24 Jul 1817: Sir, I have received Certificates that the following persons have either moved or are actually removing within the settled limits of the State (of Georgia) (viz) Lewis Crow, Jacob Crow, Levi Crow, Hugh Wilson, John Wilson, Erwin Strickland, Simon Strickland, Sion Strickland, Lazerus Strickland, Bud Mullins, John Mires, James Abercrombia Senr...

1818 HISTORY: GA, Hall County, <u>Historical Collections of Georgia</u>, by the Rev. George White, M.A., New York, Pudney & Russell, Publishers, No. 70 John Street, 1854: Hall County. Laid out by the Lottery Act of 1818. A part taken from Jackson and Franklin, 1818; part of new territory added to it, 1819. Length, 30 m.; breadth, 24 m.; square miles, 720. Named after Lyman Hall, a signer of the Declaration of the American Independence. The principal streams are, the Chattahoochee, Chestatee, Oconee, and Little rivers. The creeks are numerous. The soil is productive in some parts, in others poor. Gainesville is the seat of justice, 111 miles from Milledgeville, delightfully situated, with a climate equal to any in the world. The Sulphur Spring, six miles N. of Gainsville, is much frequented. Minerals in great variety are found in this county. Among them are gold, lead, ruby, tourmaline, cyanite, and emerald. The elastic sandstone abounds, in which a few diamonds have been found. Extract from the Census of 1850: Dwellings, 1300; families, 1300; white males, 3639; white females, 3731; free coloured males, 4; free coloured females, 3. Total free population, 7377; Slaves, 1336; Deaths, 69; Farms, 697. Value of real estate, $609,639; value of personal estate, $867,332. Among the early settlers were, Wm H Dickson, E Donegan, Joseph Wilson, John Bates, B Reynolds, R Armour, Joseph Gailey, T Terrell, John Millar, D Wafford, M Moore, W Blake, Joseph Read, R Young, J Mc Connell, R Winn, Thos Wilson, Wm Cobb, N Garrison, Joseph Johnson, John Barrett, E Cowen, A Thompson, Jesse Dobbs, James Abercrombie, Solomon Peake.

1818 HISTORY: GA, Hall Co, <u>The History of Hall County, Georgia</u>, Volume I, 1818-1900 by James E Dorsey, SLC, 975.8272 H2d, V1, page 10: Early Artisans and Tradesmen: While most of the people living in Hall County in the 1820s were farmers, some did have other occupations to supplement their **1818 LAND:** GA, Hall Co, Letter written by Annie L Ewald, 4007 Conn Ave NW, livelihoods. an appendix to the 1820 census contains a listing of "Manufacturers and Merchants," including data on investments, products, employees, costs and profits and provides an interesting glimpse into some of the activities of pioneer life in the area. While the exact location of these individuals is not given, it does appear that most lived in the eastern part of the county, the "Headright" section which had been settled originally as a part of Jackson and Franklin counties. This area had been divided into ten militia districts, which were not numbered but took the name of the "Captain" in charge of the militia for that area. Some of these early "Captains" included Captain McElhannon, Captain Buffington, Captain Reid, Captain Benjamin McCutcheon, Captain John V Cotter, Captain Carnes, Captain Byrd, Captain Abercrombie, Captain Elias Miller and Captain Tanner.

Sample appendix

THE ANCESTORS OF JANET GALBRAITH JOHNSON 1897-1979

PEDIGREE CHART

Number 1 on this chart is the same as no. 23 on chart no. 1

```
                                                                                  16 Daniel PURDY-187---------
                                                       8 Benjamin PURDY Sr-185-----------|
                                                         B: 12 Dec 1718
                                                         P:                             17 -----------------
                                                         M:     --52
                                                         P: Horseneck,,CT
                               4 Benjamin PURDY-78----------------  D: 28 Nov 1808
                                 B:                                 P: Manchester,Bennington,VT  18 -----------------
                                 P:
                                 M: 27 Feb 1770   --30            9 Deborah NATHAN-186-------------|
                                 P:                                 B: 19 Dec 1725
                                 D: 11 Dec 1828                     P:                             19 -----------------
                                 P: Manchester,Bennington,VT        D: 23 Jul 1804
                                                                    P: Manchester,Bennington,VT   20 -----------------
    2 Henry PURDY-76-----------------
      B: 14 Feb 1773                                             10 ---------------------------------|
      P: Manchester,Bennington,VT                                  B:
      M:    --29                                                   P:                              21 -----------------
      P:                                                           M:
      D: 10 Jul 1843                                               P:
      P: Plattsburgh,Clinton,NY                                    D:
                               5 Elizabeth BULLESS-79---------------  P:                           22 -----------------
                                 B: 18 Feb 1753
                                 P:                              11 ---------------------------------|
                                 D:  1 Jan 1822                     B:
                                 P: Manchester,Bennington,VT        P:                              23 -----------------
    1 Elizabeth PURDY-18----------------                            D:
      B: 20 Sep 1803                                                P:
      P: Plattsburgh,Clinton,NY                                                                    24 Joseph WASHBURN-198------
      M:  6 Mar 1823   --9
      P:                                                        12 Ebenezer WASHBURN-107-----------|
      D: 10 Mar 1881                                               B: Aft    1690
      P: Ticonderoga,Essex,NY                                      M: 30 Jun 1721   --32           25 Hannah LATHAM-199--------
    John MERCHANT-17---------------                                 P:
      Spouse                   6 Stephen WASHBURN-80---------------  D: Abt    1768
                                 B: 19 Feb 1734/1735                P:                              26 Stephen MILES-196--------
                                 P: New Milford,Litchfield,CT
                                 M:    --31                      13 Patience MILES-108-------------|
                                 P:                                 B: 20 Sep 1704
                                 D: Abt    1804                     P:                              27 Patience-197------------
                                 P:                                 D:     1743
    3 Martha WASHBURN-77-----------------                           P:                              28 -----------------
      B: 15 Mar 1776
      P: Manchester,Bennington,VT                               14 ---------------------------------|
      D: 17 Apr 1843                                               B:
      P: Plattsburgh,Clinton,NY                                    P:                              29 -----------------
                                                                   M:
                               7 Martha BULL-81--------------------  P:
                                 B:                                 D:
                                 P:                                 P:                              30 -----------------
                                 D:
                                 P:                             15 ---------------------------------|
                                                                   B:                              31 -----------------
                                                                   P:
                                                                   D:
                                                                   P:
```

329

INDEX OF NAMES

INDEX OF NAMES

BIBLIOGRAPHY

_____. *Ancestral File*. Salt Lake City, UT: Genealogi cal Society of Utah/Family History Library, 1992.

_____. *Directory of Professional Genealogists*. Salt Lake City, UT: Association of Professional Genealogists, 1990.

_____. *Family History Library Catalog*. Salt Lake City, UT: Genealogical Society of Utah/Family History Library, 1992.

Katz, William A. *Introduction to Reference Work*. Vol. 11, New York: McGraw Hill, 1987.

Lackey, Richard S. *Cite Your Sources: A Manual for Documenting Family Histories and Genealogical Records*. Mississippi: University Press of Mississippi, 1985.

Shull, Wilma Sadler. *Photographing Your Heritage*. Salt Lake City: Ancestry Publishing, 1988.

Sturm, Duane & Pat Sturm. *Video Family History*. Salt Lake City: Ut, Ancestry Publishing, 1989.

Turabian, Kate L. *A Manual for Writers of Term Papers, Theses and Dissertations*. Fifth Edition, revised and expanded by Bonnie B. Hongisblum, Chicago: University of Chicago Press, 1987.

Zinsser, William. *On Writing Well: An Informal Guide to Writing Fiction*. Third Edition, New York: Harper & Row, 1985.

GENEALOGY INSTRUCTOR'S CLASS OUTLINE

This book covers a sixteen week, full-semester, college course of instruction. Two lectures hours per week and three assisted lab hours per week work very well. I've taught it most successfully in a block on Saturday morning from 8-1, on Wednesday afternoons from 12-5, or in the evenings, twice a week from 7-9:30.

I try to allow lab time nearly every session so the students do not lose ground in their computer skills. This particular semester they will be learning two new computer programs: *WordPerfect*® and *GEN-BOOK*® as well as taking their records off the *Personal Ancestral File*® computer program. They need the lab time to feel comfortable with the programs and to experiment with many options for finishing their family histories.

I limit my classes to no more than 25 students when no lab assistant is available. You, of course, may find it necessary to modify the lessons to meet your individual needs but they have been tested and proven to work very well.

Just as in the other classes I've taught, my biggest problem was preventing students from trying to write the last, definitive history on their families. I try to explain to them that this is a time to learn and practice; and, in the end, to actually produce one history, on one family line, NOT **everything** on **every** family.

You may find, as I did, that out of your 25 students, you will have 20 different goals in mind for what they hope to write about. This last semester, one student transcribed a diary written in 1922 about a cross-country trip from Idaho to the Midwest. They then picked up relatives who were planning to move to California. But first the two families drove to the New England states and then drove through New Mexico and the southern route to California. *GEN-BOOK* was used to describe the two families and their relationship to each other, while *WordPerfect* provided the vehicle to record the additional notes and comments. It was outstanding.

I've included in the appendix many examples of what students have done. I wish I had thought about keeping samples of their work over the years. I've loved them all.

For your convenience, I have broken down the classes into the sixteen units I teach. Best wishes for a wonderful, wrap-it-up class.

SIXTEEN-WEEK COURSE OUTLINE

1. Registration of students; a definition of Family History objectives, confidence builders, and specific details for beginning the project including: determining your audience, identifying your problem, selecting the family to focus on, deciding on a time frame, choosing a writing style and how to use transitions, graphics, detail and conclusions effectively. It concludes with how to go about locating background materials to make those transitions or to provide support for your arguments. The lesson covers the introduction and pages 1-16. Students define their family history objectives and become familiar with the computer programs being used: *WordPerfect®*, *GEN-BOOK®* and the *Personal Ancestral File®* programs. (These were selected because they operate well on the Novell Network program, the first is already on most college computers and the others were allowed to be placed on the network system. The last two were very reasonably priced.)

2. Lesson two focuses on using *WordPerfect®* to accomplish their objectives. They are introduced to Typing Text, Word Wrap, Setting Margins, Reveal Codes, Centering, Indenting, Numbering

Pages, Copying, Moving or Deleting Blocks of Text, Finding a Word in pages of text, Replacing Words, Changing Font Sizes, Changing Font Appearance, Forcing a New Page, Changing Your Mind and Canceling Something, Saving Your Document, Combining Files or Chapters, Retrieving Your Documents, and Exiting *WordPerfect®* Without Saving a File. The lesson covers pages 17 to 37 and lab time is spent practicing and building on their skills.

3. Lesson three focuses on designing the layout of their book. They learn about margins, font sizes and types, graphics, page layout, paper and printing. This is followed with a study of binding types, covers, and costs. They continue to work on their word processing skills in lab. It covers pages 38-54.

4. This lesson explains how to pick up background materials for your history. First the need for such materials is shown. Then instruction is given on how to set goals in order to locate the best repository to solve the problem. Instruction is given on how to locate a repository, how to organize materials from an on-site visit and how to obtain information from Inter-library loan services. Covers pages 55-68. During lab time they review each week what was learned the week before and they add to that one or two more features of the word processing program.

5. The students are then taught how they might contract out some of the research if they are unable to do it themselves. They are instructed on how to find and hire professional services, and what to do in advance. They are shown what fee is charged and what to expect. Suggestions are given as to how to help the process, how to evaluate a research report, and what to do if you are not pleased with the results. This lesson covers pages 69-80 and lab time is spend practicing word processing techniques.

6. Collecting background materials for your book can also come through Oral Histories so their advantages are taught along with suggestions on whom to interview and in what order.

Sample topics are given and suggestions on how to arrange the room, length of time, type of equipment, recording and technical techniques. Finally how to transcribe the oral history and place it into your computer-generated family history is given. Covers pages 81-99.

7. Making International Connections is next covered since so many students want to start their book with their first immigrant ancestor. American clues are explained for finding the foreign-born ancestor as well as research strategies, evaluation of information, and how to send money overseas. Covers pages 100-134.

8. Research aids for international connections are given next including geographical reference tools, language aids, naming conventions and customs, and handwriting aids. Covers pages 135-151.

9. Midterm. Catch-up time on past assignments and practice on word processor.

10. The last in our three-part class on foreign documents, is entitled "Making Sense of the Documents You've Found". Many people are left with foreign documents which they don't know whether to keep or throw away. Even individuals fluent in 20th century foreign languages, find it impossible to read the old script, so the basic techniques for reading foreign paleography is taught. Answers are given to the foreign translations before the index in this book. German Paleography, Scandinavian Gothic Script, British Isles Court Handwriting, and calendaring challenges are given. Covers pages 152-178.

11. With the advent of so many more electronic research sources, this chapter covers, "Computer-Aided Genealogical Research" and the techniques to use them effectively all the way from organizing materials to original research. Covers pages 152-198. Students learn how to directly pull out supportive data for their hypothesis from other electronic formats.

12. Lesson eleven provides instruction on how to convert records from PAF Family Records to a Printed Family History using several conversion programs including, Pafability, KinWrite, and GEN-BOOK. Draft copies of their own family records conversions are done in class and various numbering systems are taught. Information on skanning materials into the family history is also covered. (NOTE: Skanning materials is really not cost or quality effective at this time, but the technology is taught to the students so they will be prepared for the future.) Covers pages 199-235. Students also learn how to generate an index with GEN-BOOK. Appendix should be used to show examples of other student books.

13. Lesson twelve prepares students to produce video histories. Preliminary preparations are covered including visuals, music, length, narrative, type of equipment, and background environment is covered. Covers pages 236-250.

14. Other forms of Family Histories are covered including Health Histories, calendar ideas, photo histories and art histories. More instruction on polishing of the final product is given for lab. Covers pages 251-262.

15. Lesson fourteen covers "Publishing the Final Product". How to locate a publisher, submit your manuscript, and how to share your research if you don't care to publish is covered. This lesson covers pages 263-280. Student are also taught how to create a permanent electronic record and how to send their information to the Library of Congress, local historical and genealogical societies, family organizations and the Ancestral File. During lab they will use the program to correspond with a publisher or printer. They will submit their final draft of their family history as though it were an interim report to a researcher. Teacher will grade in class, give suggestions, and help student turn in final book next week.

16. Final and turn in family history project.

Answers to Page 173

1. (Christopher) Xpofer = given name

2. (Ann) An = given name

3. Eliza

4. The XVIIth of Maye = 17 May

5. The IXth of June = 9 June

6. His wife

7. The ninthe daie of August

8. Potter

9. Sonne (son) of

10. So. (son) to

11. Mary daughter of William Foster of Wilston bourne the fifth of October 1656

12. Anna the daughter of John Dunston was baptized the XXXIth of March

13. 5 July was bap(tized): Susanne daughter of John Brooke

14. John Harison sonne of Richard Harison

15. Ellinor his wife in Grayes Inn

Answers to Page 174

1.	H	26.	Ä	51.	O
2.	D	27.	h	52.	F
3.	A	28.	i	53.	R
4.	C	29.	k	54.	5
5.	R	30.	p	55.	5
6.	P	31.	M	56.	10
7.	V	32.	D	57.	10
8.	W	33.	P	58.	10
9.	A	34.	1	59.	z
10.	N	35.	o	60.	z
11.	J	36.	r	61.	P
12.	B	37.	m	62.	6
13.	N	38.	m	63.	S
14.	1/2	39.	n	64.	5
15.	0	40.	n	65.	Ö
16.	0	41.	N	66.	w
17.	w	42.	E	67.	x
18.	a	43.	Q	68.	y
19.	c	44.	s	69.	e
20.	Ö	45.	j	70.	Æ
21.	L	46.	r	71.	Q
22.	C	47.	h	72.	H
23.	O	48.	g	73.	T
24.	3	49.	g	74.	O
25.	Æ	50.	g	75.	6

76.	s	101.	T
77.	t	102.	U
78.	u	103.	W
79.	2	104.	R
80.	2.	105.	N
81.	R	106.	ä
82.	I	107.	10-1/2
83.	U	108.	Ä
84.	P	109.	6
85.	o	110.	N
86.	1		
87.	6		
88.	h		
89.	2		
90.	P		
91.	S		
92.	T		
93.	V		
94.	Q		
95.	g		
96.	p		
97.	e		
98.	a		
99.	d		
100.	c		

Answers to Page 175

vigde	med
son	dräng
Lysning	Novemb:
Födde	Barn
ifrån	Hustru
piga	och
dotter	Åhr
Döde	Månad
Döpte	år
på	åboen
fader	jag
moder	Namn
	Anno

INDEX